Fat Boys

A Slim Book

Sander L. Gilman

UNIVERSITY OF NEBRASKA PRESS

LINCOLN AND LONDON

© 2004 by
the University of
Nebraska Press. All
rights reserved. Manufactured
in the United States of America ∞

Library of Congress
Cataloging-in-Publication Data

Gilman, Sander L.
Fat boys : a slim book /
Sander L. Gilman.
p.   cm.
Includes
bibliographical
references and index.
ISBN 0-8032-2183-5 (cloth :
alk. paper) ISBN 978-0-8032-7123-4
(paper : alk. paper)
1. Overweight men.
2. Obesity—Social apsects.
3. Body image in men.
I. Title.
RC552.025 G54 2004
616.3'98'0081—dc21
2003014544

For Zhou Xun in Respect and Admiration

Contents

Preface   ix

Introduction: *Fat Is a Man's Issue*   1

1. Fat Boys in the Cultural History of the West   35
2. Fat Boys Writing and Writing Fat Boys   63
3. Patient Zero: *Falstaff*   111
4. How Fat Detectives Think (And Fat Villains Act)   153
5. Fat Ballplayers and the Bodies of Fat Men   193

   Conclusion: *Cutting into the Future of Fat Boys*   227

   Notes   241

   Index   295

Preface

This is a slim book about a large topic. Covering the cultural and medical discourses about obesity and masculinity should be a much more extensive task than that accomplished by the rather slim volume of case studies I present here. They are not exhaustive, but they do illustrate the complexity associated with the fat man. From discourses about normality to the playing fields of baseball, from Greek male beauty to the fat detective, I have tried to examine and illustrate how cultures, medical and otherwise, have imagined and represented the fat boy. In turn I believe that these cultural images provide powerful models for the self-representation of fat men. The two categories I hesitate to define in this book, notions of "fat" and "men," are fraught with the conflicts that all perceptions of difference and normality contain. They constantly define and redefine themselves in the West, as this history suggests.

Take this volume as I offer it — as a tentative exploration of the world of male body fantasies. Be aware, however, that these are not "merely" representations; they alter how men relate to their own (male) bodies and to the bodies of others — both men and women. The fat boy is characterized as hypersexual as well as asexual. He is represented as the epitome of health and as a walking time bomb. The illustrations I use here are marginal; they stand on the edge of the literary and medical discourses of any given age. Yet they are not inconsequential. The figures or tropes I describe — from the ugly fat man with the beautiful thin man trapped inside, to the smart fat boy, to the aging body desirous of rejuvenation — appear and reappear in different guises throughout Western culture. The marginal case defines the oft-praised center of any belief system. The history of dietetics, for example, often retold, is rarely concerned with fictions about the male body; indeed, except in rare cases, neither are the literary studies that examine "freakishness." Obesity is a case so huge it seems invisible. Today we in the United States (and soon in Europe) speak glibly of an obesity epidemic. Obesity is seen as one of the major public health problem of our day, the number of gastric bypass surgeries increasing exponentially. In this context the meanings associated with the obese body seem to be natural, seem to be given. They are the habitus, the constructed but naturalized world, through which the obese, male body is seen and treated. These contexts are slippery; they change over time and with the function of the image of the obese male in culture and medicine. Yet they demand at any given moment to be seen as permanent and universally true.

The chapters of this book reflect the construction of images of the normal and the obese male body within the West. The introduction looks at core questions in culture, medicine, and law. Chapter 1 follows with the beginning of a history of the fat male body in the West, from the Greeks through to the Enlightenment. The second chapter looks at the autobiographical and fictional representation of the obese male body from the Renaissance to the end of the nineteenth century, drawing on the paradigmatic models offered in the initial chapter. Chapter 3 follows the odd history of the soldier and courtier Falstaff from the seventeenth century to the present. While in no way exhaustive, it examines some of the permutations of this most important of fat boys and his heirs. The fourth and fifth chapters deal with two further case studies of fat boys: the fat detective and the fat ballplayer. As does the story of the fat soldier Falstaff, they represent gendered categories of obesity; women are simply not to be found in these studies. (In the course of the history of such images the bodies of women soldiers, women detectives, and women athletes become part of the tale, but that is for another history of the body.) The conclusion tries to imagine the future of the fat boy in Western culture as the object of surgical intervention.

Much of the material for this study comes from the medical literature on obesity from the Greeks to the present, as well as from high and popular culture. In addition I have looked at the moral and theological literature dealing with the fat body to present a continuation of the debates from the medical literature to other forms. For this reason I have also incorporated discussions of health and the body from the extensive premodern and modern literature on longevity.[1] Coded into this literature is an obsessive concern with the collapse and decay of the body that clearly parallels the medical and cultural discourse on obesity. Obesity is seen as antithetical to a long life, thus standing for moral as well as purely medical failures. Teasing out the implications of this complex idea of the obese male body in these literatures often demands a set of readings of texts from both high and mass culture, not because of a desire to point at sources but to show the common manner of representing the obese male body within a wide range of cultural objects. How and in which direction influence flows is oftentimes difficult if not impossible to determine, which may also mean that in some cases what the reader observes is a simultaneous incorporation of cultural images in a wide range of textual sources.

I have taught seminars on this topic at the University of Chicago, the University of British Columbia, the University of California at Irvine, Cornell University, and the University of Illinois–Chicago. I have lectured on it on three continents. I am grateful to those who disagreed with me as much as to those who helped supply new materials for this study. Dana Rovang and Robyn Schiffman aided me in researching and quote checking. I am grateful for their help. Carol Sickman-Garner elegantly copyedited the manuscript.

Fat Boys

Introduction *Fat Is a Man's Issue*

A WOMAN'S ISSUE?

Since the rise of the women's movement in the 1960s the standard model for the study of the relationship between gender and obesity has focused on women's bodies. The theme of much of this work has centered on how patriarchal society (men) abhors fat women and thus causes all women to hate their own bodies.[1] In this rhetoric no woman's body could be slim enough. Fat, as Susie Orbach wrote thirty years ago, is a feminist issue![2] Kim Chernin coined the phrase "tyranny of slenderness" to reflect American society's growing preoccupation with thinness and the attendant issues for the fat female body.[3] The view that obesity is a women's issue dominated even the political reaction to the diet culture. The NAAFA (originally the National Association to Aid Fat Americans, later changed to National Association to Advance Fat Acceptance) was founded in 1969. It splintered in 1973, and members of the Los Angeles chapter founded the Fat Underground, a collective of fat activists with strong ties to the radical therapy, lesbian, and feminist communities. They published the "Fat Liberation Manifesto," a document outlining the collective's political ties to other oppressed groups, its antidiet stance, and its demand for equality in all areas of life for fat women.

Seeing obesity as a woman's "problem" is a means of locating where the "danger" of obesity lies in society. This danger, however, is not a universal truth but rather a historical artifact. One can note that obesity was not always seen as an American problem. The American neurologist S. Weir Mitchell noted in 1877 that he was startled by "those enormous occasional growths, which so amaze an American when first he sets foot in London."[4] For him this was a good thing. The British now see themselves as the most obese people in Europe, with the Germans close behind. The British director Mike Leigh in his film *All or Nothing* (2002) presents the case of a family captured by the hopeless, numbing poverty of the London council flats. The plot is triggered when Rory (played by James Corden), the obese, unemployed teenage son of the family, has a heart attack that brings the family together. The solution to the boredom of poverty seems, in Mike Leigh's 2002 version, to be family love and dieting. The film has been a great hit among middle-class viewers in London and abroad. Yet French philosophers as well as American epidemiologists have recently labeled obesity a specifically American problem.[5] Whatever the truth in this, it is always the case that stigmatizing pathological categories are distanced from the observer. For American middle-class scientists today this "American problem" is a class problem. Obesity in the Americas is often equated with poverty.[6] Obesity, however, was a problem of the nobility in prerevolutionary France, where the rallying cry was "the people against the fat."[7] By 1922, when the Prix de Goncourt went to Henri Béraud's *The Martyrdom of the Obese Man*, it had become a problem of the bourgeoisie. Béraud, later infamous because of his collaboration with the Nazis, has his fat man travel all over Europe, commenting from his obese and French perspective on the bodies of the British and the Bavarians.[8] As with other visible and stigmatizing categories, such as the syphilitic, the obese person needs to be further defined by national identity. Obesity as an American feminist issue is a reflex of a specific time and place. Obesity is a category, and categories are always self-limiting to groups that are clearly defined. Thus it can be defined by both gender and nationality in different ways at different times and in different circumstances.

In the United States this emphasis on fat as a feminist issue created a self-awareness of obesity among women, and they became the major activists in this arena. In 1973 Carolyn Soughers brought the first (but unsuccessful) size-discrimination lawsuit. She had been denied employment with a county civil service agency on account of her size. It was only in 1993 that the federal Equal Employment Opportunity Commission ruled that "severely obese" people could claim protection under federal statutes barring discrimination against the disabled. A "friend of the court" brief based on this ruling was filed in the case of *Cook v. Rhode Island*, a suit brought by a Rhode Island woman, Bonnie Cook, who accused her state of illegally denying her a job on the basis of "perceived disability" because of her size. As obesity became a disability, women were the first clear advocates for acceptance of their size.

By 2000 San Francisco, Washington DC, Santa Cruz, and the state of Michigan had passed ordinances that added height and weight to the same antidiscrimination codes that included race, religion, sex, gender, sexual orientation, disability, and place of birth.[9] Indeed, the various permutations of NAAFA, such as the Chicago Size Acceptance Group, have turned the tables, it is claimed, on the diet culture by allowing women to take pride in their size. But as one of the fathers of a member said: "Though these people raise the issue of discrimination, they're really encouraging each other to get bigger. My daughter has gained weight since she got involved. Jeanine tells me I'm a fat bigot, and I laugh. I respect the wishes of others, but some of what this movement's about makes no sense to me."[10] Over and over again the issue of size and the issue of diet have been seen as primarily of concern to *women*.

There have been very few detailed studies of the complex history of the relationship between *men* and fat because of the assumption that fat is purely a feminist issue. Yet in terms of the widest range of historical and cultural interest, it was the fat boy who claimed center stage in the obsession about fat bodies for most of Western history. As Hillel Schwartz, certainly the most perspicacious critic of the history of fat, notes, "Although we now associate dieting most immediately with women, the classical texts of dieting until the twentieth century were written by men who had made a drastic change in their habits in midlife. The archetypal public dieters were more often male until late in the nineteenth century, despite that stoutness so praiseworthy in Victorian rhetoric about men."[11] Indeed, we can almost date the shift in focus from an interest in the obese male to the obese female body. At the close of the nineteenth century any discussion of health and obesity focused on the obese male. In an anonymous 1873 article on health in *Godey's Lady's Book* it was noted that "some men drink so absurdly of spirits and bitter beer, that they become lazy and indolent. They distend visibly before your eyes, get big, and bloated, and fat. The muscle of the heart gets less muscular and more fatty. The moral of this is for men not to take heating, fattening things, unless, indeed, they are cold and thin; to prefer food to stimulant; and, if there is any tendency to indolence or obesity, to prefer claret or water to beer and spirits."[12] The author evokes the older humoral model for obesity, which is addressed in chapter 1. No matter what the model used, however, fat men were the classic examples for the dangers of obesity even in texts written for women readers.

In 1924 the editors of the *Journal of the American Medical Association* published an editorial entitled "What Causes Obesity?" In it they argue, following a powerful antipsychological strand in obesity research that began in the late nineteenth century, for its etiology in malfunctions of normal metabolic processes. See obesity as a "scientific problem," they write, and that will free the "fat woman" from the stigma that she "has the remedy in her own hands — or rather between her own teeth." Thus the new object of scientific interest became the fat woman, who had been charged with carrying "that extra weight about with her unless she so wills."[13] In 1927 Harold Dearden, in his *Exercise and the Will*, appended a chapter on obesity in which he states, "To a man the affliction is grave enough, but to a woman! — who save a woman shall attempt to measure its really dread significance."[14] By the 1950s the die had been cast. "Women," states Robert Kemp in 1959, "care a great deal, very few men care at all. . . . Indeed secretly such men often think that not only is it quite normal to be stout after middle life, but that the figure is one of dignity, satisfaction and even strength."[15] When Elmer Wheeler proposed to write *The Fat Boy's Diet Book* in the late

1940s, he was told by his publisher: "What man will buy a book on dieting? That's women's stuff."[16] By 1950 obesity had indeed become purely "women's stuff."

The fat male body generates multiple meanings, many of which present a quite different set of images than do those of the fat, female body. These meanings are complex, often contradictory, yet unexamined historically. Few scholars have actually wrestled with the history of the version of masculinity that the obese male body seems to represent. Many of the existing studies simply mirror feminist rhetoric about patriarchal society and its impact on female bodies. Thus Laura Kipnis looks at contemporary culture and sees a feminine, maternal softness on the one hand and a solid, patriarchal gigantism on the other.[17] Recently Lynn Daroff summarized this view: "Certainly excess weight is just as damaging to men's health as to women's, but for men to attract women, they don't need to be fit, or healthy, or even have hair. They just need to be men. Rich, successful men choose from the cream of the crop, discarding and replacing, as each mate ages and fattens."[18] Or they place the male in precisely the same position of powerlessness as they imagine for the female. *The Adonis Complex*, perhaps the most widely reviewed study of male bodies, stresses the beautiful, highly shaped male body as the product of an obsessive concern with perfection generated by the impossible goals of masculine body shaping in our society.[19] The reduction of the complexity of the fat boy to the category of the patriarchal or the powerless forces it to lose much of its subtlety and complexity. This is certainly the case in the few books on male obesity as a social or a cultural "problem" existing only in contemporary America.[20]

The general view is that men have a problem, but it is not as much a problem as the anxiety that women have about their bodies. By interviewing a selected group of undergraduates at comparable American and Australian universities, Marika Tiggemann and Esther Rothblum tested the "social consequences of perceived weight."[21] When asked about their ideal weight, the women on average wanted to be nine pounds thinner while the men wanted to be one pound heavier. While only 20 percent of the participants actually were overweight, 50 percent felt themselves to be so, and women made up the majority of this percentage. The second part of the project examined to what extent stereotypes about the obese are prevalent in Western society. On average fat men and women were perceived by all participants as being warm, friendly, lazy, and less self-confident and not as attractive as their thinner counterparts. The authors conclude that women have "higher public body consciousness" (85) than men and that stereotyping persists, possibly leading to social adjustment problems. Yet this view seems to contradict the anxiety model in which the scope of men's body problems mirrors that of women. "When I look in the mirror," one young man said, "I see two things: what I want to be and what I'm not. I hate my abs. My chest will never be huge. My legs are too thin. My nose is an odd shape. I want what *Men's Health* pushes. I want to be the guy in the Gillette commercials."[22] And, it goes unsaid, I really am not fat! This denial makes therapy for obesity more difficult. Concerns with whether men have it good or have it just as bad as women are, of course, misleading. Masculinity is not simply a parallel construct to femininity but has its own complex history, as do the meanings attached to the fat boy's body.

Indeed, some of the recent biologically oriented literature on obesity has become gender sensitive. In a recent study of childhood nutrition Youfa Wang of the University of Illinois at Chicago claims that girls who experience sexual maturity between eight and fourteen are more likely than other girls to be obese, while in boys early developers are less likely to be obese. According to Wang, the gender differences observed in the association between sexual maturity and obesity are likely related to differences in biological development. In boys, for example, early developers were found to be significantly taller, but not heavier, than their average- or late-maturing counterparts. By comparison, early sexual maturity in girls was associated with both increased height and weight. If there is a difference it may well lie in how energy is used during maturation. With men energy is used to grow taller, but this is not the case with women.[23] Fat boys may well be different from fat girls from conception! They are certainly different in terms of the meanings attached to their bodies.

The phrase "fat boy" will serve as shorthand in this study for the obese male. Elmer Wheeler pointed out that his rather obtuse (and rotund) publisher initially objected to his title: "I straightened out the publisher. Fat boys, I told him, have a habit of calling to each other, 'Hey, fat boy!' " In the medical literature of the mid–twentieth century on obesity the phrase of course appears in discussions of childhood obesity.[24] By the turn of the twenty-first century the fat boy had solidly entered American pop culture. Elton John and Bernie Taupin memorialized his unhappiness in their 1976 song "Fat Boys and Ugly Girls." In 1984 the Fat Boys, a rap group, had a smash single entitled (what else) "Fat Boys." But the fat boy has a much longer history, as we shall discover. The fat boy is not the nineteenth-century successful "fat man," who was often the subject of *New York Times* reports in 1887 about the various dinners and clambakes of New York's Fat Man's Association (9 September 1887). "Fat boy," rather, is a phrase redolent of the difference ascribed to men who are understood to be extremely fat, morbidly obese, large, corpulent, immoderate in body size. The terms shift from age to age, but the references are always clear. The fat boy defines something very concrete yet simultaneously very amorphous. Being obese, fatter than fat, changes what the culture represents as male. The fat boy is "Lardass, Snotface, Ugly Pig, Warthog, Stupid, Stinkbomb, Fart-tub, Greasebag," according to the brother of the protagonist of E. Annie Proulx's *The Shipping News* (1993).[25] Quoyle's "great damp loaf of a body" is the inheritance of his ancestors: "Some anomalous gene had fired up at the moment of his begetting" (2). In Peter Carey's dystopic account of an experiment using "fat men" as guinea pigs, " 'fat' entered slyly into the language as a new adjective, as a synonym for greedy, ugly, sleazy, lazy, obscene, evil, dirty, dishonest, untrustworthy. It was unfair. It was not a good time to be a fat man."[26] Obesity eats away at the idealized image of the masculine just as surely as it does at the idealized image of the feminine. In this world of deviant masculinity "thinness has become synonymous with beauty, and fatness with ugliness."[27] It is not "mere" fat, however, that shapes the images of these bodies. They are imagined at the far, pathological end of the spectrum of body size. They are "obese."

The word *obesity* has an odd double meaning. The Latin *obesus* refers to a body that is eaten away and lean as well as one that has eaten itself fat. It is the past participle of *obedere*, to devour. It seems to be introduced as a "vulgar" medical term equivalent to the Latin medical term *adiposa* in the seventeenth century, though Celsus and Roman medicine had used the term *obesitas*, a term also used by the poet Suetonius. (As we shall see in our discussion of Cervantes, this shift to the vernacular also occurs in other European contexts. Still, a slippage between "medical" labels for the fat body and popular, pejorative ones is also evident. The medical terms quite often become the popular ones, since they are already invested in a certain set of stigmatizing qualities.) Fat is both devoured and devours the body, making it unreadable and overly interpretable. Fat changes what we understand as male, distorts it, and then turns upon itself to give the fat body positive meanings. *Obesity* itself is a recent term, introduced into English in the seventeenth century with all of the overtones of the horridly expanded, already mirroring anxiety about the fat body.

It is of little surprise that the term *obesity* antedates (in English) the adjective *obese*. *Obesity* appears first in a French-English dictionary in 1611 as a translation of the "new" term *obesité*.[28] Tobias Venner's early seventeenth-century handbook of humoral good diet and health, where one of the first uses of the term *obesity* appears, notes that "a fat and grosse habit of body is worse than a leane, for besides that it is more subject to sicknes, it is for all corporall actions farre more unapt. They are more sickly that have grosse and full bodies, not onely because they abound with many crude and superflous humors, but also because they lesse (by reason of the imbicillity of their heat) resist extrinsicall and intrinsicall causes that demolish their health."[29] For Venner, a physician in Bath, lean is less evil, but "betweene these two habits there is a mean, which is neither too fat, nor too leane, or extenuated, and that verily is the best" (197). We fear obesity because we fear the meanings associated with fat. And these meanings have always been gendered. Indeed, by the nineteenth century the fear had a name — lipophobia.[30] It was a fear shared by men and women alike, but with different forms and different implications.

A FAT MAN IN A THIN CULTURE

Richard Klein has stressed the perversity of a culture that has so much food stressing the thin body as an ideal.[31] It is not merely thinness that is our ideal, however, but also a specific notion of masculinity. Always there has existed a need to draw

10

the distinction between acceptable and unacceptable fat, and acceptable and unacceptable masculinity. According to Peter Stearns, one of the best historians of fat, until the twentieth century "plumpness was associated with prosperity. In a period historically when most people were not assuredly prosperous, this was a key index. Second, plumpness was associated with good health in times when many of the most troubling diseases were wasting diseases like tuberculosis. And finally, plumpness was historically associated with good character, with cheerfulness, with balance."[32] For every glorification of "plumpness" before the twentieth century, however, there was also fear and anxiety about morbid obesity, about a plumpness gone out of control.[33] It is no accident that every classificatory system of medicine since Hippocrates has included the category of "morbid obesity," either as symptom or as etiology. In each of these systems the boundary also exists between the acceptably plump and the overtly obese. It is drawn at every stage of Western history. Yet it is also always different, with different contours, different borders, and different meanings given to both sides of the divide. Michel Foucault notes that the goal of all social control is to maintain the "permanent measure of a gap in relation to an inaccessible norm and the asymptotic movement that strives to meet in infinity."[34] This is the permanent gap that society imagines between healthy plumpness and morbid obesity. The gap, however, is what is real. These two categories are constantly shifting in relationship to one another. At certain points pleasing plumpness becomes morbid obesity, and a new body standard of plumpness is created. The gap is maintained.

Thus in popular positive representations the powerful are never obese, no matter what their actual body shape or weight. Fat, perhaps, as Henry VIII and Thomas Cardinal Wolsey were, as Edward VII and William Howard Taft were, but never obese. Louis XIV padded his body to look imposing, but in the twentieth century the idea that fat was either the cause or the result of low self-esteem separated the idea of power from the image of the truly fat man. Fat was permitted, but excess, as among the Greeks, was seen as a sign of weakness, not of strength. As William the Conqueror became obese in his old age, his grandson Henry II became a compulsive hunter and hawker to stave off the extreme size of his grandfather. Power and obesity seem incompatible in men.[35] At the same moment there are clearly cases of rulers whose fat bodies demand therapeutic interventions, for being too fat (in reality or myth) is detrimental to being seen as a leader. Sancho I, better known in history as Sancho the Fat, became King of Leon in 958 A.D. Deposed by his people, who felt that his fat made him unfit to rule, he appealed to Hisdai ibn Shaprut, the physician at the Court of Cordoba. Hisdai prescribed opiates that had the side effect of causing weight loss, and thus Sancho was able to regain his throne.[36] In the early fourteenth century John Gavalas, commander of the fleet of the Byzantine emperor, was advised to lose weight if he wanted to marry. He had to have "his Belly . . . go down and . . . appear slimmer and worthy to love because . . . he appeared disgusting with the asymmetry of his flesh." He hired an Italian physician who prescribed the Galenic method of baths (see chapter 1), emetics, exercise, and a diet excluding bread and meat.[37] He came to believe the image of himself as ineffectual because he was pilloried as obese.

The representation of the ruler as obese rather than fat is a comment on the ruler's character. The comic figure of the Whig politician Charles James Fox (1749–1806), portrayed in James Gillray's (1757–1815) caricatures as a latter-day, nasty Sancho Panza, is paired in the 1780s and 1790s with the rotund Prince of Wales (later George IV) as an emblem of dissolution and obesity.[38] Indeed, the writer and critic Leigh Hunt spent 1813 and 1814 in prison for writing in 1812 (among other things) that the Prince of Wales was a "fat Adonis of Fifty."[39] Gillray portrays the all-consuming misgovernment of the Prince Regent in the obese body of the ruler. In one image, *A Voluptuary under the Horrors of Digestion* (2 July 1792), the prince lies recumbent over the remains of a huge meal, literally bursting out of his already too tight clothes. He picks his teeth with a fork. Behind his chair a chamber pot overflows with some unnamed effluent onto a stack of unpaid bills. Behind him, on our right, stands a collection of jelly glasses, among them a small pot labeled "For the Piles." At his feet lie several books, including one entitled "Debts of Honor unpaid." Above him is hung a portrait of Luigi Cornaro, discussed in greater detail later in this book, who lived to be ninety-nine by abstemiously sipping water. Such obese figures of the time are juxtaposed with the figure of John Bull, stout but never obese in British representations, yet portrayed in contemporary French caricatures as an obese, all-devouring ogre.[40]

Being a truly fat man means more than merely not fitting into a culture of slim gymnasts and XXX movie hunks. It means not quite fitting into society as a whole. And society keeps on shifting the line between unhealthily fat and pleasantly plump. Hillel Schwartz writes: "Our sense of the body, of its heft and momentum, is shaped more by the theatre of our lives than by our costume. Our furniture, our toys, our architecture, our etiquette are designed for, or impel us toward, a certain kind of body and a certain feeling of weight."[41] We all sense that our society makes the obese or fat or corpulent body more visible because it does not fit. Yet this visibility is seen to have multiple, often conflicting meanings.

How has society defined the obese man? How has it represented his body and his soul? Is there a history of the medicalization of "fat" that can help us understand the meaning of the fat *male* body? All of these questions have a place in this study; all are central because much of the scientific work done on obesity over the past centuries makes clear gender distinctions. Medicine is "instrumentally symbolic," as Jean Comaroff observes, as it actively produces social categories. Medical representations, such as obesity, serve as metaphors, symbols, and icons to order experience and construct social and cultural boundaries both within and beyond the culture of medicine.[42] The meaning of the fat male body in the general as well as the medical culture seems to define the "problem" of fat in quite different ways than it does for the body of the woman.[43]

FAT AS DISABILITY

How slippery the concept of obesity truly is can be judged, perhaps, from the following thought experiment.[44] Let us look at the question of what a *disability* is. Obesity is now considered a disability, though for a long period of time it was not. The Americans with Disabilities Act (1990) states that impairment is a state that substantially limits major life activities. (Analogous definitions are used in the Canadian Charter of Rights and Freedoms [1994], the British Disability Discrimination Act [1995], and the Swedish Act Concerning Support and Services for Persons with Certain Functional Impairments [1993].) Obesity certainly does limit such activities. The obese, as we shall see, "continually encounter various forms of discrimination, including outright intentional exclusion, the discriminatory effects of architectural, transportation, and communication barriers, overprotective rules and policies, failure to make modifications to existing facilities and practices, exclusionary qualification standards and criteria, segregation, and relegation to lesser services, programs, activities, benefits, jobs, or other opportunities."[45] Under the regulations promulgated to enforce this act, "morbid obesity," defined as body weight more than 100 percent over the norm, is "clearly an impairment."[46] This rather arbitrary line means that to be covered by the Americans with Disabilities Act an individual cannot just be too overweight for a specific occupation. In one case the court held that the male "plaintiff cannot demonstrate that he was regarded as disabled on the basis of a specific job of his choosing."[47] What that means is that the question of defining obesity as a disability still remains fluid.

The definition of a disability seems to be rather specific even if the Supreme Court has recently been altering and limiting it. The World Health Organization, in its 1980 *International Classification of Impairments, Disabilities, and Handicaps*, makes a seemingly clear distinction among impairment, disability, and handicap. Impairment is an abnormality of structure or function at the organ level, while disability is the functional consequence of such impairment. A handicap is the social consequence of an impairment and its resultant disability. Thus cognitive or hearing impairments may lead to communication problems, which in turn result in isolation or dependency. Such a functional approach (and this approach was long the norm in American common and legal usage) seems to be beyond any ideological bias. This has changed very little in the most recent shift to the idea that disability is to be redefined on a scale of "human variation" that postulates the difficulties of the disabled as the result of the inflexibility of social institutions rather than their own impairment.

When, however, we substitute "obesity" for "cognitive impairment" in the functional model, there is suddenly an evident and real set of implied ethical differences in thinking about what a disability can be. What is obesity? While there is a set of contemporary medical definitions of obesity, it is clear that the definition of those who are obese changes from culture to culture over time. Obesity is more than the body-mass index (wt/ht²), because even this changes in meaning over time.[48] Today in the United States and the United Kingdom people with a body-mass index between 25 and 30 kg/m² are categorized as overweight, and those with a body-mass index above 30 kg/m² are labeled as obese. Yet when the National Health and Nutrition Survey in 1999 recorded a 55 percent increase in obesity over three decades in the United States, it retrospectively used a body mass index of 30 to compute this figure.[49] What is fat and what is obese (the survey's two categories) shift over time.

Let us apply the rather straightforward World Health Organization standards of disability to the world of the obese. Is obesity the end product of impairment, or is it impairment itself? If it must begin with impairment, what "organ" is "impaired"? Is it the body itself? Is it the digestive system? Is it the circulatory system? Or is it the mind, the obese suffering from that most stigmatizing of illnesses, mental illness? Is obesity a mental illness that is the result of an addictive personality (where food is the addiction)?[50] Is addiction a sign of the lack of will? Is obesity a physical dependency, like heroin addiction? Is it a genetically preprogrammed "error" in the human body that expresses itself in psychological desire for food or the inability to know when one is no longer hungry?

Is the impairment of obesity like lung cancer in that it is the result of the voluntary consumption of dangerous substances like fat and carbohydrates? Certainly the World Health Organization believes this. Having struggled against tobacco consumption, it is now intent on launching a campaign against the rising levels of obesity by persuading manufacturers of processed foods to limit the amounts of added sugar.[51] Is such

16

food "addictive" like nicotine, or is it merely an interchangeable sign in society for those things we all desire but most of us can limit? Surely it is not possible to go without food, as one could go without cigarettes. Is the obese person mentally or physically disabled? On the other hand, can you be obese and mentally stable? Is obesity a disease of "civilization" caused by too fat or too rich or too well-processed food? Is its "cure" a return to "real" food or the rejection of food in general? Has it become the new "epidemic" to be charted by epidemiologists and combated by public health organizations?[52] If it is an epidemic, is it contagious or ubiquitous? Or is it a disease at all? Being "too fat is not usually regarded as a real 'disease' by most people — even those who are — those same people would probably rather pop a pill to reduce than go on a strict regime of diet and exercise."[53] As if diet and exercise were the sole cure for the myriad definitions of obesity. Is the social consequence of obesity isolation or a central place in society? Where on the scale of "human variation" are you placed in a world completely shaped by and for those who are not fat? Is obesity exogenous, or is it endogenous? Are you in the end treated like a social pariah or Santa Claus?

Many years ago Tristram Engelhardt, a leading medical ethicist, noted that "deciding what counts as health requires a decision about what counts as an appropriate goal for man. And to be sound, such a decision requires clear logic, breadth of reasoning, and creative sensitivity with respect to ethical issues. These are philosophical problems as much as they are medical problems."[54] I would add that these are cultural and historical problems as well and that obesity can serve as an elegant object of study for negotiating the complexities of defining the "healthy" and the "ill." The study of obesity in its cultural and social contexts provides a wide range of interlocking questions about the cultural construction of the body.

The role that gender plays is one further variable in the study of the cultural representation of the obese body. And this is true throughout the ages. In 1620, in the first use of the word *obesity* in an English text, Tobias Venner notes: "Those that feare obesity, that is, would not waxe grosse, be carefull to come often to our Bathes: for by the often use of them, according as the learned Physician shall direct, they may not only preserve their health, but also keep their bodies from being unseemingly corpulent."[55] This is a specific direction for men, as Venner immediately follows it with the statement that such baths are "also singularly profitable to women, for they helpe them of barrennesse, and of all the disease and imperfections of the matrice." For Venner the exemplary obese patient is male. This is of little surprise, as most pathological states (with the exception of those associated with gynecology and obstetrics) are seen as impacting on men to a greater degree, or at least in a different manner, than on women. It is the fat boy who is at the center of Venner's concern.

The concept of obesity thus implies in its very structure a focus on the male body. Yet for every question that we can ask about the meaning of obesity, a parallel one can be asked about gender. Who is a man? Is masculinity a biological or a cultural artifact? Can one choose or change one's gender? Does one's gender (or at least one's gender role) shift when one has same-sex partners? How do nation-states create ideal males and to what purposes? Is "masculinity" merely a sham, to be invested with whatever qualities you think are possible and able to shift from time to time and place to place, or does it have some limitation in gender roles or sexual anatomy? Can you be less than a man? Can you be more than a man?

The question of how the masculine is defined is not unimportant in the few contemporary studies of obesity. According to Jeffrey Sobal and his colleagues at Cornell, there is a high correlation between being married and being overweight, primarily in the case of men.[56] Using the results of the National Survey of Personal Health Practices and Consequences administered in 1979–80, they suggest that married men are more likely to be obese than single men or married women. The cause may well be the persistence of traditional masculine gender roles, as men may be less physically active in marriage and "eat more regularly and abundantly" (920) than when they were single. They comment that weight control often emerges as an important tool in mate selection for men, so that once they are no longer on the "marriage market," there is substantially less interest on their part in diet and exercise. The authors suggest that one of the implications of this study might be felt in the treatment of fat men. If "marital status influences obesity" (920) for men, therapeutic methods might take into account the marital role and in turn be more successful in helping patients lose weight. Fat married men are different from unmarried men, and both are different from their respective female counterparts. The unmarried Immanuel Kant prefigured this argument in his essay "Von der Macht des Gemüts, durch den blossen Vorsatz seiner krankhaften Gefühle Meister zu sein" (Overcoming unpleasant sensations by mere reasoning; 1797) when he wrote that most of the long-lived people he read about or knew were married but that unmarried people preserve, for the most part, their youthful appearance longer.[57] Marriage keeps you alive (if fat), but bachelordom preserves your vitality.

If, once married, men do not seem to need to remain attractive and have access to the means of gaining weight in their home life, then the very notion of a hobbled masculinity seems to be built into the image of the fat man. He is now beyond desire, except for food. Yet the image of the heterosexual male as defining the obese man is a cultural trope. The protagonist of Kingsley Amis's *One Fat Englishman* (1963), Roger Micheldene, is concerned with "keeping hidden the full enormity of his fatness" when he is off to seduce women: "Recent experience suggested that that belly, exposed in a moment of inattention or abandon, could cause total withdrawal of favours previously granted."[58] In Salman Rushdie's first novel, *Grimus* (1977), a fantasy work centering on a quartet of misfits, one of them, Virgil Jones, "gross of body," is in love with the hunchbacked Dolores O'Toole: "They loved each other and found it impossible to declare their love. It was no beautiful love, for they were extremely ugly."[59] When they finally do make love, their "disfiguration [is] transformed into sexuality" (50): "Her hands grasping great folds of his flesh. . . . It's like making bread, she giggled, pretending to work his belly into a loaf" (50). Only the disfigured may love the disfigured, and in the rhetoric of the novel the fat boy is as disfigured as the hunchbacked woman.

The image of deviant bodies attracting can also be seen in American popular culture, as in the first season of the TV series *Ally McBeal*. In the episode "The Promise" (air date 27 October 1997) the overweight attorney Harry Pippen (Jay Leggett) collapses in court and is revived by Ally McBeal (Calista Flockhart) in her most anorexic mode, by mouth-to-mouth resuscitation. Pippen falls in love with her and walks away from his upcoming marriage to his fiancée, Angela (Rusty Schwimmer), a very large woman who accidentally cracks Ally's back when she hugs her to thank her for saving Pippen. After much confusion the episode ends with their marriage. Angela notes, "Sometimes when you hold out for everything, you walk away with nothing." Marriage seems to her better than nothing. Sexuality thus may be purposefully eliminated from the image of the fat boy.

The quintessential fat boy's novel in American literature is

John Kennedy Toole's *A Confederacy of Dunces* (1980). Toole's protagonist, Ignatius J. Reilly, opens the novel waiting for his mother and "shifting from one hip to the other in his lumbering, elephantine fashion . . . [sending] waves of flesh rippling beneath the tweed and flannel, waves that broke upon buttons and seams."[60] Reilly's New York, Jewish, college girlfriend Myrna Minkoff had failed in her many attempts to seduce him because "my stringent attitude toward sex intrigued her; in a sense I became another project of sorts" (137). Are fat men asexual, or are they perceived as asexual, or are they made asexual by marriage? Is their sexuality damaged by their fat, or does their fat damage their sexuality? Are all fat men heterosexuals or merely repressed homosexuals hiding under a veil of obesity?

FAT GODS AND THE NORMAL MAN ON THE STREET

What happens when we try to imagine a body that is both "fat" and "male"? Most representations of the godhead in the West are of the ascetic male body of God, as in the battered, pierced, emaciated body of Christ in Mathis Grünewald's *The Isenheimer Altar* (1513–15). But there is another side to the image of the godhead (or *his* manifestations): "fat" or huge or gargantuan male gods, ranging from the image of the divine body in the kabala, to the enlightened Buddha sitting under the Bo tree, to, at least, Thomas Nast's fat Santa Claus. (There is of course also a radically starved Buddha — the Fasting Bodhisattva — whose thinness mocks that of the ascetics.) St. Nicholas, then Sint Nikolass, then Sinterklass in the Old World, were, to a greater or lesser extent, figures of wrath, never afraid to leave coal and soot for misbehaving children. St. Nicholas was a thin, wan figure, becoming fat only in the United States with Clement Clarke Moore's poem "A Visit from St. Nicholas" (1823): "He had a broad face and a little round belly, / That shook when he laughed like a bowlful of jelly. / He was chubby and plump." It should come as no surprise that "it was in America that Santa put on weight."[61] This beneficent, tamed, secular American Santa Claus, whom no one needs to fear, is very different from the images of the drunken and sexual Selinus and Bacchus, whom one did need to fear. They in turn provide a classical gloss on the "fat god," but these are but aspects of a male godhead seen as obese and out of control. Santa Claus cannot be such a fat boy. Santa has none of the licentious sexual attributes that are usually attributed to the fat gods of the West. Indeed, when this meaning is transgressed, a conflict arises in society's response. Thus in Milos Forman and Oliver Stone's film *The People versus Larry Flynt* (1996), one major criticism of Larry Flynt's (Woody Harrelson) disrespectful attitude toward American icons is his treatment of Santa Claus. The prosecuting attorney opens his questioning of Flynt with this image (my transcription):

PROSECUTING ATTORNEY: What you are about to see is going to take your breath away. *Hustler Magazine* depicts men and women posed together in a lewd and shameful manner. *Hustler Magazine* depicts Santa Claus posed in a lewd and shameful manner.

DEFENSE ATTORNEY: What is he talking about?

LARRY FLYNT: (*whispers in his ear*)

DEFENSE ATTORNEY: Jesus Christ, Larry.

PROSECUTING ATTORNEY: Mr. Flynt, could you turn to page 77? Could you describe to this jury what is on page 77, please, sir?

LARRY FLYNT: It is a picture of Santa Claus.

PROSECUTING ATTORNEY: What is Santa Claus doing?

LARRY FLYNT: He's talking to Mrs. Claus and holding in his hand what appears to be a large erect penis.

PROSECUTING ATTORNEY: And would you read the caption beneath the cartoon, please?

LARRY FLYNT: It says, "This is what I've got to ho-ho-ho about."

The sexual taboos about the fat male body are real, and they evoke a range of responses. The offense here is that the iconic image of Santa Claus has been sexualized. An analogous case is the 1921 scandal surrounding the accusation that Roscoe "Fatty" Arbuckle had ruptured a young woman's bladder because of his weight while having sex with her. Arbuckle had "capitalized on his fat to enter the neutral realm of the child" in his cinema roles.[62] It was impossible to imagine him (or Santa) as a sexualized fat boy.

It is hard to imagine a sexual fat man in modernity. At the beginning of the twentieth century, in Edna Ferber's "The Gay Old Dog" (1917), Jo Hertz, an old bachelor, is condemned to a single life by his demanding sisters and mother.[63] At fifty he was fat, his body rebelling in "his fat-encased muscles" when he tried to look youthful (12). After a love affair destroyed by the demands of his family, he falls into a bachelor's life as his sisters move on to their own married or professional lives. He becomes "a rather frumpy old bachelor, with thinning hair and a thickening neck" (19). At the beginning of the Great War he is watching the troops march down Michigan Avenue as they go off to war when a voice behind him shouts, "Let me by! I can't see! . . . You big fat man! My boy's going by — to war — and I can't see!" It is his former lover, now married, whose son is marching. He sees the boy — "picked him assuredly as his own father might have" (26). He returns home, where his sisters confront him about his social life, and he turns on them: "You two murderers! You didn't consider me, twenty years ago. . . . Where's my boy! You killed him, you two, twenty years ago. And now he belongs to somebody else. Where's my son that should have gone marching by today?" (27). Jo is rendered impotent by his family, his boy the public sign of his thwarted reproductive drive.

At the end of the century, in Eddie Murphy's 1996 remake of Jerry Lewis's *The Nutty Professor* (1963), Buddy Love, the svelte Hyde to the obese Professor Sherman Klump's Jekyll, is hypersexual. Indeed, his first action when he is transformed into a thin, sexy man is to look down and say, "Shit, I can see my dick." Hypersexuality is a quality ascribed to the premodern fat boy, but repressed in modernity. If God can be an unsexed fat boy, what other meanings can fat male bodies have?

Both these questions, of what fat is and what a man is, assume the existence of a "normal" ideal of both weight and masculinity. It is no surprise that in common law the "normal" is male. The law has exhibited "an unwillingness or inability to recognize that theorizing a relation between masculinity and law may have any intellectual validity in the first place."[64] Yet it is assumed that there is a creature who is the definition of the "normal." (I avoid here the more technical term *normate*, coined by Rosemarie Garland Thompson to refer to people typically considered "normal.")[65] He is the reasonable man. The reasonable man is a "fictional" or "notional" person.[66] As Justice J. A. Laidlaw aptly describes him, he is "a mythical creature of the law whose conduct is the standard by which the Courts measure the conduct of all other persons and find it to be proper or improper in particular circumstances as they exist from time to time."[67] In 1856 Baron Alderson (the Victor Frankenstein of law?) created the reasonable man by furnishing the common-law world with a definition of negligence: "Negligence is the omission to do something which a reasonable man, guided upon those considerations which ordinarily regulate the conduct of human affairs, would do, or doing something which a prudent and reasonable man would not do. The defendants might have been liable for negligence, if, unintentionally, they omitted to do that which a reasonable person would have done, or did that which a person taking reasonable precautions would not have done."[68] In English law the reasonable man, the American "man on the street," has been described as "the man on the Clapham omnibus."[69] His Australian counterpart is "the man on the Bondi tram," and in Canada he may well be "the person on the Yonge street subway."[70] Yet even with this slightly more gender-neutral formulation, he remains male. In fact, A. P. Herbert, in his caricature of the reasonable man, goes further by attributing a personality — and perhaps neuroses — to the man who already has a form of transport. He writes of the reasonable man that he never "swears, gambles, loses his temper, . . . does nothing except in moderation, and even while he flogs his child is meditating on the golden mean. Devoid, in short, of any human weakness, with not one single saving vice, sans prejudice, procrastination, ill-nature, avarice, and absence of mind, as careful for his own safety as he is for that of others, this excellent but odious creature stands like a monument in our Courts of Justice, vainly appealing to his fellow citizens to order their lives after his own example."[71]

Thus, while the reasonable man is merely an imaginary character, the various descriptions and embellishments by the judiciary and the commentators attribute to him characteristics and personality traits that in turn can be used to further flesh out the identity of the reasonable man. His body cannot be that of a fat man; rather, it is the archetypal body that defines the normal male.

The fat boy remains a problem of our twenty-first-century culture. The normal body defines what the male should be and how the male body is seen. There is a fat identity that exists in contemporary culture. But how do people come to think of themselves as "fat" and thereby adopt a "fat" identity? And how do individuals cope with the problematic interactions that arise with the adoption of a fat identity? According to Douglas Degher and Gerald Hughes, the movement toward the realization that one is fat occurs in several steps.[72] One goes from being teased in school (being called "chubby"), to identifying as "chubby" (one may not have thought about it before), to resigning oneself to being "chubby." In turn various coping behaviors are used, such as avoidance (I am simply not going to think about being fat) and compliance (I will diet to please my mother/father/boyfriend/girlfriend, but not for myself). At that point one is obese but not yet a fat boy.

Stephen Gray, of Nottingham Trent University, examined more than two thousand men in a study on male obesity. He concluded, "The reality is that men's bodies are taking a turn for the worse, as they overtake women in the battle of the bulge, piling on the pounds faster than ever before and becoming more and more round shouldered." Fat men's bodies seem to be "readable" to everyone but fat men themselves. Gray scanned three-dimensional images of ten male volunteers to show them how they appeared. Only four correctly identified their own image. Gray notes that fat men deceive themselves in terms of their appearance: "Men tend to stand in front of the mirror and pull in their stomachs, and then think they look okay. When the men were shown their 3D images, some were aghast because they really did not know what they looked like."[73] Fat men are invisible even to themselves, for who wishes to embody unreasonableness? This would be "merely" a problem of self-perception, perhaps of interest to psychologists dealing with various forms of "body dysmorphic disorder," if it did not correlate to self-images of health. In the science of obesity it has been assumed that illness is the necessary correlation to fat: "The obese, therefore, inevitably becomes a sick person and an invalid. According to hereditary predisposition, his soil, his habits and surroundings, he will suffer from all the disorders caused by the slackening of the nutrition. He may suffer from fatty diabetes, gouty hypertension, from hepatitis or enteritis, from cardiac, varicose or renal troubles, have eczema or psoriasis, or Basedow's disease, be neurasthenic or have the neurosis of fear; but he will *always* be an old man before his time, having shortened his life by nearly half."[74] One early twentieth-century diet book states simply, "A fat man is an unhealthy man."[75] This also has a moral dimension — true even in the seventeenth century when Richard Browne states, in an even more basic manner, "Health with Virtue, and Diseases with Vice, run parallel."[76] The moral dimension has rarely been hidden; today we see it clearly if we study many of the representations of the obese male.

The reality seems to be that if you see yourself as fat, as stated in a recent study by Kenneth F. Ferraro and Yan Yu, you will also see yourself as ill. This is true of both genders and of African-American and White subjects. Self-rating of health by fat boys is always pathological, while extremely thin people show no such self-evaluation.[77] Today's fat boys understand illness as appropriate to their self-image. Yet this self-image seems to be more treatable in men than in women, as Hillel Schwartz notes: "The exogenous fat man, cheerful and responsive, was easier to treat. He was a familiar figure, a companionable creature of the sensuous moment, and his diet could be abbreviated without fearing for his health. Reducing his weight was a matter of will, conviction, and the restraint of impetuosity. Prescribe lean beef, laxatives, and golf. The endogenous fat woman was much harder to treat. She was haunted by history. She could not be held fully responsible for an inherently weak metabolism. Her plight was depressing."[78] The illness of the fat boy, as we shall see, has a quite different quality because of his gender, but ill he is and ill he remains until he reforms his body.

The French critic and philosopher Jean Baudrillard, in an attempt to understand the social configurations of fat in America, imagines the fat person's body as invisible in its intense visibility.[79] We can no longer see the body that seems to have no limits. It is a body now without shame. It is beyond ridicule. The fat body becomes a sign of a very human disease, for "there are no obese animals, just as there are no obscene animals" (30). But Baudrillard slides in seeing the "excessive superfluity" as sexless and diseased. There are no fat boys in Baudrillard's world — only fat ill people. They are metastases (quoting Franz von Baader) whose bodies are in revolt "as in cancer" (32). The fat person is beyond the rational, "in a total delirium" (33). The fat person is ill but "exceeds his own pathology. This is why he escapes both dietetics and psychopathology" (34). The reality is that the fat male body is defined by the world of medicine. The reasonable man is also the healthy man; the fat boy is neither of these. Clearly, it is in the world of dietetics that the link between the fat and the male body, perhaps sexless but certainly gendered, is made.

"I am fat. I am disgustingly fat. I am the fattest human I know. . . . Flesh drips from me like hot fudge off a sundae. . . . That fat is in itself above bourgeois morality. . . . We must train ourselves to confront the obese without judging, without thinking this man's fat is first-rate fat and this poor wretch's is grubby fat." So states Woody Allen in his "Notes from the

Overfed (after reading Dostoevski and the new 'Weight Watchers' magazine on the same plane trip)."[80] The monologist, parodying Dostoevski's madman, finds his lost god in food: "succulent chocolates, vegetables in sauce, wines, fish, creams and noodles, éclairs, and wursts totaling in excess of sixty thousand dollars." He ends with the claim that "fat is life, and fat is also death."

This would be parody except that in 2002 Southwest Airlines began charging overweight passengers for two tickets if they spilled over into their neighbor's seat. "We sell seats, and if you consume more than one seat, you have to buy more than one seat," said Beth Harbin, a Southwest spokeswoman.[81] Fat people's fat does have meaning. It is a sign of their extraordinary consumption of everything, including space. The response was immediate and direct. "It's just discriminatory and it's mean-spirited," said Morgan Downey, executive director of the American Obesity Association. "This is singling out a group that's been very heavily stigmatized rather than making some accommodations in their cabins." Tiny seats for large passengers. Neither excessively tall nor excessively smelly but only excessively fat people are impacted. Fat does indeed seem to have meaning as a sign of the imposition of bodies on one another.

FAT BOY'S POETRY

Let us look for a moment at two poems, both written by mid-twentieth century American poets. John Ciardi's "Washing Your Feet" is an interior monologue attempting to reflect on what a fat male must sense when he is no longer in control of his own body: "Washing your feet," it begins, "is hard when you get fat."[82] Washing one's feet and those of others is part of ritual and art, Ciardi notes: "To touch one's own body anywhere should be ritual."[83] Yet this is a ritual that fat has taken from the fat man; in the end "It is sad to be fat and to have dirty feet." The physician-poet Jack Coulehan's poem "The Six Hundred Pound Man" sings of the "six hundred pound man on two beds."[84] Now dead, he has become myth: "I see him now, rising in the distance, / an island, mountainous / and hooded with impenetrable vine." Where Ciardi's fat man is sad and dirty, Coulehan transforms the fat man into nature with his own insight: "I discover him beautiful." Yet fat men "wheeze" (Ciardi), and Coulehan's fat man "grunts." They are pathological cases, whether embodying negative or positive stereotypes. Neither would fit comfortably on the Clapham omnibus, the Bondi tram, the Yonge street subway, or even the Southwest Airlines seat. The fat boy or the fat man is an exception even to the law. The "normal" is a cultural standard to be found in all aspects of society from the law to medicine. The fat boy is not reasonable even in the implied claim that his masculinity is the default definition in law of the human being as the male. He is not normal; he is not a reasonable man. The body of the reasonable man is not a fat body. J. G. Fleming, for instance, argues that the reasonable man "is the embodiment of all the qualities we demand of a good citizen: and if not exactly a model of perfection, yet altogether a rather better man than probably any single one of us happens, or perhaps even aspires, to be."[85] Obesity is not one of the qualities that society sees in the model citizen, who must be healthy — at least not since the concept of the reasonable man strolled (upright and with due care and prudence) into the legal world. Moreover, if the reasonable man is better than most of us are, he is not fat, for we, the normal, the average, the acceptable, do not consider ourselves to be obese. We may be fat or corpulent or overweight or big-boned, but never obese. As A. L. Linden remarks: "The law has required of everyone a minimum level of performance, whether they are capable of it or not. It is not enough for an actor to be pleased that he did 'the best he knew how,' for the law 'does not attempt to see men as God sees them.' This may be hard on the dull and awkward person, but the general welfare of society demands reasonable conduct from everyone."[86]

The sense of physical activity connoted by the terms *performance, actor,* and *conduct* is inherent to the man on the street. Those for whom Linden suggests such standards are perhaps unattainable are the dull and awkward, the very words that might well be used to describe the obese. They are the modern, secular version of what Augustine would have recognized as persons guilty of slothfulness caused by gluttony. Body size and movement are read as having meaning. In our modern age the obese body is no longer overtly read as sinful; now it is tied to an image of the fat boy as condemned to a life of clumsiness, illness, and unhappiness. What, if not dull and awkward, is Jack Coulehan's "Six Hundred Pound Man" or the fat narrator of John Ciardi's "Washing Your Feet"?

ILLNESS AND FAT BOYS AGAIN

The fat boy's body is different from a normal body. He bears what Leslie A. Fiedler decries as the "grosser physiological abnormalities that have for so long haunted us." Now (as Fiedler wrote in the 1970s) these bodies "disappear forever — prevented, repaired, aborted, or permitted to die at birth[;] those of us who are allowed to survive by the official enforcers of the Norm will be free to become even more homogeneously beautiful."[87] This scenario of aesthetics and health has now targeted fat, the epidemic of the twenty-first century, replacing in America and Europe the public fascination with HIV/AIDS that dominated the past decades of our public concern. Indeed, in the world of HIV/AIDS the fat boy's body has come to be a marker of health![88] Thinness, as Tom Hanks showed in his role in Jonathan Demme's *Philadelphia* (1993), became a marker, a sign, for the appearance of the new disease. Julien Murphy quotes one mother speaking of her son: "Hardest of all was watching a young, healthy man turn into a gaunt, old one, fumbling and shuffling, uncertain and confused. I watched his hair, eyelashes and eyebrows grow sparse and dull. I watched him get so thin that it was too painful to sit on a chair."[89]

This was a thinness that evoked other historical moments of emaciation: "The AIDS body photographed as bone-thin and languorous in yellow light, appeared as haunting and eerie much like images of other gaunt and terrorized bodies — victims of famine, the bubonic plague, and Auschwitz survivors."[90] Thinness, not obesity, marks illness here, very much in line with images of consumptive diseases (tuberculosis or cancer) in Western history. The very image of the ill person with tuberculosis is tied to an unnatural (and inherently ugly) image of emaciation.[91] This thinness imposed on the body is the sign that marks the body of Franz Kafka's "The Hunger Artist" (1922). This man starves not because he wills himself thin but because he cannot find any food to his taste! Fat in this historical context marked a healthy body, but this fat was healthy plumpness, not chronic, morbid obesity.

Yet we can simultaneously speak of an epidemic of fat. Philip James, head of the International Obesity Task Force, observes: "This pandemic of obesity is remarkably recent. It pervades the whole world and it is escalating at an alarming rate. The actual practical causes may differ indeed, but we now know that there is obesity in practically every country we've been to and assessed. It's quite astonishing and we're now seeing all of the ghastly consequences of it."[92] But the "ghastly" fat boy has always been with us. He has always been a focus of fascination, concern, horror, interest, and that obsessive interest exists not primarily because of any "real" concern for men's health but because it presents the outer limits of the performance of masculinity. When we contemplate the fat bodies of formerly slim males, whether Elvis Presley, Orson Welles, or Marlon Brando, it is not the spectacle of declining health that horrifies us but the very collapse of our fantasy about the male body. The fat boy marks an anomalous state that rereads the body of the male in contradictory ways. The concern is a cultural one, but one that mirrors itself in law and medicine.

Fat Boys in the Cultural History of the West

Fat has been a pathological category in the West from the earliest state of medical culture. In ancient Greece it appears in texts ascribed to Hippocrates (440–340 B.C.E.). Hippocrates — or at least the approximately sixty texts of the Hippocratic corpus attributed to him — based his notion of health and illness on the balance of the humors, the *chymoi*. According to this view, these four crucial bodily fluids, blood, yellow bile, black bile, and phlegm, were found in all individuals, producing health when in balance and illness when one dominated the others. They also produced the visible aspects of the body that could be measured by the physician: blood made the body hot and wet, choler hot and dry, black bile cold and dry, and phlegm cold and wet. They were also correlated to the four ages of man — infancy, youth, adulthood, and old age — and to the essential aspects of the world: air, fire, earth, and water. The physician could affect the domination of one or the other humors by intervening, often with lifestyle or regimen changes, which entailed changing the food or activities of the patient. The humors were also the key to bodily shape and physique. Thus, a natural predisposition to phlegm resulted in fat. Each humor also determined temperament; the phlegmatic person (who was also fat) was pale, lazy, inert, and cool in character — as well as, of course, phlegmatic. Phlegm was "naturally" of water and old age. In humoral theory fat could either be a sign of indisposition, with the domination of phlegm to be treated by hot and dry foods, or a constitutional status (as in aging) in which your phlegmatic nature could be mitigated but not altered. In the first instance one was a fat patient, but not in the latter. Greek medicine was rooted in the practice of *diatetica*, the diet as the primary therapy, or to use a more modern phrase, "eating as healing." Greek physicians therefore also believed that there was a one-to-one relationship between foods and their effects. Dionysus of Carystus (in Euboea), who practiced in the fourth century B.C.E. and was known to the Athenians as the "younger Hippocrates," argued, like Hippocrates, for a completely causal relationship in dietetics.[1] Certain foods were not only healthful but also curative, just as a surfeit of others was the cause of illness; a central illness was obesity.

For the followers of Hippocrates fat and thin could be either "natural" antitheses or signs of illness in terms of the balance and unbalance of the humors. Thus fat reflected a pathological state of the body caused by imbalance. For the sufferer from fat as a sign of disease, there was also a clear distinction between fat men and fat women: "When unnaturally fat women cannot conceive, it is because the fat presses the mouth of the womb, and conception is impossible until they grow thinner" (*Aphorisms* V, XLVI).[2] But men "who are constitutionally very fat are more apt to die quickly than those who are thin" (*Aphorisms* II, XLIV), abandoning their families and their role in society, both paramount responsibilities in the ancient world. In all cases extreme fat fell in the realm of medicine: "Repletion too, carried to extremes, is perilous," Hippocrates observes (*Aphorisms* I, IV). Hippocrates does acknowledge that corpulence gave one a slight advantage over febrile diseases, but this was greatly outweighed by its pathological effects. Greek medicine, in seeing the dominance of phlegm as pathology, also evolved the concept of *polysarkia*, too much flesh. This term was reintroduced into Roman medicine by the North African Caelius Aurelianus in the fifth century c.e. in his *De morbis acutis et chronicis*. *Polysarkia* was the result of the imbalance of the humors, but also a quality of temperament. Thus lazy, phlegmatic persons also consumed too much food. They lived in a concomitant state of slothfulness and stupidity.[3] Such people violated the principle of constraint in all things. Constraint, Socrates frequently reminded his listeners, is the greatest good, and in complex ways the obese male violates this dictum.[4]

The line that the Hippocratic corpus assumes between acceptable fat and excessive fat (extreme repletion) is the difference between life and death. In Aristotle's essay on longevity fat is the quality that preserves warmth. Animals (including human beings) are "naturally moist and warm, and life too is of this nature, whereas old age is cold and dry, and so is a dead body."[5] Aristotle (384–22 b.c.e.) continues: "Fatty things are not liable to decay because they contain air . . . [and] air like fire does not become corrupt."[6] Animals that are "bloodless" are protected by their fat: "In animals the fat is sweet; for this reason, bees are longer lived than other larger animals."[7] Here too the line is assumed between acceptable "fatness" and pathological obesity.

Pathological obesity, not simple fatness, also redefines masculinity. In Act I of Aristophanes' *The Frogs* (405 B.C.E.) the fat role of the male is defined when the character of the parodied god Dionysus is called "pot-bellied" (*gastrôn*, or "fat-guts") by Charon (l. 199). Later on the character of Xanthias uses the word *gastêr*, which refers to Dionysus's wide girth (l. 663). The "guts" in question are comic because the word is a play on Dionysus's identity as a man. In the Greek *gastêr* — paunch or belly — combines with the word *pherein*, meaning to bear a child. At least in the second instance Greek allows for a suggestive linguistic link between a fat male body and the female body.[8] The association between unmanliness (even in a god) and fat stems from the notion of the fat male body as not man enough. It is a body out of control. In the Greek text *The Regimen of Health* the appropriate foods are prescribed for the appropriate seasons to reestablish the inner balance of the humors. The results of obesity were gender specific. For men obesity led to a shortened life span, for women the curse of infertility.[9] In ancient Greece men were defined by their ability to work and women by their ability to reproduce. Fat makes both difficult, if not impossible. Work for men, however, is not only physical labor but also entails the ability to think rationally. In the *Timaeus* Plato (427–347 B.C.E.) argues that there are four separate souls and that the highest soul (located in the head) was isolated from that of the belly so as to limit gastronomic impact on rational capabilities (70e).[10] Plato contrasts the false feelings of the stomach with the power and purity of reason (71a). Listen to your gut, he says, and you will submit to the base and the carnal.

Moreover, for the Greeks fat was *ugly*! Both Plato and Xenophon agreed to this but stressed that fat men were particularly unpleasant to see. Thersites was not only proverbial for his ugliness and sharp tongue but also, according to legend, the fattest warrior among the common Greeks who besieged Troy. Every reader of the *Iliad* cheers when Achilles, of beautiful body and spirit, strikes him down after he mocks Achilles' sorrow at the death of Penthesilea. Indeed, the compendium of Spartan laws collected under the name of Lycurgus outlawed obesity, stupidity, and ugliness. The Greek idea of ugliness connected with the fat body has a long history. In *The Symposium* Plato, or at least Alcibiades, likens Socrates to an ugly Silenus. Michel de Montaigne (1533–92) wrote, "It grieves me that Socrates, who was a perfect pattern of all great qualities, should, as reports say, have had so ugly a face and body, so out of keeping with the beauty of his soul, seeing how deeply he was enamored of beauty, how infatuated by it! Nature did him an injustice."[11] The Enlightenment explained Socrates' ugliness by reference to Cicero's tale of his encounters with the physiognomist Zopyrus. Socrates' face struck Zopyrus as that of someone who was inwardly dull, brutish, sensual, and addicted to the vice of drunkenness. Socrates agreed with this assessment, Cicero notes, but stated that he was able to raise himself above his temperament through the persistent pursuit of learning.[12] Ugliness and its internal parallel, bad character, can be checked by the autonomous individual's determined effort to change himself.

Obese ugliness was the antithesis of the beauty of the male as presented in classical Greek sculpture.[13] Works such as Lysippos's fourth-century B.C.E. "Farnese" Herakles, or Praxiteles' Apollo Sauroktonos, from more or less the same period, present the ideal body of the male on display. These statues were both male but were also exempla of masculinity; this was the way the "real" man should appear. Here the warrior and the athlete's bodies merge into the hard, sculpted body of the perfect (indeed, too perfect) male. One must remember that Greece was an *askesis* society, a society built around exercise. The Olympic games, recorded as early as 776 B.C.E., antedate the earliest written records of Greek medicine. The male of the age (and those who inherited the tradition) saw his body as a process in which the humors had to be balanced to achieve, if not the perfection of the sculptures, then at least the sense of beauty and health that the culture demanded.[14] These were the amateur athletes of the day, but their bodies were constantly on display and compared with the "functional" bodies of professional athletes. Being "fat" was simply unacceptable within this world of *askesis*. (One can note that these ideal bodies reappear as models for masculinity with the work of Johann Joachim Winckelmann and his contemporaries in the eighteenth century. The key example, as Gotthold Ephraim Lessing shows in his essay of 1766, is the early first-century *Laocoon*, attributed to Athanadoros, Hagesandros, and Polydoros of Rhodes. Somehow what had been an "ideal" type came to be admired as the typical body of the "beautiful" male in the post-Enlightenment world.)

Here we should remind ourselves, as the nineteenth-century German sociologist Georg Simmel does, that "nature is never ugly. It becomes ugly only when the person conceiving nature gives natural objects certain pretensions. The ape is ugly the moment one anthropomorphizes it."[15] This reading is a powerful one, even though a recent book looking at this issue assumes that animals are inherently different rather than imagined as different.[16] We make obesity ugly by giving it meaning. For the Greeks it was associated with all forms of misshapenness. In nature, of course, the large male body does not have meaning. We associate the vision of the beautiful with the healthy body and the imperfect, ugly body with a lack of virtue.

Strength, health, and beauty are the "virtues" of the Platonic body. It is the beautiful athlete who is admired as the image of perfection. And this even though (or because) Plato was fat! It is no accident that one of the most important commentators on diet in the ancient world was Herodicus of Selymbria, a trainer of athletes who used gymnastics to cure his own fat body.[17] Hippocrates stressed that "in athletes a perfect condition that is at its highest pitch is treacherous. Such conditions cannot remain the same or be at rest, and, change for the better being impossible; the only possible change is for the worse. For this reason it is an advantage to reduce the fine embonpoint quickly, in order that the body may make a fresh beginning of growth" (*Aphorisms* I, III). Here it is the professional *athletae* competing in the games, rather than the *agonistae* seeking health and strength through gymnastics, who needs to be thin. And the cure for the fat body was diet and exercise.

Early Roman medicine likewise saw obesity as pathological. Articulated in the works of the Alexandrian physician Celsus (fl. 30 C.E.) is the assumption that there can be a natural predisposition to fat. It is a sign of disease: "The obese, many of them, are throttled by acute diseases and difficult breathing; they die often suddenly, which rarely happens in the thinner person."[18] (Celsus uses the phrase "Obesi plerumque acutis morbis.") Its indicator (and all meanings of fat for Celsus are associated with very specific physical and moral signs) is too loose skin. It is as if the body were asking to be filled with fat. Celsus suggests tepid salt-water baths, hard exercise, food of an austere kind, and restricted sleep.[19]

More important is the shift undertaken in the first century when Galen (129–c. 216 C.E.) began to rethink the basic categories of Hippocratic medicine. He dismisses mere "empiricism," as per the Hippocratic method, and demands a theoretic underpinning to medical knowledge. While the Hippocratic physicians used foodstuffs to treat the imbalance of the humors, Galen sees the natural world as the very source of the illness from which human beings suffer. It is not the weak will of the phlegmatic individual that leads to *polysarkia*, but the very nature of food itself. For Galen, in "On the fat and lean mode of life," the causes of illness lie in those things that are *res contra naturum* (non-natural; i.e., not the humors): *aer* (light and air), *cibus et portus* (food and drink); *motus et qies* (movement and rest), *somnux et vigilia* (sleeping and waking), *exkreta et sekreta* (metabolism), and *affectus animi* (affect).[20] This argument places "nurture" as equivalent to "nature." Galen suggests "quick exercise" as a cure for obesity. He provides food, "but not of a very nourishing description," to be consumed only after exercise.[21] The cause of obesity lies in the natural products of the world consumed in excess. All are necessary and natural, but used improperly they can create illness. Following Galen, in the seventh-century writings of the Alexandrian physician Paul of Aegina, obesity is a problem only when it is "immoderate." Since "warm temperament renders the body lean," it is this state that should be created in fat people: "Active exercise, an attenuated regimen, medicines of the same class, and mental anxiety bring on the dry temperament, and thereby render the body lean." Paul of Aegina also recommends that diuretics and small amounts of food (in proportion to exercise taken and preferably only once a day) should be prescribed.[22]

With Galen, what had been the theory of the bodily fluids became a means of speaking about natural tendencies inherent in the body and the way that the body interacts with the world. At the beginning of the nineteenth century Edward Dickinson could write in his *Regimen of Health and Longevity: A Poetical Invitation*:

The *mens sana in corpore sano*
From temp'rance, labour, and contentment, flow,
From genial fruits of garden, orchard, field —
Milk, honey, water recently distill'd;
Which no vile salts, no caustic oils display.[23]

These notions about the relationship between food and health did not vanish with the rise of modern science and medicine in the late nineteenth and twentieth centuries. The food critic Jeffrey Steingarten notes that today there are "three related beliefs: first, that all foods are either poisons, which make you fat and feeble, or medicines, which make you sleek and lovely; second, that raw vegetables, including salad and crudités, fall into the medicine category; and third, that the plant kingdom has been put there by some benign force for man's pleasure and well-being."[24] Another critic has labeled this "healthism," where the "healthiness of food has become more important than its taste. . . . According to such 'healthism,' thinness equals health, whereas fatness equals illness."[25] Galen would have been quite comfortable with that formulation but very ill at ease with Steingarten's deconstruction of its implications.

The complex traditions of Hippocratic and Galenic medicine form the medieval view of the obese body. In the medical school at Salerno, in the thirteenth century, the *Regimen sanitatis salernitanum* (Salernitan regimen of health) was composed. A book of verses attributed to Arnald of Villanova (1240–1311), it provides practical guidelines for good living but also definitions of the healthy and pathological bodies. Extraordinarily popular, it summarized and formed much of the later view of obesity. In a seventeenth-century English translation it provides a snapshot of the humoral obese body:

> Men that be flegmatik, are weak of nature,
> Most commonly of thick and stubbed stature.
> And fatnesse overtaketh them amain,
> For they are slothfull, and can take no pain.
> Their sences are but dull, shallow and slow,
> Much given to sleep, whence can no goodnesse grow,
> They often spet: yet natures kind direction,
> Hath blest them with a competent complexion.[26]

Thus the phlegmatic fat man is also not much of a man. He cannot stand pain, he is lazy, and he is nonproductive. There is, however, a healthy fat that dines on "sweet wine, delicious meats, eggs that are rare / Over ripe figs and raisins, these appear / To make the body fat, and nourish nature, / Procuring corpulence, and growth of stature" (7). This fat can itself become pathological but is of a different nature, because of a different source, than the inherent obesity of the phlegmatic body. Food can cause illness, as Galen states, but a "healthy" fat is the result of eating without overindulgence. The cure for overindulgence is to eat foods with the antithetical humoral traits from those of the fat person. Thus drinking vinegar (which is dry and cool) as therapy for the obese body (wet and cool) "unto fat folks, greatly doth no good" (19).

For the Greeks (and perhaps still for many of us) humoral theory informed the temperament, and fat was an aspect of the entire personality as it interacted with the world. Galen follows Aristotle's law of the golden mean — everything in moderation — but he understands this medical rule as applicable on a case-by-case basis and not to all human beings.

44

Each person is different in regard to his or her interaction with the world, and one must seek one's own golden mean. All philosophy since Aristotle, states the German-Jewish philosopher Franz Rosenzweig, has dealt with death, desiring to transcend it through universal reason.[27] The golden mean in classical medicine is one further aspect of this goal. Come to an understanding of how you can control the body, and you will live, if not forever, then longer than everyone else. This is presumably done by implementing the idea of the golden mean in one's life, thus influencing one's interaction with the world and how one is viewed within the world.

The ancient literature on longevity and other forms of body control incorporates concerns with the dangers posed by obesity. Thus the idea of the normal and the reasonable continues to haunt the image of the fat man. The quality of personality most closely associated with fat in the historical literature is stupidity. Today young children describe obese children shown in silhouette as "lazy," "dirty," "stupid," as people who "cheat" and "lie." Physicians are not much better than the children. They describe their obese patients as "weak-willed, ugly, and awkward."[28] These power images seem to be part of the cultural vocabulary of male obesity.

FAT BOYS AMONG THE JEWS

Historically, the Jews spent relatively little time focusing on the representation of the fat male body. Such a body is evoked by the biblical figure of Eglon, King of Moab, who oppressed the children of Israel for eighteen years.[29] His fat male (*ish bari me'od*) body was destroyed by the left-handed hero Ehud (Judg. 3:17, 22). Indeed, the Old Testament even describes how Eglon's fat closes about the blade when he is pierced. Ehud smuggles his sword into the presence of the king by wearing it on the "wrong-side," or at least the wrong side for right-handers. Ehud is "treacherous and sneaky; perhaps the culture of ancient Israel thought those descriptions to be synonymous, at least stereotypical."[30] As for the fat king, his guards do not even notice that he has been disemboweled until they smell his feces. Is this a case of one deviant body destroying another? The Talmudic fat male body was a deviant one, but not particularly a dangerous one. Rather, there was a sort of fascination with this body. The Talmud even asks whether very fat men, such as Rabbis Ishamel ben Yose and Eleazar ben Simeon (second century), could ever reproduce because of their huge bellies. (We will see more of the Talmudic representation of fat rabbis in chapter 4.) Jewish attitudes toward such obesity, however, were clearly defined by the model of the lack of self-control. Not yet a "sin," obesity was a sign of the lack of self-discipline appropriate for a real man, a real scholar, and could be punished.[31] In the classic work of the twelfth-century Iberian physician-philosopher Maimonides on dietetics, the *Regimen of Health*, there is no sense that obesity was a moral or even a medical problem (at least for the rulers for whom Maimonides wrote), while sexual overexertion is noted as such a problem.[32] However, it was still viewed as an important health issue with repercussions for the body of the individual; Maimonides treated the condition of "obese old men" with medication, exercise, massage, and baths.[33] His work provides a synthesis of Galenic medicine and the work of the Arabic physician Ibn Sina (Avicenna, 980–1037), whose *Kitah al-Quanun* (The canon) includes a detailed discussion of obesity in its fourth book.

It was only in modernity that the Jew's body came to represent all of the potential for disease and decay associated with the modern body of the fat boy. In modern medicine there has been a preoccupation with a claimed Jewish predisposition to diabetes. The nineteenth-century practice of labeling Jews as a "diabetic" race was a means of labeling them as inferior. The Parisian neurologist Jean Martin Charcot, in the fall of 1888, described to Sigmund Freud the predisposition of Jews to specific forms of illness, such as diabetes, stating that "the exploration is easy" because the illness was caused by the intramarriage of the Jews. Jewish "incest" thus left its mark on the Jewish body in the form of diabetes, as well as on the Jewish soul. (Indicative of his depreciatory attitude in regard to the Jews, Charcot's letter to Freud uses the vulgar "juif" rather than the more polite "Israélite" or more scientific "sémite.")[34] However, there were further views of why Jews were predisposed to this illness. The British eugenicist George Pitt-Rivers attributed the increased rate of diabetes among the Jews to "the passionate nature of their temperaments." He noted that by the 1920s diabetes was commonly called a "Jewish disease."[35]

Over and over again, however, the obesity inherent in the Jew's body (and soul) was seen as the cause of the illness. Often the power of the racial model overwhelmed any specificity of gender, even though the seemingly ungendered term *Jew* in this context was always understood to be the male Jew. Fat Jews are assumed to be fat Jewish men unless otherwise stated. The "Oriental races, enervated by climate, customs, and a superalimentation abounding in fats, sugar and pastry will inevitably progress towards the realization of fat generations, creating an extremely favourable soil for obesity."[36] Even in the Diaspora the assumption was that the Jew was diabetic because of his predisposition to fat: "All observers are agreed that Jews are specially liable to become diabetic. . . . A person belonging to the richer classes in towns usually eats too much, spends a great part of his life indoors, takes too little bodily exercise, and overtakes his nervous system in the pursuit of knowledge, business, or pleasure. . . . Such a description is a perfectly accurate account of the well-to-do Jew, who raises himself easily by his superior mental ability to a comfortable social position, and notoriously avoids all kinds of bodily exercise."[37] Jews inherited their tendency toward fat because of their lifestyle: "Can a surfeit of food continued through many generations create a large appetite in the offspring; alternatively, can it cause a functional weakness of their weight-regulating mechanism?" asks W. F. Christie. He answers: "Take, for instance, the Hebrews, scattered over the ends of the earth. Probably no race in the world has so apparent a tendency to become stout after puberty, or is more frequently cited as an example of racial adiposity. It is also probable that no nation is so linked in common serfdom to their racial habits and customs. [Elliot] Joslin says of the present generation of Jews: 'Overeating begins in childhood, and lasts till old age.' The inheritance of large appetites and depressed weight-regulating mechanism may exist in them, although they show no other signs of the latter; whereas the inheritance of fat-forming habits is certain."[38] Thus, Jews inherit the compulsive eating patterns of their ancestors and are therefore fat already as children. Their obesity and their diabetes are a reflection of their poor hygienic traditions, precisely the opposite of the claims of nineteenth-century Jewish reformers who saw Judaism as the rational religion of hygiene. Indeed, the "oriental" Jew presents the worst-case scenario for this line of argument. Max Oertel, perhaps the most quoted authority on obesity at the beginning of the twentieth century, states, "The Jewesses of Tunis, when barely ten years old, are systematically fattened by being confined in dark rooms and fed with farinaceous articles and the flesh of dogs, until in the course of a few months they resemble shapeless lumps of fat."[39] Here the fantasy about the "oriental" body in the West is heightened by the Jews feeding their daughters nonkosher food, much like Luther's fantasy of the Jew's body and food that we shall discuss later.

From the nineteenth century diabetes had been seen as a disease of the obese, and in an odd set of associations the Jew was implicated as obese due to an apparent increased presence of diabetes among Jews. According to a turn-of-the-century specialist, mainly rich Jewish men were fat.[40] Rather than arguing for any inborn metabolic inheritance, however, he states that the predisposition is the fault of poor diet among the rich — too much rich food and alcohol, this being yet another stereotype of the Jew. Yet the other side of the coin was amply present. At the beginning of the twentieth century scientists began to explore the relationship between the predisposition of the Jews to diabetes and the assumed relationship between diabetes and obesity. One physician noted that "one in twelve obese Gentiles develops diabetes, [and] no less than one in eight obese Jews develop it. This, it is suggested, is to be explained by the fact that a fat Hebrew is always fatter than a fat Gentile, and that it is the higher grade of obesity which determines the Semitic preponderance in diabetes."[41] The assumption about fat and the "oriental" race is one that would come to haunt discussions of the meaning of fat.[42] When William Sheldon developed his "somatotypes" in the 1940s (see chapter 5) he observed that Jews show an exaggeration in each of his body types. Thus fat Jews are somehow fatter than fat non-Jews.[43] More recent studies of obese Jews look at the complex behavior patterns that occur when religious demands for fasting and the psychological predisposition of the obese come in conflict.[44]

Today the general consensus is that diabetes is not particularly a Jewish illness. Research now follows the so-called thrifty genotype hypothesis suggested in 1964. Simply stated, it has been observed that when mice are transferred from a harsh to a benign environment, they gain weight and are hyperglycemic. Thus the assessment of first-generation groups of immigrants to the United States in the late nineteenth century or to Israel today finds a substantially higher rate of diabetes. The initial groups, for example, the Yemenites, who immigrated to Israel from a harsh environment, showed an extremely low index of diabetes when they arrived in Israel. This index, however, skyrocketed after just a short time of living in their new environment. Thus, diabetes and obesity seem to be an index of a failure to adapt rapidly to changed surroundings.[45]

Yet fat still is imagined as a Jewish issue. The columnist David Margolis, writing in the *Los Angeles Jewish Journal* in 2002, observes: "A lot of people also consider fat a Jewish issue. According to a recent survey in the New York City area, Jewish families consume 'almost double' the amount of cake and donuts that non-Jewish families do and more than twice as much diet soda and cottage cheese. A professional in the eating-disorder industry claims that Jews tend to choose food over addictions to other substances. Food is just another drug, after all, the cheapest, most easily available, most socially acceptable mood-altering substance. Is it merely a coincidence that Alcoholics Anonymous was founded by two Christian men, while Overeaters Anonymous was founded by two Jewish women?"[46] The image of the overfed Jew, central to the culture that needed to see the "oriental" disease of diabetes as an essential aspect of the corrupt Jewish soul, now has a place in American popular culture about the Jewish body. Yet here it is transformed into the body of the Jewish woman, as "fat" in the United States "is a feminist issue."

Between the biblical and the modern discussions of the fat Jewish male came the powerful tradition of early Christian (Pauline) attitudes toward the body. Medical notions of the ill body of the Jew were impacted by this tradition.[47] Health became a powerful metaphor in early Christianity, especially in terms of the relationship between the newly healthy body of the Christian and the sick body of the Jew.[48] With Christianity (most readily seen in St. Augustine's *Confessions*) the submission to the temptation to overeat was written on the body in the form of fat. *Gula* is one of the seven deadly sins for *all* people, men and women, yet it seems to have a special place in the world of men.[49] Yet Augustine, as a man, writes that he struggles each day with the desire to eat and drink even more than he does with sexual lust: "In the midst of these temptations I struggle daily against greed for food and drink. This is not an evil which I can decide once and for all to repudiate and never to embrace again, as I was able to do with fornication."[50] For the seduction of food and what it signifies, the fat body haunts Augustine's sense of himself. He sees food as both necessary for health and a force for healing, but only within strict limits: "I look upon food as a medicine. But the snare of concupiscence awaits me in the very process of passing from the discomfort of hunger to the contentment, which comes when satisfied. For the process itself is a pleasure and there is no other means of satisfying hunger except the one, which we are obliged to take. . . . Health and enjoyment have not the same requirement" (236). The desire for food is itself the Devil present in the body. He cites Paul's assertion that "we gain nothing by eating, lose nothing by abstaining" (1 Cor. 8:8). This is a basic struggle to control desire and the very form of the body. Augustine makes the ideal body the body divine;

as in the Platonic notion of beauty it is beyond the material.

In his *City of God* Augustine links the carnal pleasures of the flesh to sins of the soul. They are the same. He condemns with equal verve the Epicurean philosophers who "live after the flesh, because they place man's highest good in bodily pleasure," and the Stoics "who place the supreme good of men in the soul, live after the spirit." The Epicureans also claim that "pleasure is very largely a matter of physical health" and the Stoics that "only the wise are beautiful."[51] Augustine quotes Paul over and over again on the need to control carnality and the fallen nature of the soul. The ideal body is to be found only in heaven, Augustine describing heavenly bodies as possessing "a wondrous ease of movement, a wondrous lightness."[52] Here the image of the perfectly light and slim divine body is in contrast to the mortal and sinful one. The crucial early Christian text is again from Paul's letters (1 Cor. 8:1): "Knowledge puffs up, but love builds up." Fat, as a sign of gluttony, is a reflection of the prideful nature of humans. It is often linked to *acedia*, sloth, the deadly sin that is part of the tradition of the representation of madness in the West. The puffed-up body is also the spirit that is so unwilling to act as to be a sign of moral decay and mental instability.[53] For Augustine this is his *male* body, in which all desires seem confused and interchangeable. It is the male body that is most at risk from inaction and desire. St. Thomas Aquinas restates this limitation in Pauline terms when he preaches that when we are "meditating upon all these things, let us not give our minds to delights, but to what is the end of delights. Here on earth it is excrement and obesity, hereafter it is fire and the worm."[54] If for Paul all humans are damned by their flesh, Aquinas needs to stress this once again, seeing us trapped in our fallen bodies by our natural functions — eating and excreting.

By the early modern period the religious, ascetic castigation of the body through the refusal to eat and drink, except in minute amounts, had become a sign of moral virtue in the West. In this there is a distinction between the gigantic and the obese male body. The long history of the skinny bodies of saints, so well examined by students of "holy fasting," is paralleled by a litany of the fat bodies of sinners.[55] During the Renaissance the notion of the fat man as the condemned body on his way to Hell (as in Giotto's paintings) merges with the huge male body of Rabelais's Gargantua (1532–64). Rabelais's figure is huge, reflecting his extended (eleven-month) gestation period and the extraordinary feast of tripe that his mother consumed. In the heavy satire of the text this is how fat boys are made. It is the male giant Gargantua who first arrives on the scene. His huge body, a body that dominates the landscape, is not obese (in a contemporary pathological sense) but gigantic in all of its qualities. Rabelais was himself a physician and cites in his prologue the appropriate classical references to excess (Plato and Galen) so that his drawing of a distinction between merely large and obese would be meaningful. Thus the mock-heroic aspect of the figure of Gargantua is tied not to any pathological fatness but to a gigantism that has its purposes in the course of the text. Giants, as Lorraine Daston and Katharine Park show elegantly, are the products of excess.[56] It is excess, however, of a different order than obesity. The figures in Rabelais's world are huge because they consume everything, and they consume everything because they are huge. Food, and therefore gluttony, is central to their representation, yet they are not obese in the pathological sense. They are related to the medieval giants, who are simply oversized exempla of human beings. Here too an arbitrary line is drawn between the unacceptable and the tolerable, at least within the world of late medieval satire. It is the identical boundary to that suggested by Michel Foucault. Even in the world of the giant, one can at any point in the history of dietetics distinguish between the "merely" fat and the chronically "obese."[57] Medieval masculinity is constructed along quite different lines.[58]

The gigantic can become dangerous once it is read in Christian terms. One of the negative figures in Edmund Spenser's *The Faerie Queene* (1590–96) is the giant Orgoglio (whose name means "arrogant pride" in Italian), associated in the poem with swelling of all types (including corpulence), as his name would suggest. Introduced in the first book, he is a demonic parody of the hero, the Red Cross Knight, whom he defeats after the knight drinks from a magic fountain and loses his powers. The knight is spared only after Duessa, whom he has rescued from Sansfoy, agrees to become the giant's mistress. Redcrosse survives this confrontation but is thrown into Orgoglio's dungeon, from which he is freed by Timias and King Arthur, who in canto 8 dismember the giant. Orgoglio is in this sense the vicious twin of Gargantua. He is huge and oversexed, but unlike Gargantua evil at the core, his corpulence a sign of Christian immorality, not medieval carnival. His character is indeed mirrored in his body; even his dismemberment evokes church history. His left arm is first amputated (the Church in Bohemia), and then his right arm is cut off (the Church of England). Then he dies, as will the corrupt Church of Rome.[59]

The Reformation distinction between the merely huge and the obese is central to Martin Luther's commentary on 1 Corinthians 15, the text that established the Pauline image of the bloated body.[60] Man must bear his earthly body as a confinement for the soul. He drags his heavy paunch about with him, the mortal body symbolized by the paunch, the sack of stench, that man must endure. He stuffs himself, evacuates, discharges mucus, and suppurates as a consequence of his mortality (28:172). The ailments that plague fat bodies are sickness, misfortune, frailty, filth, blemishes, and stench (28:203), and these are always attributed to the influence of Satan. This heavy existence contrasts with the heavenly body that will move though all the heavens as swiftly and lightly as lightning and soar over the clouds among the dear angels (28:196; also 28:143, 28:188). Above all, it will be devoid of all infirmities and wants (28:172). This contrast between heavy and light bodies, which Luther occasionally employs, is common among the Greek and Latin fathers. Luther's text depicts only fat bodies this side of heaven.[61] Indeed, any of the commentary's descriptions of life on earth are bound to include mention of the paunch, of the gut that extends in front of us, a perpetual reminder of our fleshiness. This paunch eclipses the genitalia as the most salient image of carnality. However, Luther differentiates good fat from bad fat, Christian bodies from diabolical bodies.

Luther describes two distinct types of fat bodies: the bloated and the solid. Each of these bodies corresponds to a mode of being in the world. The bloated body relies on the image of the puffed-up body from Paul. When Luther observes that the opponents of Paul in Corinth claimed that they knew better than he about God, he compares them to Isaiah's audience, which he describes as "arrogant and miserly paunches" and "vexatious windbags" (28:158). Their proud bellies are expansive, but only because they are filled with air. These bodies are fat, but certainly not solid. In keeping with this image Luther continually invokes the image of the pig, which, although bulky, has a reputation as perhaps the least solid of all animals. It waddles on stubby legs, fat jiggling, and resembles a curious balloon more than a mass of solid flesh. Invoking this fat flimsiness, Luther makes an explicit connection between the pig and the arrogant, bloated body (28:148). "Swinish" becomes his preferred adjective for this type of existence. For Luther the swinish man stuffs his paunch until it covers his penis, thereby eliminating his sexuality.

It is of little surprise that Luther, in texts written shortly before his death, also attributes such bodily qualities to the Jews, whom he sees worshipping the pig in a motif that has its roots in the Middle Ages.[62] In *Von den Juden und ihren Lügen* (On the Jews and their lies; 1543), he curses the "damned Jews" who "dare to apply this earnest, glorious, comforting word of God so despicably to your mortal, greedy belly, which is doomed to decay, and [who] are not ashamed to display your greed so openly." He uses the image of the Jews worshipping the pig and eating its excrement: "You should read only the bible that is found under the sow's tail, and eat and drink the letters that drop from there. That would be a bible for such prophets, who root about like sows and tear apart like pigs the words of the divine Majesty."[63] This is the appropriate food for the swinish nature of the Jews and their decaying and bloated bodies. The pig is traditionally associated with images of male gluttony. This can be seen in an illustration to Psalm 102 in a 1475 psalter from Poitier, now in the Morgan Library in New York City (manuscript M. 1001). In the illustration a large-bellied man is depicted astride a pig, food and drink spilling over him and a ham under his arm. He is labeled "Glotonie." The bloated body is what Julia Kristeva evokes when she writes of anti-Semitism that "the Jew becomes the feminine exalted to the point of mastery, the impaired master, the ambivalent, the border where exact limits between same and other, subject and object, and even beyond these, between inside and outside, and disappearing — hence an Object of fear and fascination. *Abjection itself.*"[64] Abjection is here the truly obese, now clothed in the body of the Other.

The opposite of this puffy, bloated figure of false belief is the fat but solid body. These are healthy bodies. Every human being, without exception, gains weight for the slaughter (i.e., death), when Satan will devour us. The difference is that the swinish herd actively fatten themselves while true Christians passively endure being stuffed by Satan. Luther writes of the bloated ones: "Let those people go their way with their mocking, their carousing and swilling and living like swine that wallow around among the husks and fatten themselves until they are slaughtered" (28:164). But regarding the Christians he writes: "Satan dispenses no other food than pestilence and every other sickness and pours no other wine of drink than pure poison. Therefore we can expect nothing else than that he will fill us with this and then butcher and flay us" (28:111–12). The bloated body and the solid body acquire their fat differently. Thus the fat means something quite different. True Christians possess a remedy for Satan's poisonous edibles, and that is nourishment from God's Word. Unlike the bloated glutton who is always looking for food to consume, the Christian (again passively) receives sustenance from God. Luther writes: "See to it that you remain in the Word. By it God wants to bear you up and sustain you, so that you will not be lost" (28:75). The Christian has access to God's nourishment through the Word and is thereby given a healthy supplement to his or her diabolical diet. For Erik Erikson this passivity is a return to the mother, who "taught him to touch the world with his searching mouth and his probing senses." He writes, "I think that in the Bible Luther at last found a mother whom he could acknowledge: he could attribute to the Bible a generosity to which he could open himself, and which he could pass on to others, at last a mother's son."[65] A mother with her suckling child (Mary and Jesus) is Luther's crucial image for establishing a healthy relation to the Word. Above all, the solid constitution is characterized by its passive relation to external powers, both to Satan who inflicts disease and to God whence flows the maternal milk of the Word. Thus the moral order of Pauline Christianity and its image of the fat body are converted into a diet culture rooted in belief and sustenance.

THE FAT BOY ENTERS MODERNITY

When Peter Paul Rubens, the master of representing fat female bodies as voluptuous and erotic, imagines the fat male body it is anything but erotic. His *Drunken Silenus* (begun in 1610) and his various versions of the *Bacchanal* present a grotesque fat boy who is both sexual and unerotic. (The biblical equivalent is found in images of the drunken Noah.) While Silenus has his roots in Virgil's account of him in the sixth *Ecologue* as the drunken creator of song and therefore literature, Rubens's Silenus is all gut. Rabelais evokes Silenus in the preface to his work as his patron god, the parodic evocation of Virgil's fat god placing him in the world of still acceptable fat men. For Rubens (and later artists such as Jusepe de Ribera in 1628), Silenus's grotesque fat is a sign of the real world of sin and voluptuousness, now written as decay on the body.[66] This is not the ugly body hiding the good soul, as we have in the depictions of the ferociously ugly Socrates, but a body that is in complete agreement with the corruption present in the soul. Thus in Rubens's extraordinary portrayal of souls on their way to hell, painted in 1620, all of the damned are obese. The fat gut becomes the representation of obesity in all of its Christian theological implications and is now projected back into the classical world.

By the age of Rubens, the seventeenth century, a specialized literature of good and bad foods had been created, such as Johann Sigismund Elsholtz's *Diaeteticon* (1682).[67] His tabulation of every possible food and drink that was (or could be) consumed for its healthy and unhealthy properties had become a standard for the classification of foods. Indeed, Elsholtz quotes Galen to the effect that every physician should become knowledgeable in the art of cooking (Xx2). Toward the end of his book he offers advice on the appropriate diet for men — they should combine eating with work or exercise, such as fencing. He also ends with a warning, following Hippocrates, that the athletic body of the man can more easily age and become ill when he overeats (345). A religious obsession about moral corruption had come to be the stuff of the science of dietetics, dealing with pathology — not that dietetics had ever vanished, as we shall see in the next chapter. The meaning of the fat male body, however, came to be the focus of science, with all of the moral quality now ascribed to secular questions of health and illness rather than to moral readings of gluttony and obesity.

The moral questions remained but slowly were loosed from the overt religious rhetoric of obesity. Jean de La Bruyère presented a series of portraits of men who are types, or "characters," in 1688. Among them is Clito, who "had, throughout his life, been concerned with two things alone: namely, dining at noon and supping at night; he seems born to digest; he has only one topic of conversation: he tells you what entrées were served at the last meal he was at, how many soups there were and what sort of soups." He is "the arbiter of good things." But sadly, La Bruyère notes, "he was giving a dinner party on the day he died. Wherever he may be, he is eating, and if he should come back to this world, it would be to eat."[68] *Gula* has become gormandizing, but the result is the same — death.

By the Enlightenment, Christoph Wilhelm Hufeland had captured in his extraordinarily popular *The Art of Prolonging Life* (1796) the "good" and "moral" aspects of the physical nature of man.[69] Fat was simply bad for Hufeland and the Enlighteners because most people eat much more than they need. "Immoderation" is one of the prime causes of early death (2:43). Invoking the golden mean, eating too much and eating too richly will kill you. "Idleness" is also a cause of death (2:64). Human beings have lost their natural ability to determine how much they need through childhood overindulgence. Natural man, notes Hufeland, in plowing the fields has purpose, exercise, and food appropriate to long life: "His son becomes a studious rake; and the proportion between countrymen and citizens seems daily to be diminished" (2:217). The fat child is now the father (and mother) of the fat adult. Indeed, Hufeland places at the very beginning of his list of things that will certainly cause early death a "very warm, tender, and delicate education" in which children are stuffed "immoderately with food; and by coffee, chocolate, wine, spices, and such things" (2:9). Not sin but middle-class overindulgence began to be seen as the force that creates fat boys. In the nineteenth century the "science" of diet seemed to replace the morals of diet. The hidden model, however, remained the same: the normal, reasonable man is always contrasted with the fat boy and always to the fat boy's detriment. And the reward for the thin man is life, life extended (and if Augustine is to be believed, life eternal), while the fat man dies young and badly.

Immanuel Kant, in his essay "Overcoming unpleasant sensations by mere reasoning" (1797), argues that dietetics will only become philosophy "when the mere power of reason in mankind, in overcoming sensations by a governing principle, determines their manner of living. On the other hand, when it endeavors to excite or avert these sensations, by external corporeal means, the art becomes merely empiric and mechanical" (371). This is his direct answer to Hufeland's empiricism.

Hufeland had sent him his book on diet and longevity in the winter of 1796, and Kant recognized in it Hufeland's attempt to fulfill Kant's demand that the physical (and physiological) aspects of the human being be treated "morally." Kant acknowledged that Hufeland's argument for prophylaxis was to avoid illness, rather than to use specific foods for treatment in a philosophy of moral life. He relates this to the Stoic notion of "endurance and moderation" (375).

Kant's essay is highly autobiographical. His discussion of diet is tangibly tied to his awareness of his own aging body (383). He compares himself to men in their prime and defines aging specifically in gendered terms. He speaks of the increased amount of liquid that "aged men" seem to need to drink, which then disturbs their sleep. For Kant the power of the rational mind to avoid illness rests not only in the control that the mind has over what one ingests but also in the control of breathing and the body. It is the will that controls the body. Part of this rationale is explained in Kant's final footnote, in which he speaks of the blindness in his one eye and his anxiety about the failing sight in the other. He distances this fear by asking whether the pathologies of vision are in the eye or in the processing of the data in the brain, wondering if he has actually felt the loss of the blind eye. Unlike diet, which can be manipulated to control the health (and weight) of the body, the aging body seems to have its own rate of decline for which there is no control, even in rationality. Kant's essay, which begins with Hufeland's dietetics, ends with the aging, half-blind philosopher ruminating on the irresistible but fascinating decay of his own body.

The beginning of a "modern" (i.e., materialist) science of medicine saw the development of the view that human beings proceed along an arc of development, with a specific moment where the (male) body is most at risk from obesity. Thomas

Jameson in 1811 felt that the period from the twenty-eighth to the fifty-eighth year was the height of male perfection.[70] Kant would have agreed with this. Yet this is also the age of the most danger, as "we . . . find corpulency steals imperceptibly on most men, between the ages of thirty and fifty-seven. In many instances the belly becomes prominent, and the person acquires a more upright gait" (90). Yet this is not necessarily a bad thing, as "a moderate degree of obesity is certainly a desirable state of body at all times, as it indicates a health condition of the assimilating powers" (91). Obesity "also diminishes the irritability of the system, since fat people are remarked for good humour, and for bearing cold better than those who are lean, on account of the defensive coat of fat surrounding their nerves" (91). But fat can become dangerous: "When the heart and great vessels are so oppressed with fat, as to render the pulse slow and feeble, and the respiration difficult, the cumbrous load becomes of more serious import to the health" (92). The "prominent belly" is "considered as the first symptom of decay, particularly as it is generally observed to continue through a great part of old age" (105). Here again the shadow of the Greek humors reappears to claim that the phlegmatic body and the aged body have the same underlying pathology, that of obesity.

By the early modern period the outline of the fat boy's body is fixed. The discourses of medicine, theology, and the encompassing culture have generated and manipulated the image of fat boys for multitudinous purposes. Much attention has been given to defining and redefining how fat impacts his masculinity and how his masculinity rereads his fat. His profile is set. Now the inner contradictions and anomalies in the medical representations of the obese male come to be internalized in the lives of "real" fat boys and in the fantasies and parodies of the fat boy in the world of literature.

Fat Boys Writing and Writing Fat Boys

The meanings associated with the fat male body are produced in the spheres in which fat and masculinity are often seen as incompatible. These meanings are not freely floating, existing as stereotypes of failed masculinity. They are attached to real bodies and to real men. How these men respond to their being seen as fat boys is a measure of the power of these images of failed masculinity and how specific systems, such as medicine, are empowered by them to deal with the fat boy's body. By the beginning of modernity the body of the fat man carries a specific set of meanings in the world of health and illness. The fat male becomes a pathological case, so much so that when there is stress on the female obese body, it is often placed against the background of an assumption of the masculinity of fat. This is true well before Rubens. What is most striking is that these fat boys are often garrulous about their bodies, or at least make them visible, talking about them when they begin to see themselves regaining control. It is perceived that within each fat, diseased body, a thin, healthy person is hidden that can be willed into being revealed. As Edward Jukes, the self-promoting inventor of the stomach pump, observed at the beginning of the nineteenth century, the "most corpulent man or woman may with the aid of diet and exercise be reduced to their natural size."[1] The natural versus the unnatural, the thin versus the obese, is the model of the Doppelgänger, spied in the fun-house mirror. The model these unnatural bodies take is that of medicine, and they often see themselves in collaboration with the world of medicine that defines their bodies by illness and their minds as mad.

Certainly, the earliest and most influential text of this conventional model that still has a readership today is the autobiography of the Venetian Alvise (Luigi) Cornaro (1464–1566). His elegantly written Italian text *Discorsi della vita sobria*, variously translated in English as *Discourses on a Sober and Temperate Life*, *The Art of Living Long*, and *The Temperate Life*, first appeared in 1558.[2] Begun in 1550 when he was eighty-three, the final installment appeared when he was ninety-five. It became an instant best seller. According to the Renaissance physician Girolamo Cardano, it was immediately "in everybody's hands."[3] Cardano states that he would not "disdain to make use of the example of his life and the *experimentum* of his work, even though Cornaro did not profess humane letters or medicine" (80). Cardano wrote an account of his own fat, illness, and diet in *On the Usefulness to Be Gained from Adversity*. His text seems to have been shaped by his reading of Cornaro, even though the illness he reports took place four years before the publication of Cornaro's text (88) and was seen by him as quite separate from his own extensive medical works on diet and health. Its authenticity lay in the nature of the fat boy's confession, leading Cardano, as a physician, to see the autobiography as an example of good medicine and thus as the redemption of the fat man. As a virtual contemporary of Rabelais, his view is that of an "insider," a fat man desirous of showing that he can control those passions that so dominate Rabelais's gargantuan world.[4]

Cornaro confesses to the reader that at middle age, he was dissipated by forty years of gluttony and overindulgence in sensual pleasures. He was at death's door. For him gluttony was a killer, not merely a sin, for it "kills every year . . . as great a number as would perish during the time of a most dreadful pestilence, or by the sword or fire of many bloody wars" (41). In the depths of his illness he turned to the physicians. They advised him to be temperate. He thus cured his obese body through a strict limitation of his diet. While the cure was for him proof of the beneficence of God, it was equally proof that living longer allows one to develop those "splendid gifts of intellect and noble qualities of heart" (42) that can evolve once the demands and desires of youth are met. In a sense the evidence for God's grace and the best use of his gifts come at the end of life with a "natural death," at the time when one's vital powers have diminished and one dies well — peacefully and without struggle.

Cornaro's text is a handbook for a good life (and death). Its power lies in its autobiographical — indeed, confessional — mode, which echoes Augustine's. Cornaro observes, and carefully chronicles, his symptoms as a younger man from his perspective as an old, healthy, thin man. He was certainly ill with many of the diseases attributed to obesity in the Galenic tradition: "I had pains in the stomach, frequent pains in the side, symptoms of gout, and, still worse, a low fever that was almost continuous; but I suffered especially from disorder of the stomach, and from an unquenchable thirst" (43–44). He had also lost his ability to reject temptation, having become addicted to eating and drinking. He turned to the physicians, whose advice was quite clear; they "declared there was but one remedy left for my ills — a remedy which would surely conquer them, provided I would make up my mind to apply it and persevere in its use. That remedy was the temperate and orderly life" (44). This is what the physicians admonished and what the patient followed to success.

Sobriety after a life of indulgence is a cure for the physical effects of obesity, not obesity itself. Cornaro sees himself as typical of the men of his age. The riches of their lives have led them to the brink of death as a result of what he identifies as the three evil customs or sins widespread in sixteenth-century Italy: "adulation and ceremony . . . heresy and . . . intemperance" (40). Only through the good counsel of the doctors did he find a cure for all three. Gluttony is understood as the cause of the list of infirmities found in the fat man. The overindulgence of the man in his best years is the cause of his fat, and his fat is the sign of his sick body. A strong moral tradition existed that owed its form to Paul and the Christian abnegation of the body. The society in which Cornaro lived, however, did not understand this simple rule:

> These false notions are due entirely to the force of habit, bred by men's senses and uncontrolled appetites. It is this craving to gratify the appetites which has allured and inebriated men to such a degree that, abandoning the path of virtue, they have taken to following the one of vice — a road which leads them, though they see it not, to strange and fatal chronic infirmities through which they grow prematurely old. Before they reach the age of forty their health has been completely worn out — just

the reverse of what the temperate life once did for them. For this, before it was banished by the deadly habit of intemperance, invariably kept all its followers strong and healthy, even to the age of fourscore and upward. (41)

It is not knowledge of the world that cures, but simplicity and temperance. Cornaro bemoans the fact that "friends and associates, men endowed with splendid gifts of intellect and noble qualities of heart, . . . fall, in the prime of life, victims of this dread tyrant; men who, were they yet living, would be ornaments to the world, while their friendship and company would add to my enjoyment in the same proportion as I was caused sorrow by their loss" (42). He has been cured of his illnesses and fat by his strict regimen.

The world of simplicity may have its roots in the advice of physicians, but when Cornaro, at the age of seventy, was in a carriage accident and dislocated an arm and leg, he rejected his physician's suggestion that he be bled. He was convinced that his now healthy body would heal itself, and according to his account, it did. As a result of his own diet, he believes he knows his body so well that he is aware of what it needs to evince a cure.

Moderation has become his model for men to regain again their manhood, a manhood defined by longevity. And Cornaro was long-lived. This indeed was the key to his claim to authenticity in writing his autobiographical text. However, another level of anxiety about the body and masculinity also haunted Cornaro's world. The now moderate Cornaro was long a member of the circle around Cardinal Pietro Bembo that also included the poet-physician Girolamo Fracastoro. This particular group was especially concerned with the plague that was stalking Europe at the moment, a plague that was seen by most of its contemporaries as punishment for the sexual excesses of the age. Fracastoro gave it its name: *syphilis* — a disease of men (caused by women). Cornaro was explicitly interested in the public health of Venice, in the unwholesome air of the fetid swamps near Codovico, where he had his home. Fracastoro too was convinced that such air bred what he christened "germs." Cornaro's anxiety about controlling the world (of food) in order to control his body had its roots to no little extent in the syphilophobia of his age. The attitude of sufferers, such as Ulrich von Hutten — who died in 1523 and whose autobiographical "Dialogues with Fever," written shortly before his death, parallels Cornaro's work in surprising ways — was that a cure could be found in the restoration of natural balance.[5]

The anxiety about sexuality that coupled it with suffering, death, and damnation was a leitmotif of Christianity. After the beginning of the sixteenth century and the spread of syphilis, this anxiety was heightened. Cornaro's rejection of excess in food parallels Augustine's anxiety that gluttony was even worse than sexual license, for one did not have to fornicate (to use Augustine's concept), but one did have to eat. But what is excessive in the intake of nourishment for one man may not be for another. One can eat anything one wants, but in moderation: "I began to observe very diligently what kinds of food agreed with me. I determined, in the first place, to experiment with those, which were most agreeable to my palate, in order that I might learn if they were suited to my stomach and constitution. The proverb, 'whatever tastes good will nourish and strengthen,' is generally regarded as embodying a truth, and is invoked, as a first principle, by those who are sensually inclined. . . . In it I had hitherto firmly believed; but now I was resolved to test the matter, and find to what extent, if any, it was true. My experience, however, proved this saying to be false" (46). Since we must eat, as Augustine noted, we cannot suffer only to eat those things that give us pleasure, for that will only make us more gluttonous. Appetite is but a form of desire. Cornaro translates this into the discourse of health and illness. Eat for pleasure, and you will become ill. It is also clear, however, that the ability to eat exactly those things that he wants is linked with his idea that certain foods are simply healthy.

Those foods, such as meat and fish, clearly evoke the wealth that was part of the temptation of Cornaro's youth. A member of the powerful Cornaro family of Venice, he could earlier afford to be gluttonous, and now he can afford to eat fish:

> Of meats, I eat veal, kid, and mutton. I eat fowls of all kind; as well as partridges and birds like the thrush. I also partake of such salt-water fish as the goldney and the like; and, among the various fresh-water kinds, the pike and others. . . . Old persons, who, on account of poverty, cannot afford to indulge in all of these things, may maintain their lives with bread, bread soup, and eggs — foods that certainly cannot be wanting even to a poor man, unless he be one of the kind commonly known as good-for-nothing. Yet, even though the poor should eat nothing but bread, bread soup, and eggs, they must not take a greater quantity than can be easily digested; for they must, at all times, remember that he who is constantly faithful to the above-mentioned rules in regard to the quantity and quality of his food, cannot die except by simple dissolution and without illness. (87–88)

Cornaro resolved to restrict his diet drastically. Initially it was reduced to a daily intake of twelve ounces of food and fourteen ounces of wine. Eventually, however, it was reduced to a single egg a day. However, he also understood the relationship between the outward manifestation of the body and its spirit. He resolved to control his temper and the "melancholy, hatred, and other passions of the soul, which all appear greatly to affect the body" (48). Assuming that he was in fact born in 1564 (contesting some accounts that claim his age at death was 103), Cornaro lived to be 98, and according to his autobiography, it is accomplishments in old age that reveal the character of man. He muses on what it is to be old and healthy. This is defined by his ability to work and to concentrate on questions of private as well as public health:

> My greatest enjoyment, in the course of my journeys going and returning, is the contemplation of the beauty of the country and of the places through which I travel. Some of these are in the plains; others on the hills, near rivers or fountains; and all are made still more beautiful by the presence of many charming dwellings surrounded by delightful gardens. Nor are these my diversions and pleasures rendered less sweet and less precious through the failing of sight or my hearing, or because any one of my senses is not perfect; for they are all — thank God! — most perfect. This is especially true of my sense of taste; for I now find more true relish in the simple food I eat, wheresoever I may chance to be, than I formerly found in the most delicate dishes at the time of my intemperate life. . . . With the greatest delight and satisfaction, also, do I behold the success of an undertaking highly important to our State; namely, the fitting for cultivation of its waste tracts of country, numerous as they were. This improvement was commenced at my suggestion; yet I had scarcely ventured to hope that I should live to see it, knowing, as I do, that republics are

slow to begin enterprises of great importance. Nevertheless, I have lived to see it. And I myself was present with
the members of the committee appointed to superintend
the work, for two whole months, at the season of the
greatest heat of summer, in those swampy places; nor
was I ever disturbed either by fatigue or by any hardship
I was obliged to incur. So great is the power of the orderly life which accompanies me wheresoever I may go!
Furthermore, I cherish a firm hope that I shall live to
witness not only the beginning but also the completion,
of another enterprise, the success of which is no less important to our Venice: namely, the protection of our es-
tuary. . . . These are the true and important recreations,
these comforts and pastimes, of my old age, which is
much more to be prized than the old age or even the
youth of other men; since it is free, by the grace of God,
from all the perturbations of the soul and the infirmities
of the body, and is not subject to any of those troubles
which woefully torment so many young men and so
many languid and utterly worn-out old men. (69–70)

Cornaro's autobiography is at its heart a handbook of dietetics
to reform the body of the fat boy and turn him into a healthy
and abstentious man who can in turn create a healthy world.

Yet by 1526 Erasmus had already turned many of these
guidelines borrowed from Galenic medicine into parodied
rules for the reformation of the Church's fasting require-
ments.[6] Like Cornaro, he saw "adulation and ceremony . . .
[and] heresy," if not "intemperance," as the greatest failings of
his age. His criticism of the obligatory days on which only fish
could be eaten, so familiar to many before Vatican II, has Erasmus turn first to the notion of health and eating. The eating of
fish is, for Erasmus, an evil because it typifies the false prac-

tices of the Church. The eating of fish also presents real physical dangers: "Men's bodies are corrupted and filled with putrid humors from eating fish, which causes fever, consumption, gout, epilepsy, leprosy, and many other diseases" (277). The fishmongers violate the natural flow of the seasons by insisting on selling their stinking wares in summer, "corrupting the infancy of the springing year by bringing old age upon it. When nature is busy purging the body of unwholesome juices and making it fresh to bloom anew, you throw into it stench and corruption" (279). Likewise, in the 1620s Tobias Venner urges his readers to avoid fish for health reasons "because fish increase much grosse, slime, and superfluous flemge, which residing and corrupting the body, causeth difficulte of breathing, the Gowte, the Stone, the Leaprie, the Scurvie, and other foule and troublesome affects of the skin" (69). "Fish," according to the thirteenth-century prototypical scientist Roger Bacon in a seventeenth-century translation, "sometimes breed bad Humours" and should be avoided by aging men.[7] By the beginning of the seventeenth century audiences would have well understood the severity of Hamlet's insult in act 2 when he calls Polonius a fishmonger.[8]

Despite health concerns regarding fish, Erasmus's purpose is not the dietetics of the body but of the soul. He quotes the "prophets who portrayed God as abhorring their fasts, rejecting their gifts, and desiring a people of circumcised hearts. The Lord Himself confirmed the prophecies by holding forth to the Disciples His Body and Blood, as is stated in the New Testament" (283). Cornaro's eating of meat and fish places him on the side of a conservative Church, in opposition to reformers. Where Erasmus's eaters of fish make themselves ill because of the sickness that is present in the body of the Church, Cornaro's diet reforms the body so that it can be a productive part of society. For the scientist Johannes Baptista van Helmont, in the middle of the seventeenth century, the fish is again the chemical model for purity. (Helmont's views on obesity will come to play an important role in eighteenth-century high culture, as we shall see.) The fish is able to transform pure water into its "fat, bones and flesh." "Fish is, in material form, nothing more than transformed water and can therefore be transformed through art [*Kunst*] into water again." This is the reason that fish is healthful and easily digested, but now only to the believing Christian.[9]

The cult of Cornaro was a long-lasting one, reaching into the present, and often the model presented was an autobiographical account of the rescue of the thin, healthy man from fat. Leonard Lessius, the Belgian writer, in 1613 wrote his own *Hygiasticon*, which simply repeated Cornaro's life as his own. Rescued from a world of dissipation and fat after the physicians had given him up as lost, he found the simple pleasures of sobriety and self-limitations, which enabled him to become manlier in his deeds and actions.[10] Leonard Lessius not only mirrors the autobiography of Cornaro but also cites St. Augustine's struggle with the pleasures of gluttony as one of his models (20–21). Lessius paraphrases Augustine, stating that "Lust knows not where Necessitie ends," which is, for Lessius, why one may grow fat (21). He stresses that, like Augustine, we must all control our desire to "feast and banquet" (85). We can do this by imagining food as disgusting and bad smelling. If we do not we shall certainly die, as almost all diseases come from taking more food into the body than "nature requires" (103). Lessius continues by amplifying the arguments of Cornaro about longevity and diet, as well as echoing the theological and moral underpinnings of his text.

Cornaro's account of the extended lives of men had its prophets through the centuries. Joseph Addison praised it in *The Spectator* on 13 October 1711 as the key to a better life for men in London. Real men, "farmers, gardeners, hunters, soldiers and sailors," according to Christoph Wilhelm Hufeland's *The Art of Prolonging Life* (1796), can live to 150 years of age; Hufeland cites Cornaro in his introduction.[11] Hufeland's contemporary Benjamin Franklin proposed his own approach in *The immortal Mentor; Or, Man's Unerring Guide to a Healthy, Wealthy, and Happy Life*, which was republished together with Cornaro's autobiography in 1796.[12] Edward Jukes provided a potted account of Cornaro's life in his own 1833 account of why people should live abstemiously (and if not, why their physicians should use the stomach pump on them!).[13] And Friedrich Nietzsche, sick with syphilis, turned to Cornaro in the 1880s as part of his attempt at self-cure. In Nietzsche's case, the cure clearly did not work, as he fell into syphilitic madness in Turin on 3 January 1889. He died on 25 August 1900, a little more than half a century old.

In a world living under Cornaro's promise that thin, abstemious men would live to be a hundred years old, short, fat, gluttonous men came to be seen as marking the boundary between acceptable and unacceptable masculinity. In dying young they destroyed the promise of masculinity, which included the responsibility to live to an age beyond desire and thus be of greater service to the Church and the State. This belief, or its antithesis, is echoed in all forms of literature during the day.

If there is one moment in the modern novel where classical body types are parodied in fiction, it is in the first book of Cervantes' *Don Quixote* (1605). It is here that Cervantes introduces the thin knight and his servant, Sancho Panza (Mr. Gut).[14] Mr. Gut has "a big belly, short body, and long shanks" (77) — at least in the virtual illustration of him that Cervantes imagines illustrating the tale. The original is even more strik-

ing — "la barriga grande, el talle corto y las zancas largas" —
and suggests the popular, nonmedical terms for aspects of
Sancho Panza's remarkable, obese body with its exaggerated
belly (the same word exists in contemporary Spanish).[15]

In stark contrast Quixote is the mad, thin man who does
not eat (often) because the books of knighthood he has read
never show the knights actually eating. He emulates them and
becomes as thin as his horse, "so long and lank, so hollow and
lean, stiff . . . and so far wasted so like one wasted in consumption" (77). His servant, on the other hand, "a poor yokel,"
lives to eat and drink. He leaves stealthily with the knight,
"without Panza saying goodbye to his wife or children" (66),
when Quixote promises him that he will be governor of his
own island kingdom. Sexual desire is conquerable, as Augustine said, but gluttony one must face each and every day —
and as often as not Panza succumbs. Sancho Panza's "stomach
was full" with eats and drinks while his master fasts (70). Cervantes presents the thin man and the fat man not as a healthy
thin man hidden within an obese, but as both equally be-
trayed by their bodies and minds. What for Cornaro and the
diet cult of sobriety is the revelation that healthy thinness
trumps unhealthy fat is for Cervantes a world in which body
types provide faulty clues to the inner lives of his characters.

By the second volume of the novel, published in 1615, Sancho Panza has become unhealthy — at least within the new
self-reflexive satire of the novel. In the second installment of
the novel it seems to all concerned that Quixote is "mad."
His mental state is the ironic representation of a madness that
reveals the truth — or at least the substance behind the illu-
sion of reality. Many critics who have examined the juxtaposition of the first, non-self-reflexive volume and the second, in
which the characters read about themselves in Cervantes'
novel, agree concerning Quixote's "illness."[16] Indeed, the

good knight has even been diagnosed retrospectively with at least one contemporary syndrome (if not more).[17] On the other hand, Sancho Panza's corporeality has not been read as revealing any hidden truths about epistemology or textual manipulation. Mr. Gut is simply fat and funny. Yet Cervantes may well have the last laugh on Cornaro.

Sancho Panza follows Don Quixote because of Quixote's promise of a governorship for him, and through a series of misadventures he actually makes good on this promise. However, being in the service of the state has certain disadvantages. In the forty-seventh chapter Sancho Panza is only finally able to reap the benefits of his new office: "Immediately upon his entrance into this room the clarions sounded and four pages came in to bring him water for his hands, which Sancho received with great gravity. Then the music stopped and he took his seat at the head of the table, for there was no other seat besides and no other place laid" (764–65). He begins to eat, but every time he takes something from a plate, the plate is automatically removed from the table. This happens over and over again, and the bounty is itself parsimony. He complains to the individual overseeing the banqueting hall, who reveals himself to be Doctor Pedro Recio de Aguero, placed in charge of the good health of the governor:

> "It must merely be eaten, Lord Governor, according to the manner and custom of other isles where there are governors. I, sir, am a physician, and I am salaried to act as doctor to the Governors of this isle. I am much more careful of their health than of my own, studying day and night and sounding the Governor's constitution to find means of curing him if he should fall ill. My principal duty is to be present at his dinners and suppers, not to

let him eat what seems to me harmful and be injurious to his stomach. This is why I ordered that dish of fruit to be removed, it being far too moist; and the other dish I had removed because it was too heating, containing many spices which increase the thirst; for one who drinks much kills and consumes the radical humour wherein life consists."

"At that rate," said Sancho, "the dish of roast partridges over there won't do me any harm. They look very tasty to me."

To which the physician replied, "The Lord Governor shall never eat of them whilst I live."

"Why not?" asked Sancho.

"Because our master Hippocrates," answered the physician, "the pole-star and light of medicine, says in one of his aphorisms *'omnis saturatio mala, perdicis autem pessima,'* which means all surfeit is bad, but that of partridges is the worst." (765)

This is, of course, a brutal form of irony aimed against the cult of moderation. Repletion, as we well know, is bad for the body because it leads to fat and disease. The humoral Sancho Panza of volume 1 soon gives way to a medicalized one. Cervantes is careful to have the doctor use the technical term for "adiposa," obesity, for Sancho Panza ("rolliza"), indicating that his fat is much more than merely a reflection of his character. It can be read only as disease.[18] But Dr. Recio adds to the Hippocratic corpus the worst type of obesity: repletion with partridges! In the classical authorities cited in the seventeenth century, from Galen to Martial, the partridge is praised as a particular delicacy. In the *Regimen sanitatis salernitanum*, for example, the "perdix" should be "eaten with wisdom as we ought to do" as a healthy food.[19] Roger Bacon, in his book on longevity, argues that partridges are appropriate for "old men," for "old men's meats ought to be of good juice, hot and moist, that they may be quickly and easily digested, and descend from the Stomach . . . their Flesh should be that of Pullets, Kids, sucking Calves, young Geese, Lambs, Partridge." (His seventeenth-century commentator adds, "the younger the better.")[20] Partridges are particularly easy to digest, says Everard Maynwaringe at the end of the seventeenth century.[21] Yet Cornaro notes that he eats partridges because he can afford them! Tobias Venner sees them as very welcome in a diet "and very acceptable to the stomacke" (58). They are "only hurtfull to Country-men, because they breede in them the Asthmatick passion, which is short & painfull fetching of breath, by reason where of they will not be able to undergoe their usual labours" (59). The common man, that is, Sancho Panza, cannot tolerate such rich food. It would make him ill. Van Helmont sees the partridge as one of the most delicate of foods, used to tempt ill soldiers and poor folks to eat specifically because they rarely have access to them (86). Partridges, however, at least according to one seventeenth-century German source, are a rich and healthy dish, especially favored by the Spaniards eaten hot.[22] Partridges are fine as the food of the rich and the exotic but will indeed make the servant now transformed into a governor ill.

The medical reference is one that educated readers of the time would have known; there is, however, a long-standing belief that Cervantes was himself the son of a physician and may well have had some medical education. His Quixote is quick to offer Sancho Panza proverbial guidelines (à la Polonius) to eating that are simultaneously tips for social behavior and medical advice: "Do not eat garlic or onions; for their smell will reveal that you are a peasant. Walk leisurely and speak with deliberation; but not so as to seem to be listening to yourself, for all affectation is bad. Be temperate in drinking, remembering that excess of wine keeps neither a secret nor a promise. Take care, Sancho, not to chew on both sides of your mouth, nor to eruct in anyone's presence" (741). To eat in moderation is given exactly the same weight in this topsy-turvy world as not belching at the table. Knowing what to eat that will not mark you as a man of the lower classes is of equal importance to the quality of the food that preserves health. Sancho soon learns that the guidelines of healthy eating are part of the obligation of the male citizen.

Sancho is in the service of the state. What is good for him must be good for the nation, a point that Cornaro had already elaborated upon. Thus when the duke warns Sancho Panza of an imminent attack on the island, his response is to order the doctor locked up, "for if anyone may kill me it will be he, and that by the most lingering and worst of all deaths, hunger" (768). He needs food, and he needs food that is safe. He is warned that nuns may have poisoned the food — "as the saying goes, behind the cross stands the devil" (768). The doctor urges that he eat nothing but pure, unadulterated food, and in spite of himself Sancho Panza agrees. As a result he turns to Cornaro's diet: "So for the moment let me have a piece of bread and some four pounds or so of grapes. There can be no poison in them. For really I can't hold out without eating, and if we have to be ready for these battles they threaten us with we must be well nourished, since guts carry heart and not heart guts" (768). (Here too Cervantes puts the vernacular about the body in the mouth of his character: "porque tripas llevan corazón, que no corazón tripas" [1431].) One thinks with one's gut even when it is filled only with bread and grapes — peasants' food, precisely — which sharpen the mind and heal the body of the fat man. Of course, Mr. Gut remains fat and survives his term in the service of the state, while the gaunt Don Quixote dies at the close of the novel. If the moral of Cornaro's account is that the thin man within not only survives but also flourishes once he is rid of fleshly desires, then Cervantes reverses this completely, for it is the fat man who survives and flourishes in his happy corporality. Cervantes is convinced that reading the character — or perhaps more accurately, reading the fate of characters — in terms of their bodies is without any merit. Sancho Panza lives at the conclusion of the novel, while the lean and mad Quixote expires. Fat preserves; Sancho Panza lives on to spawn an entire literature (and filmology) of paired thin and fat men.[23]

One example will have to suffice, as it picks up a thread about the obese body of the Jew that haunts Western culture and medicine with the advent of Christianity. The image of the fat buddy in literature following Cervantes shows how Sancho Panza becomes a model for the later association of obesity and a type of effeminacy. In the first modern Yiddish novel, Mendele Mosher Seforim's *The Travels and Adventures of Benjamin the Third* (1885), the pairing of the thin and fat protagonists — so well-known both from fictions (Quixote and Sancho Panza) and from autobiographical, overcoming-adversity narratives (I was fat and now I am thin) — is repeated with meaningful variations.[24] Here the obese figure is clearly defined with overt attributes ascribed to the feminine in Yiddish popular culture. Mendele's Sancho Panza, Senderel, is "simple minded, unassuming" (37), and is often the butt of jokes in the synagogue. His wife supports him, and he takes over the wifely duties in the kitchen. Indeed, he is called Senderel "die Yiddine," the housewife (39). Our Quixote, Benjamin, "always found it a pleasure to talk to him. It's quite possible, too, that Benjamin took into consideration Senderel's lack of resistance; Senderel would be bound to agree to his plan" (39). Like Quixote, Benjamin convinces Senderel to leave his family and go with him on an adventure. When they leave home, Senderel is dressed in "a skirt made of calico and a woman's headgear" (48). Cervantes' pairing of fat and thin has so pervaded the culture that, by the time of Mendele, there is no longer even any need to evoke body type. It is assumed that Benjamin has a body like that of Cervantes' protagonist and that his Sancho Panza is again "Mr. Gut." But as with the image of the Jewish obese body in the diabetes literature of the time, this image of the feminine male has contemporary resonance.

This is the male Jew as woman. The assumption of nineteenth-century culture was that Jewish males were effeminate. The image of the male Jew was feminized even in the work of Jewish scientists of the period. Indeed, in accepting the view that the Jews are a single race in 1904, the Elberfeld Jewish physician Heinrich Singer comments that "in general it is clear in examining the body of the Jew, that the Jew most approaches the body type of the female."[25] Hans Gross, the famed Prague criminologist (and father of the psychoanalyst Otto Gross), can comment with ease about the "little, feminine hand of the Jew."[26] These medical views echoed the older anthropological view, such as that of the Jewish ethnologist Adolf Jellinek, who stated quite directly that "in the examination of the various races it is clear that some are more masculine, others more feminine. Among the latter the Jews belong, as one of those tribes which are both more feminine and have come to represent [*repräsentieren*] the feminine among other peoples. A juxtaposition of the Jew and the woman will persuade the reader of the truth of the ethnographic thesis." Jellinek's physiological proof is the Jew's voice: "Even though I disavow any physiological comparison, let me note that bass voices are much rarer than baritone voices among the Jews."[27]

The association of the image of the Jew (here read: male Jew) with that of the woman (including the Jewish woman) is one of the most powerful to be embedded in the arguments about race.

Thus Mendele's feminized Senderel seems to be very much in character. Yet the pairing with the emaciated Benjamin provides, within the model provided by Cervantes, an answer that sets these characters off from all other Jews. They are not representative but anomalies, part of the parodic world in which the Jewish body can be displayed. However, the special relationship of the obese body to the feminized male is here used to refute the assumption of the "oriental" fat boy that haunts the image of the Jew in the West. These paired antiheroes employ the "fat buddy" as a means of characterizing male-male relationships and thus defining masculinity. The literary figure and the autobiographical accounts are cut from the same cultural cloth.

STERNE AND CHEYNE

Certainly the most important of Cervantes' offspring in the British tradition is Laurence Sterne's *Tristram Shandy* (1759–67).[28] Sterne knew the Cervantes novel better than virtually any other novel of his time. He understood that the diet Mr. Gut is forced to follow is to control his passions: "Was I left like Sancho Pança, to chuse my kingdom, it should not be maritime — or a kingdom of blacks to make a penny of — no, it should be a kingdom of hearty laughing subjects: And as the bilious and more saturnine passions, by creating disorders in the blood and humours, have as bad an influence, I see, upon the body politick as body natural — and as nothing but a habit of virtue can fully govern those passions, and subject them to reason — I should add to my prayer — that God would give my subjects grace to be as WISE as they were

MERRY . . . " (298). It is the humors that need to be controlled in order to create the happiness of the public and the state. Sterne knew, ironically, that disorder in the body demands some type of control. His irony makes it impossible, however, to imagine a body over which one could actually have that sort of control!

In *Tristram Shandy* the fat man is also present, but only peripherally. The dichotomy between the fat man and the thin man (that odd version of the story of dieting and recuperation in which the thin becomes the fat becomes the thin) is transferred to another aspect of the body. What fat means for Cervantes, the shape of the nose means for Sterne. How bodies are read is at the center of both satires, but the body parts are different. Sterne's two fat characters are the notorious Dr. Slop, the man midwife, whose badly used forceps alter the shape of Tristram's nose, and the tubby little drummer lad at the gates of Strasbourg. Slop is "a little, squat, uncourtly figure . . . of about four feet and a half perpendicular height, with a breadth of back, and a sesquipedality of belly, which might have done honour to a Serjeant in the Horse-Guards" (123). His form reflects his rather too literal and rather too Catholic mindset as his Catholic faith is central to Sterne's satire on his body. The character, based on a real physician, Dr. John Burton, a contemporary expert in obstetrics, is transformed into a Catholic to match his rather comic but dangerous physiognomy. Burton was tall and impressive; Slop can be caricatured, according to Sterne, as the antithesis of William Hogarth's ideal of beauty.[29]

Sterne's concern in the novel is not specifically with Dr. Gut and the world of the fat boy, though he evokes it; he turns at one point to a discussion of the science of longevity and good health, describing the secret of health that Walter Shandy, Tristram's intellectual father, developed:

The whole secret of health, said my father, beginning the sentence again, depending evidently upon the due contention betwixt the radical heat and radical moisture within us; — the least imaginable skill had been sufficient to have maintained it, had not the school-men confounded the task, merely (as *Van Helmont*, the famous chymist, has proved) by all along mistaking the radical moisture for the tallow and fat of animal bodies. Now the radical moisture is not the tallow or fat of animals, but an oily and balsamous substance; for the fat and tallow, as also the phlegm or watery parts, are cold; whereas the oily and balsamous parts are of a lively heat and spirit, which accounts for the observation of *Aristotle*, "*Quod omne animal post coitum est triste*." Now it is certain, that the radical heat lives in the radical moisture, but whether vice versa, is a doubt: however, when the one decays, the other decays also; and then is produced, either an unnatural heat, which causes an unnatural dryness — or an unnatural moisture, which causes dropsies. — So that if a child, as he grows up, can but be taught to avoid running into fire or water, as either of 'em threaten his destruction, — 'twill be all that is needful to be done upon that head. (351)

A healthy body is not fat but instead possesses "radical moisture." Laurence Sterne presents, from the perspective of his characters, an alternative view to the fat body of Sancho Panza. The two bodies in Cervantes, first the humoral body of the icon described by the narrator and then the doctor's image of the fat body, are contrasted here. For Sterne, of course, this passage also reflects the bizarre worldview of the family Shandy. "Real" science deals with the chemical nature of the obese body and its fat as an elemental aspect of the body.

Sterne's view rests on the movement between a metaphysical and a biochemical model of fat that evolved in the seventeenth century, by his day having come to represent the "battle of the books" in regard to fat. Johannes Baptista van Helmont (1577–1644), the early seventeenth-century Flemish chemist, had introduced a radical empiricism into medicine in his posthumously published compendium, *Ortus medicinae* (1648). He argued (following Paracelsus) against the notion that the imbalance of the humors caused illness. For him there had to be material reasons. Van Helmont imagined that there could be "wild spirits" that could neither be seen nor kept in vessels. He called them "chaos" (pronounced "gas" in Dutch). Everything, when burned, gave off different gases: *gas carbonum* from burning charcoal, *gas sylvester* from fermenting wine and spa water, inflammable *gas pingue* from organic matter. His physiology was likewise material; he believed that each organ had its own spirit, or *blas*. This view was quite different from Paracelsus's belief that a single *archeus* or spirit animated the entire body. In retrospect it is clear that van Helmont used a highly religious vocabulary to frame his materialism. It was clearly (like Newton's) informed by the religious world in which he functioned. Van Helmont's text on medicine is a seventeenth-century mix between highly speculative religious imagery and the technical medicine of his time, but it also includes a long treatise on longevity.

Anti-humorist and anti-Galenist, van Helmont developed the first notions of a medical chemistry; one of his theories deals with the difference between oil and fat. In his *First Three Principles* he argues that elementary water is made into oil in vegetables, animals, and sulfurs; likewise, all oil is easily reduced to water. The first principle is that such things cannot be exchanged for each other or cease to be that which they were before. Oil is an elementary property. But it is present as a form of seed (*Samen*), which can be transformed into a combustible substance (143).

Oil is not body fat. Van Helmont provides a case study to illustrate this. In his treatise "The law of the double nature of man" van Helmont presents the case of an extremely fat person whose fat he transformed into a watery substance, which he evacuated through the bladder (851–52). Such transformations are not the property of oil. But even though water is passed through the kidneys, van Helmont is not convinced that the kidneys have the power to transmute fat into water even if they are healthy. He ascribes this power only to the blood, which can transform itself into a solid.

For van Helmont fat seems to be granted its power through the action of the stomach. But obesity is not the result of eating. He gives the example of the Capuchin monk who fasts and thirsts but is still "fat in his body," as opposed to those who eat extremely well and still remain thin. Due to some unseen working in the flesh, fat is the result of the entire body, including the blood. The stomach he sees in the end as the "regent of digestion" (858). Its function (*blas*) is to process food. This is inherently human, for van Helmont is unable to find an analogy to its function in the animal kingdom. Yet for van Helmont the stomach is the very center of the body. His reason for this placement is theological rather than chemical, as he argues that Abraham bore the Messiah in his loins (850). The confusion between the gut and the loins is a telling one. If Sterne has Walter Shandy distinguish between the fluid that, when expended, makes all men sad and bodily fat, this distinction rests on van Helmont's view that the loins and the stomach are the avenues through which man's fluids flow, consequently diminishing him.

In van Helmont's guidelines for a long life obesity is to be eschewed. Human life can be extended by medicine, but what

God can offer is life eternal, not merely fleshly life. As a physician van Helmont saw his job as prolonging the "Life of the World." What is bad for human life is clear: carnal lust, tobacco, and mushrooms, as well as "much and unreasonable gluttony" (1241). ("Mushrooms . . . breed melancholy," according to Roger Bacon's treatise on longevity.)[30] Food remains at the core of health. Thus, deceiving the body by reducing hunger is dangerous. Tobacco seems to still hunger but ultimately doesn't; it merely makes one insensitive to the natural need for food, which itself must be controlled. So van Helmont returns to a notion of the control of food as a means of controlling the potentially obese body.

For some contemporaries of van Helmont the idea of food control needed to be augmented by a radical understanding of the body's inner workings. It was the alchemist Johann Joachim Becher (1635–82) who revised Aristotle's theory regarding the four chief elements found in nature. He suggested that minerals are composed of three constituents: *terra lapida* (stone), giving body to substances; *terra mercurialis* (mercury), providing the properties of density and luster; and *terra pinguis* (fat), giving combustibility.[31] This is his version of van Helmont's oil. This view, echoing Paracelsus's conception of the three inherent elements of nature (for him salt, sulfur, and mercury), placed "fat" as one of the new shaping forces of the universe. "Fat" is chemical, but it is intrinsic to existence and is rather different from the fleshly fat that constitutes the obese human.

Tallow, body fat, is bad — it is "cold," and what one needs for health is "radical heat." After sex, Sterne quotes Aristotle (as does his contemporary William Hogarth in a telling "before and after sex" series), a man is sad because he has released heat. Thus Dr. Slop, as cold a figure as you can find in Sterne's novel, is an exemplar of an unhealthy mind in an unhealthy body. (His German cousin is a Protestant divine, the equally stupid and bumbling hero of Friedrich Nicolai's *Geschichte eines dicken Mannes worin drei Heiraten und drei Körbe nebst viel Liebe* [The story of a fat man; 1794].)[32] This science is the science of the mean, of balance, but fat or tallow is a substance that is beyond balancing. It is a sign of illness and disruption. It is also a sign of the lack of adventure. For the "corpulent" body, according to Shandy, does not desire to move, while the thin think differently with their bodies. They are "so much of motion" (436). What was sloth has become lassitude; what was gluttony has become pathology.

Thus Father Shandy gets it quite right even if for all the wrong reasons, attributing to contemporary science a view that matches "hot" and "cold" aspects of the body in a humoral manner. Indeed, van Helmont's specific *blas* of the stomach has little relationship to any transcendental notion of fat, and Becher's *terra pinguis* has no relationship to body fat. Out of these viewpoints, certainly seen as part of popular science of the time, Sterne crafts a new version of an older view of the function of human fat. This old wine in new Helmontian bottles is his attempt to create a new science of good and bad fat. Shandy's lesson learned is not far from the platitudes of Don Quixote about diet — children should stay away from fire and water, and they will have a long life.

Sterne's "modern" evocation of fat is very much within the new mechanical physiology of Thomas Sydenham, who wrote of the "irregular motions of the animal spirits" as the cause of illness.[33] It is the unhealthiness of fat and its relationship to altered psychological states, such as melancholia, that become part of the image of "spleen," the disease of the moment. David Hume, in a 1734 letter to George Cheyne, recounts how he fell into a deep "bodily Distemper . . . the Disease of the Learned."[34] He began to suffer from a series of physical maladies, aware that he was afflicted with a disease of the soul, and this resulted in his obesity. Soon thereafter "there grew upon me a very ravenous Appetite, & as quick a Digestion, which I first took for a good symptom. & was very much surpriz'd to find it bring back a Palpitation of Heart." The resultant weight gain he saw as the direct result of his melancholy.[35] The physiology of fat espoused by the elder Shandy falls very much within the range of these theories. However, it is also indicative of a movement in the perception of the meaning of fat, from seeing it as a purely moral failing, such as gluttony, to the espousal of a more mechanical image of fat as a result of the metabolism of the body, even if cast in humoral garb.

Sterne was writing in the first real age of weight watching for men. Public weighing machines ("steelyards") were developed in France and first appeared in 1760 in London. The medical theory regarding physical weight had been developed by the Venetian Sanctorius Sanctorius in late sixteenth-century Padua. Sanctorius monitored his body weight for thirty years. He announced in *De statica medicine* (1614) that what he consumed weighed less than what he excreted and assumed that the missing weight had been perspired, a sign of health. He recommended the regular weighing of the body to promote health! In his aphorisms he argues against too rapid weight gain or loss, for "when the body is one day of one weight, and another day of another, it argues an introduction of evil qualities." However, he also implies that too great a weight gain is itself pathological: "That weight, which is to any one such as that when he goes up some steepy place, he feels himself lighter than he is wont, is the exact standard of good health."[36] Constant weight and mobility define health.

While some of the older traditions of weight loss, such as the use of the flower thrift (*Armeria maritima*), were continued, diet was the newest fad.[37] Even Dr. Samuel Johnson, whose odd-looking body was wracked by innumerable ailments, both inherited and acquired, undertook such a cure in September 1780: "I am now beginning the seventy-second year of my life, with more strength of body and greater vigour of mind than, I think, is common at that age. . . . I have been attentive to my diet, and have diminished the bulk of my body."[38] Johnson's fat was an ailment of his middle age, but he had been beset by other illnesses from early on. When he was two and a half he contracted scrofula and was taken by his mother in March 1712 to be "touched" by Queen Anne to cure what was then called the King's Evil.[39] This "cure" had as little impact on his life as did diet. Johnson, according to his comments in James Boswell's *Life*, viewed obesity as purely a product of bad diet: "Whatever be the quantity that a man eats, it is plain that if he is too fat, he has eaten more that he should have done." Boswell, by the way, disagreed with Johnson, stating that "you will see one man fat who eats moderately, and another lean who eats a great deal."[40] This remark was in response to Johnson, who had commented that he "fasted from the Sunday's dinner to the Tuesday's dinner, without any inconvenience."[41] Boswell notes that this may well have been true but that Johnson could "practise abstinence, but not temperance."[42] However, it is clear from these discussions that Johnson and Sterne lived in an age when the male, fat body was of concern.[43] Dietary manuals such as John Arbuthnot's *Essay Concerning the Nature of Ailments* (1730) and George Cheyne's *Essay on Health and Long Life* (1724) continued the debates about longevity and masculinity that were begun during the Renaissance in medical discourse about diet. It was George Cheyne, personal physician and friend to Samuel Richardson, who authored an autobiography that captured much of the anxiety about diet and longevity tied to images of the male body (including that of David Hume).

George Cheyne's (1672–1743) autobiography is appended not to his book on longevity but notably to his 1733 handbook, *The English Malady; Or, a Treatise of Nervous Diseases of all kinds, as Spleen, Vapours, Lowness of Spirits, Hypochondrical, and Hysterical Distempers.*[44] Life experience, as with Cornaro, becomes the basis for his claim to the authenticity of his understanding of how to cure the obese male body. It is also vital to realize, however, that the portrayal of Cheyne's body evoked the caricature of the fat man, such as Trulliber in Henry Fielding's parody of the novel of female sensibility, *Joseph Andrews* (1742): "He was indeed one of the largest Men you should see, and could have acted the Part of Sir John Falstaff without stuffing. Add to this, that the Rotundity of his Belly was considerably increased by the shortness of his Stature, his Shadow ascending very near as far as in height when he lay on his back, as when he stood on his legs."[45] In this depiction the fat man is a comic character, a figure greater than life that can exist only on the stage or in the comic novel. He is Gil Perez in Alain-René Lesages's extraordinary picaresque novel of manners, *Gil Blas* (1715), suspended between Cervantes and the social satires of the eighteenth century, such as Sterne. Indeed, Alexander Pope describes Cheyne in 1739 in a letter to their mutual friend Lord Lyttlelton as "a Perfect Falstaff."[46] When you are a fat boy you are seen as a literary figure. What happens when that fat man is you?

Cheyne, born in Scotland in 1673, studied medicine in Edinburgh and had established himself in London by the beginning of the eighteenth century as one of the most successful (and interesting) figures on the medical scene.[47] Wracked with self-doubt after a number of his books were either ignored or attacked, he had a massive breakdown at the age of forty-two. He undertook a rigorous diet of milk and vegetables with little wine and fewer fats only to lapse again, weighing 448 pounds by the time he was fifty-one. He then repeated the process and lived, if not to a hundred, then at least to seventy-two.

Cheyne's autobiography is presented, with all modesty, as a case study. He is aware of how "indecent and shocking" (362) it is for an author, especially a physician, to present himself as a patient. It is the very success of his cure, however, that makes this self-presentation necessary. Cheyne places himself as a follower of Cornaro, citing him in his study of longevity as a model for health. He sees the autobiographical account of the cure of his fat as the strongest proof of the efficacy of his treatment. The treatment links in very specific ways the mental and physical state of the physician and his profession. What makes a good doctor (read: male) is that which cures both his melancholy and his fat.

The cause of the ailment is clear in Cheyne's account. While he came from healthy parents, one side of his family was corpulent. He himself was not as a child, because he lived the life of the mind "in great Temperance" (325). His predisposition to fat, he states, was triggered when he moved to London, where he fell into the company of "Bottle-Companions, the younger Gentry, and Free-Livers" (325). The sole purpose of this companionship was to eat and drink. Taken up by them, Cheyne "grew daily in Bulk" and after a few years became "excessively fat, short-breathed, Lethargic and Listless" (326). He then began to suffer from a series of illnesses, each of which was more difficult to cure than the last. Fits followed fever. As he became more and more ill, his friends abandoned him, "leaving me to pass the melancholy Moments with my own Apprehensions and Remorse." Such friendships, founded on "sensual pleasures and mere Jollity," were false, as they were not rooted in "Virtue and in Conformity to the Divine Order" (328).

Forced to retire to the country, Cheyne began to diet, stripping his daily food down to the barest until he "melted away like a Snow-ball in Summer." But Cheyne also claims this was easier for him because he had been led astray rather than having given into the vices of London society. He was able to cure himself because he remained an outsider to the "Vices and Infidelity" that made up the modern, urban world. In this Cheyne sees society as the cause of his ailments and the countryside and the acknowledgement of "natural Religion" (331) as the cure. Here the piety of the body is repeated, but now in British, millenarian terms. What is piety for Cornaro is the stuff of parody for Cervantes; what is satire for Sterne becomes a means of comprehending one's life for Cheyne.

Cheyne's image of the country as the refuge from a life of dissipation and the place where the obese, ill body can be reconstituted as a healthy, male body is a reflection of the newly emerging belief that the ideal state of nature is the only place where healthy, thin, and beautiful bodies exist. This notion is reflected in the memoirs of Georg Forster, who accompanied Captain James Cook around the world in the 1770s. In 1773 Cook and Forster found themselves in Tahiti, an island that they (and the French, especially Bougainville and Diderot) saw as the perfect natural society. Food abounded, and one did not have to work for it. Therefore gluttony was impossible, as only in a society of inadequacy did the passion for food arise. Fat men were impossible in Tahiti — except, as Forster reports, while walking along the shore he saw a "very fat man . . . who seemed to be the chief of the district" being fed by a "woman who sat near him, [and] crammed down his throat by handfuls the remains of a large baked fish, and several breadfruits, which he swallowed with a voracious appetite."

His face was the "picture of phlegmatic insensibility, and seemed to witness that all his thoughts centred in the care of his paunch." Forster is shocked because he had assumed that obesity of this nature was impossible in a world where there existed "a certain frugal equality in their way of living, . . . [with] hours of enjoyment . . . justly proportioned to those of labour and rest." However, here was the proof that obesity and society were not linked, for Forster found a "luxurious individual spending his life in the most sluggish inactivity, and without one benefit to society, like the privileged parasites of more civilized climates, fattening on the superfluous produce of the soil, of which he robbed the labouring multitude."[48] This contradiction caused much consternation.

Jean Anthelme Brillat-Savarin would write as late as 1825 that "obesity is never found either among savages or in those classes of society which must work in order to eat or which do not eat except to exist." He provided a caveat, however: "Savages will eat gluttonously and drink themselves insensible when ever they have a chance to."[49] Obesity, therefore, could be an illness of natural man as well as of civilization when the bounds of power were transgressed. Hufeland recognized this when he commented that "a certain degree of cultivation is physically necessary for man, and promotes duration of life. The wild savage does not live so long as man in a state of civilization."[50]

The myth of obesity among "natural man" echoed among American explorers of the West, but it took on a specifically gendered form. In 1819 Edwin James stated that "the Missouri Indian is symmetrical and active, and in stature, equal, if not somewhat superior, to the ordinary European standard; tall men are numerous. The active occupations of war and hunting, together perhaps with the occasional privations to which they are subjected, prevents that unsightly obesity, so often a concomitant of civilization, indolence, and serenity of mental temperament."[51] But this was true only of men. John Wyeth observed in 1832 that among the tribes of the Northwest "the persons of the men generally are rather symmetrical; their stature is low, with light sinewy limbs, and remarkably small delicate hands. The women are usually more rotund, and, in some instances, even approach obesity."[52] Among "natural peoples" it was shocking to imagine an obese man, while fat women represented the locus of that illness called obesity. This is a simple reversal of the model imagined by the explorers in the civilization from which they had come.

Cheyne's cure was not limited to the countryside; he also attempted to be cured by waters at Bath and at Bristol (334). He dieted, and he regularly vomited and purged — and he lost weight. Yet he continued to have illness after illness. He finally went onto a "milk diet" suggested by one of his physicians who had used it himself. No alcohol in any form, no meats, only milk — and the physician claimed that he could play six hours of cricket without tiring. Cheyne reduced his meat and alcohol intake, adding vegetables, seeds, bread, "mealy roots, and fruit" (337). And the weight continued to come off. He became "Lank, Fleet and Nimble" (338). Riding ten to fifteen miles a day, he felt he was fit even though he continued to purge and vomit. He suddenly felt that he could add some meat, chicken, and a few stronger liquors. He also stopped exercising and soon became very ill again. He then returned to his diet for twenty years and continued "sober, moderate and plain" (342). Yet over time he fell into the habit of adding more and more foods, alcohol, meat, nuts; his weight returned, and he again became "enormous": "I was ready to faint away, for want to Breath, and my Face turn'd Black." Upon trying to walk up a flight of stairs he was "seiz'd with a Convulsive Asthma" (342). His body was covered in ulcers, and he began to suffer from gout. The pain forced him back on his milk diet. All along he suffered from "Sickness, Reaching, Lowness, Watchfullness, Eructation, and Melancholy" (346). His mental state was as bad as his physical one.

Yet he continued to practice as a physician: "I attended indeed (in a manner) the Business of my profession, and took Air and Exercise regularly in the Daytime; but in such a wretched, dying Condition as was evident to all that saw me" (348). He was persuaded at the end of 1725 to return to London, where he then met with his medical friends, who were not the dandies that had abandoned him. He tried to return to the earlier diet but suddenly became aware that the flexibility of his youth had diminished; he had to be ever more watchful and vigilant in his present state (350). This meant no meat, little alcohol, and a modicum of medicinal port. While this is a healthy diet, one only comes to it in extremity: "No one will ever be brought to such a Regimen as mine is now, without having been first extremely Miserable; and I think Common Life, with temperance, is best for the Generality, else it would not be Common" (353). What he ate is familiar to us from Cornaro and Don Quixote: "the Simplicity of the Alimentary Gospel." He avoided "onions and garlick" (355). Still, he continued to suffer from flatulence and eruction — belching — for a time. He became fit, however, able to "be abroad in all Weathers, Seasons or Times of the Year, day or Night, without much Dread or Hazard of Cold" (358). More important, when (like Cornaro) he had a carriage accident and was knocked unconscious, he was able to recover, according to him, because of the new state of his health (361).

The Enlightenment's image of the fat boy reformed places Cheyne between idealization and horror, between success and disease. In truth his is a religious text about the bounty of God and the need to control one's flesh. Daniel Defoe,

Cheyne's contemporary, preached against "the unmortified pampered Carkass" that was the source of "all these raging, tyrannizing Inclinations."[53] Like Augustine, Defoe was preaching against carnal desires, but the craving for food was very much in Cheyne's world a sin against the health of the flesh. Cheyne's dietetics preaches a personal religion of bodily reform, one quite familiar to his Scottish contemporaries and most specifically to his own religious advisor George Garden. Garden's theology of bodily control became the science of dietetics as a means to cure the soul in Cheyne. Indeed, from Cornaro to Cervantes, from Sterne to Cheyne, the underlying notion is the ability or claim to see within the soul of the unreadable body of the obese. The fat man's soul is corrupt because he is not a true man. Whether in a fantasy Tahiti or in Sterne's Britain, he is seen as deviant in complex and contradictory ways; he is unable to fulfill the true role of manliness because of his inability to move and therefore to work. For work is the boundary between the idle rich and the productive members of society — in other words, between the dandy and the doctor. The medical literature of obesity plays with its relationship to other illnesses such as gout and thus transforms it into an image of class.

THACKERAY AND BANTING

"Class corrupts" is the motto of Cheyne's autobiography, and God (and sobriety) cures. In William Thackeray's *Vanity Fair* (1847–48), the rich bachelor Joseph (Jos) Sedley is Becky Sharp's first and last target. "A very stout, puffy man, in buckskins and Hessian boots, with several immense neckcloths, that arose almost to his nose," Sedley's enormous bulk makes him into a creature of vanity only waiting to fall.[54] He sees himself and Beau Brummel as "the leading bucks of the day" (59). In fact, he is seen in the novel as a "fat gourmand, [who] drank up the whole contents of the [punch] bowl" (93). Indeed, he is called the "fat un" and likened to Daniel Lambert, the fattest man on record at that time, who died in 1809 at the age of forty, weighing 739 pounds.

Daniel Lambert was the exemplary fat man of his day. Lambert was displayed as a wonder of nature along with giants and dwarfs much against his own desires.[55] He was huge, yet the contemporary literature stresses that he neither drank nor ate "more than one dish at a meal," and after his death he was remembered as a man of great "temperance."[56] Other than his size, he was deemed to be of "perfect health: his breathing was free, his sleep undisturbed, and all of the functions of his body in excellent order."[57] In other words he was huge, but healthy and happy. His early death was bemoaned by fashionable London, which had made him one of the sights that had to be visited when you were on the town. When he died his body had to be removed from the room in which he was staying by demolishing a wall! Lambert functions here as an exemplar of great size but also of a social status that is attributable to his "freakish" character. Lambert was one of the "case studies" of obesity of the time that created much of the interest in obesity as part of the world of medical freakishness. Indeed, Dr. T. Coe's earlier 1751 letter to the Royal Society about Mr. Edward Bright, the "fat man at Malden in Essex," has a certain breathless quality about it. Bright was "so extremely fat, and of such an uncommon bulk and weight, that I believe there to be very few, if any, such instances to be found in any country, or upon record in any books."[58] According to Coe, Bright was descended from a lineage of "remarkably fat" people. Extremely fat as a child, he grew in size and weight over the years until his death at thirty, when he weighed more than 616 pounds at five feet nine inches. He was "the gazing-stock and admiration of all people" (189). He ate "remarkably" and drank much beer, a gallon a day (191). Those around him saw his "life as a bur-then, and death as a happy release" (192).

Being seen as a new Daniel Lambert in Thackeray's novel placed Sedley in the realm of the pathetic fat boy whose body mirrors his weak character. He is very different from the image of Lambert, but his body is reread in terms of the loss of moral control ascribed to the literary fat boy. Thackeray provides much more detail for Sedley's life of work. He had been in India in the East India Company's Civil Service for twelve years and was well-known and successful there. He worked at a completely isolated station, a "fine, lonely, marshy, jungly district," and it was only because he developed a liver complaint that he returned to England. There he was transformed into a "gay young bachelor" (59). Spoiled by being part of the fashionable life of the city, he became "lazy, peevish, and a bon-vivant." When he returned to India and afterward, he saw this moment as the defining period of his life. Returning again to England he would try to diet in "a desperate attempt to get rid of his super-abundant fat; but his indolence and love of good living speedily got the better of these endeavours at reform and he found himself again at his three meals a day" (59). Thackeray continues to provide the reader with incredible de-tail about Sedley's life: "Like most fat men, he would have his clothes made too tight and took care they should be of the most brilliant colours and youthful cut" (59). Each detail pro-vides a sense of the role that class has in defining his (and everyone else's) role in *Vanity Fair*.

Becky Sharp, the novel's protagonist, knows what she is doing when, addressing his vanity, she calls Sedley "a very handsome man" (60). The adventures with Becky, however, end in Brussels, at the moment of the Battle of Waterloo, when Sedley decides that "warriors may fight and perish, but he must dine." The more he eats the happier he is: "Jos's spirits rose with his meal" (368). At least until the moment when the cannons on the battlefield are heard and he flees ignominiously. Thereafter, "our worthy fat friend Joseph Sedley returned to India not long after his escape from Brussels" (451). Here he remains to the very end of the novel, returning to Brussels one last time as "Waterloo" Sedley. Having rewritten that part of his life, dressing the part of the dandy and eating himself across the countryside wearing "gorgeous waistcoats of all sorts, or silk and velvet, and gold and crimson" (684), he dies just one page before the end of the novel, in Brussels. It is hinted that Becky is responsible. Sedley never reforms. His is a weakness of the will, a disease thought typical of the age.

Diseases of the will made up a category well loved by philosophers as well as professionals in the mental health field by the nineteenth century.[59] Central to this view was John Locke's belief that the will was "the power that the mind has to order the consideration of any idea, or the forbearing to consider it."[60] Immanuel Kant gives his own aged body as the best example of a will to health. Youth, he states, can "eat what it wants, infirm age demands control" (384). Thus old *men* want to drink more and more water, but "thirst is but a habit." Kant has trained himself to drink less, showing how reason can control the desire for food and drink! (The Scottish writer on longevity John Sinclair learned from this in the early nineteenth century that "the fat and unwieldy, ought to abstain from liquids as much as possible; for great drinkers are more apt to be corpulent than great eaters. Even water is fattening.")[61]

In the nineteenth century faculty psychology began to focus on people as capable of truly voluntary acts, in which (according to Thomas Reid) "every man is conscious of a power to determine, in things which he conceives of to depend upon his determination."[62] This faculty to determine could become ill, and pathologies of the will resulted. The major psychiatrists wrote of this, from J. E. D. Esquirol to Theodor Ribot and Henry Maudsley. The psychiatric category that resulted was "abulia," the inability to execute what one wants to do, without any sign of physical impairment. (Today we speak of obsessive-compulsive disorders or addiction.) With this condition there is no ability to move from motive and desire to execution. Fat men suffer from abulia once they acknowledge their impairment. "Obesity," as Brillat-Savarin states in his handbook on food and diet at the beginning of the nineteenth century, "is not actually a disease, it is at least a most unpleasant state of ill health, and one into which we almost always fall because of our own fault."[63] By the middle of the nineteenth century it had become a sign of a disease of the will, but a disease more of men than of women. It affected the strength of men and the beauty of women disproportionately, according to Brillat-Savarin. This was the new illness that was ascribed to the obese, and it was in the promise of execution, of being able to act, that the fat man now showed his masculinity.

Autobiographical texts by fat men are found in the medical literature of the early nineteenth century. William Wadd presents a series of them as an appendix to his study of obesity, beginning with an "extract of a Letter from ——, Esq," in which the author gives an autobiographical account of his plight.[64] (Of all the cases Wadd tabulated only one is that of a woman.)

In 1863 William Banting sat down and penned his own autobiography accounting for his obesity and how he overcame it. In doing so he showed his mental as well as physical health. His *Letter on Corpulence Addressed to the Public* is an account of how a successful, middle-class undertaker and coffin maker (he had actually supplied the coffin for the Duke of Wellington) overcame his fat.[65] He was not fat because of inaction or lassitude: "Few men have led a more active life — bodily or mentally — from a constitutional anxiety for regularity, precision, and order, during fifty years' business career . . . so that my corpulence and subsequent obesity was not through neglect of necessary bodily activity, nor from excessive eating, drinking, or self-indulgence of any kind" (10–11). Yet, at the age of sixty-six, he stood at about five feet five inches tall and weighed 202 pounds. He sensed that he had stopped being corpulent and had become obese. A "corpulent man eats, drinks, and sleeps well, has not pain to complain of, and no particular organic disease" (13). Obesity, however, was now a source of illness. He developed "obnoxious boils" (15), failing sight and hearing, and a "slight umbilical rupture" (16). He could neither stoop to tie his shoes "nor attend to the little offices humanity requires without considerable pain and difficulty" (14). Indeed, he was "compelled to go down stairs slowly backward" (14). All of these pathologies were seen by Banting (and his physicians agreed) as the direct result of his obesity rather than his aging. In the appendix to the second edition, like the first distributed for free, Banting states: "I am told by all who know me that my personal appearance is greatly improved, and that I seem to bear the stamp of good health; this may be a matter of opinion or a friendly remark, but I can honestly assert that I feel restored in health, 'bodily and mentally,' appear to have more muscular power and vigour, eat and drink with a good appetite, and sleep well."[66] Health is beauty.

Most galling for Banting was the social stigma: "No man labouring under obesity can be quite insensible to the sneers and remarks of the cruel and injudicious in public assemblies, public vehicles, or the ordinary street traffic. . . . He naturally keeps away as much as possible from places where he is likely to be made the object of the taunts and remarks of others"

(14). Underlying Banting's desire to lose weight is the fact that he was seen as a fat man and his body was perceived as useless and parasitic. One of his critics saw this as the core of Banting's personal dilemma. It was not fat but a "morbid horror of corpulence" and an "extreme dislike to be twitted on the subject of paunchiness" that were at the core of Banting's anxiety about his body.[67] He was certainly not alone, however. Brillat-Savarin tells the story of Edward of New York, who was "a minimum of eight feet in circumference. . . . Such an amazing figure could not help but be stared at, but as soon as he felt himself watched by the passersby Edward did not wait long to send them packing, by saying to them in a sepulchral voice: 'WHAT HAVE YOU TO STARE LIKE WILD CATS? . . . GO YOU WAY YOU LAZY BODY . . . BE GONE YOU FOR NOTHING DOGS . . . and other similarly charming phrases."[68] Stigma, as much as physical disability, accounted for Banting's sense of his own illness.

Having been unable to achieve weight loss through the intervention of physicians, Banting was desperate. One physician urged him to exercise, and he rowed daily, which gave him only a great appetite. Another told him that weight gain was a natural result of aging and that he had gained a pound for every year since attaining manhood (13). Indeed, the medical literature of the mid–nineteenth century had come to consider obesity a problem of medical therapy; it condemned self-help: "Domestic medicine is fraught with innumerable evils — it is false economy to practice physic upon yourselves, when a little judicious guidance would obviate all difficulties" (20). He took the waters at Leamington, Cheltenham, and Harrogate; he took Turkish baths at a rate of up to three a week for a year but lost only six pounds in all that time and had less and less energy. Nothing helped.

Failing a treatment for his weakened hearing, he turned to William Harvey, an ear, nose, and throat specialist and a Fellow of the Royal College of Surgeons, in August 1862. Harvey had heard Claude Bernard lecture in Paris on the role that the liver played in diabetes.[69] Bernard believed that in addition to secreting bile, the liver also secreted something that aided in the metabolism of sugars. Harvey began to examine the role of various types of foods, specifically starches and sugars, in diseases such as diabetes. He urged Banting to reduce the amount of these in his diet, for, he argued, "certain articles of ordinary diet, however beneficial in youth, are prejudicial in advanced life, like beans to a horse, whose common food is hay and corn" (17). The aging body could not use the common diet and needed much less sugar and starch.

Banting's body finally began to shed its excess weight. He lost thirty-five pounds, could walk downstairs "naturally," could take ordinary exercise, and could "perform every necessary office for himself"; his rupture was better, and he could hear and see (22–23). Equally important, however, his "dietary table was far superior to the former — more luxurious and liberal, independent of its blessed effect" (21). He remained at a normal weight until his death in London in 1878 at the age of eighty-one. Not quite one hundred, but not bad either.

Banting's pamphlet became a best seller and initiated serious scientific concern as to the meaning of obesity. It was actually one of a number of such pamphlets of the day. One, by A. W. Moore, published in 1857, cited Cornaro as the prime case of someone who was able to lose weight and become healthy.[70] Watson Bradshaw, a physician who had written on dyspepsia before Banting's pamphlet appeared, countered it in 1864 with his own work on obesity, warning people against "rash experiment upon themselves in furtherance of that object."[71] For Bradshaw the ideal of the fat body in cultures such as China and Turkey, where the "ultima thule of human beauty is to possess a face with a triple chin, and a huge abdomen," had become impossible in the West. It was impossible because the "assimilative function has changed its character — the absorbents have varied their duties — fat forsakes the lower extremities and other parts of the body; and persists in concentrating itself in the abdomen, giving rise to what is called 'Corpulence'" (6). Corpulence is a condition of the modern, Western age and, concentrated as it is in the gut, a quality of men. It is clear that this was a pathological state to Bradshaw, but he saw only the extreme cases as diseased. In a pamphlet of 1865 "A London Physician" wrote about "How to Get Fat or the Means of Preserving the Medium Between Leanness and Obesity."[72] He begins by noting that the one question everyone asks is, "Have you read Banting?" This has "invaded all classes," he says, "and doubtless, will descend to posterity" (7). "Corpulence is a parasite, . . . the parasite is a disease, and the close ally of a disease, and the said parasite has been exposed and his very existence threatened" (7) by writers such as Banting and William Harvey. This pamphlet then turns to the emaciated body, which is seen as equally at risk and in need of diet and reform.

Banting's text, however, became the most popular because it was sold as autobiographical. People spoke of "banting" when they tried to shed weight. Even today the Swedish term for "to diet" is *bantning*. S. Weir Mitchell in 1877 noted that " 'Banting' is with us Americans a rarely needed process, and, as a rule, we have much more frequent occasion to fatten than to thin our patients."[73] The obese patient was the subject of reform, and for a rather long time that patient was seen as a European one. Banting's mentor, William Harvey, turned to this topic in 1872, spurred on, he wrote, by Banting's success. Harvey stressed that the new scientific advances in "physiology and animal chemistry" (vi) meant that one could treat obesity as a disease. To that point he cited the case of Daniel Lambert and suggested that there seemed to have been no attempt to "arrest the progress of the disease" (viii). Banting began his pamphlet with the argument that obesity was a "parasite affecting humanity" (7). Suddenly, sufferer and physician saw obesity alone as the product of forces beyond the will. Harvey agreed with Banting, however, that until this stage of pathology was reached, "persons rarely become objects of attention; many have even congratulated themselves on their comely appearance, not seeking advice or a remedy for that which they did not consider an evil" (ix). One of Banting's severest contemporary critics, William E. Aytoun, observed: "We are acquainted with many estimable persons of both sexes, turning considerably more than fifteen stone in the scales — a heavier weight than Mr. Banting ever attained — whose health is unexceptionable, and who would laugh to scorn the idea of applying to a doctor for recipe or regimen which might have the effect of marring their developed comeliness."[74] Is fat a definitive sign of disease? Even Daniel Lambert was seen as healthy until his death.

Banting and Harvey needed to redefine obesity as a physiological disease rather than as a fashion or a moral failing. Yet Harvey could not make a sufficient leap between his knowledge and the actual mechanism by which "respiratory foods" (carbohydrates) caused obesity and other ailments. Felix Niemeyer, from Stuttgart, had argued that the ingestion of more or less pure protein would reduce the toxic effects of sugars and starches.[75] All believed that the body — in light of the views of materialists such as Johannes Müller — was a collection of chemical processes. Questions of will and its attendant diseases were eliminated.

Yet the disease from which Jos Sedley and William Banting suffered was not merely one of excessive corpulence. It was a disease of their manliness. Having people help you with your evacuations or mock you on the street meant that you were not quite a man. Joshua Duke knew this well when in 1885 he wrote his screed *Banting in India with Some Remarks on Diet and Things in General*.[76] Duke was surgeon-major with the Third Punjab Cavalry, on duty in Kashmir in 1884, when he wrote his book. *Banting in India*, written some four decades after Thackeray and almost two decades after Banting's pamphlet, called for the radical reform of the British in India. They had become exemplars of "effeminacy, unmanliness" as "represented by the Esthete and Estheticism" (10). The soldiers had become "gentle and good." This was a rather sad state of affairs for real men. Even "flogging is now considered unnecessary in our army and navy" (10). Time in India had "altered . . . the sturdiness and doggedness" of the British (11). Duke's is the same view as that of Rudyard Kipling, who, in the *National Observer* in 1890, made the starved, half-naked Gunga Din a better man than the average white English soldier because of his pluck. And the sign of the unmanliness of the British soldier in India was his obesity! It could be seen in the "enormous enlargement of the omentum and the condition called Potbelly" (32). This "omental fat" impedes breathing and eventually impacts on the heart.

Brillat-Savarin, whose 1825 account of food and its pleasures was also a study of corpulence and its dangers, stressed the physiognomy of obesity. He wrote in an autobiographical mode about his sense of his obese body:

There is one kind of obesity which centers around the belly; I have never noticed it in women: since they are generally made up of softer tissues, no part of their bodies are spared when obesity attacks them. I call this type of fatness Gastrophoria and its victims Gastrophores.

I myself am in their company; but although I carry around with me a fairly prominent stomach, I still have well-formed lower legs, and calves as sinewy as the muscles of an Arabian steed. Nevertheless I have always looked on my paunch as a redoubtable enemy; I have conquered it and limited its outlines to the purely majestic; but in order to win the fight, I have fought hard indeed: whatever is good about the results and my present observations I owe to a thirty-year battle.[77]

He was commenting on his struggle with a disease of the will in the form of his own obesity. The stomach, Cervantes' Mr. Gut, began, however, to take on a life of its own. The potbelly became a major indicator of the potential for illness for the observers of masculine obesity in the late nineteenth century. Indeed, of the 163,567 overweight men in the United States and Canada identified between 1870 and 1899 (for insurance purposes), abdominal obesity (the waist being of greater circumference than the chest) was present in about 13 percent.[78] This was taken as an absolute sign of increased morbidity and mortality. The projected deaths of these individuals were almost one-third less than their actual death rate. "Omental fat" in the disease of Gastrophoria (potbelliedness) came to represent the bloated unmasculine over time.

Joshua Duke's example of the pathological effect of "omental fat" was the gastrophore Daniel Lambert, who died at the age of forty. Yet Lambert's huge body was fat from his legs to his neck. In contrast to Lambert, Duke's positive case study was the gastrophore William Banting, who overcame his "omental fat" to become a productive member of society (35). According to Duke, in order to restore the manliness of the soldiers of India, such as Colonel W——, it was necessary to reduce weight, and the most direct manner of doing this was to follow the diet prescribed by Banting, eschewing starch and sugars (35). As a last thought, Duke suggested that one could add a "comparatively new drug 'Cuca.' It is obtained from Peru, and is chewed by the Indians when going on long and exhausting journeys" (55). With a strict diet and much cocaine, one could accomplish wonders. With the work of Duke, the move from the secularization of the fat boy's body to its medicalization was complete. Yet at every step the fat boy struggles with the meanings attached to his body.

The world of Banting is the world of fat boys. The literary versions that haunted the nineteenth century, as we have seen and will see, are powerful representations of the differences perceived in the obese male. As indicated in the introduction, the addition of further categories, such as "race" (in the sense of nineteenth-century racial theory) and "class," also altered how the representation of the fat boy was understood. By the end of the nineteenth century the heirs of Cornaro and Cervantes were still slightly anxious about the impact of the obese body on masculinity. In the eighteenth century, from Sterne, Samuel Richardson, and Henry Fielding to Tobias Smollett, the fat boy was at the very heart of fiction. Indeed, Smollett translated both *Don Quixote* and *Gil Blas*, and he even modeled *Roderick Random* on the latter. The nineteenth-century fiction of Charles Dickens, as we shall see, continued this tradition. Each writer brought images of the fat boy into fiction and into the lived experience of obese men.

Patient Zero *Falstaff*

If there is an exemplary fat boy who links the world of high culture and that of medicine it is Shakespeare's Sir John Falstaff. As a literary character he moves from a bragging soldier in the *Henry IV* plays (1598–1600), a close relative of Plautus's *miles gloriosus*, to a pathetic and comic old man in *The Merry Wives of Windsor* (1602). Falstaff is part of a long line of comic or pathetic fat men on the English stage. He is a comic figure whose very presence on the stage is seen to evoke some type of real or potential danger. Stuart M. Tave notes that "English comedy and even English farce and comic epilogues . . . were a vital national bulwark against the ever waiting terrors of lunacy, melancholy, spleen. . . . Laughter had always been recognized as an excellent therapeutic that fattened the body and healed the mind: 'A merry heart doeth good like a medicine'

(Proverbs 17:22). The Prologue of *Ralph Roister Doister* is one of many appeals to the same commonplace. The compilers of jestbooks, to go no further, were, and still are, able to exploit it in advertisement."[1] The comic fat man simultaneously alleviated and provided a bridge to the causes of the terrors associated with the freakish and therefore dangerous body.

Falstaff's antecedents are indeed to be found in Nicholas Udall's *Ralph Roister Doister* (1553), as well as in Ben Jonson's "humorous" plays *Every Man in His Humour* (1598) and *Every Man out of His Humour* (1599). There the enactment of the classical humors, including the phlegmatic knight Bobadill in the former play and the vainglorious knight Puntarvolo in the latter, provide models for the satiric function of the *miles gloriosus* in Elizabethan drama. As he matured, Jonson came to see himself as a "fat boy writing." In his autobiographical poem of 1619 or 1620, "My Picture Left in Scotland," he represents himself as an aging man with a substantial paunch and pockmarked face:

> Tell me that she hath seen
> My hundred of gray hairs,
> Told seven and forty years
> Read so much waste, as she cannot embrace
> My mountain belly and my rocky face.
> . . .
> And all these through her eyes have stopp'd her ears.[2]

Here the self-image of the aged fat boy is as a sexually depleted male, who like William Shakespeare's Falstaff is no longer attractive to the women about him. Jonson's "rocky face" as well as his paunch point in the visual culture of the time to the reason for his lack of attractiveness.

The dramatic braggart becomes the corrupt, desexed fat man in his transformation from the Henry plays to *The Merry*

Wives of Windsor. In the Henry plays Falstaff still bears the remnants of the highly sexualized, mocking braggart of the older tradition. His comic turn in *The Merry Wives of Windsor*, however, is no longer as part of a court that is in transition; he is now firmly, if unhappily, ensconced in the middle-class world of Windsor. Here he poses a danger rather than comic relief to the established order of the new society.[3] His fat male body represents these two differing and competing stages and lays the foundation for what would become the exemplary fat man in later literary and medical examinations. This view, that his fat defines Falstaff's character, is an old one, perhaps best presented by William Hazlitt in 1817.[4] But what is the actual quality of character that this fat male body represents on the stage?

According to Shakespeare's worldview, Falstaff's collapse into the fat, comic figure is a collapse redolent of pathological decay — more specifically, the decay of age — as he moves from soldier to comic braggart. During the Renaissance such decay, according to Robert Burton, was associated with corrupt living and most specifically with sexually transmitted diseases, which necessarily result from such a life.[5] The internal state of being, the character of Falstaff, reflects this diseased nature. The diseased soul is encapsulated by the fat body. Falstaff's decline into fat is simultaneously the progress of the disease. In old age he suffers consequences from the "pox" of his youth (*Henry IV, Part 2* 1.2.242–43).[6] But the presence of syphilis, read as causing and being caused by the character of Falstaff, reflects an older moral tradition.[7] Given that syphilis was seen as a "new" disease, its reading within older moral categories was particularly powerful proof of the divine nature of its cause. This association was also made by analogy with the corrupt body of the false Christian, following the model of Augustine.[8] The older Christian category of "gluttony," one of the seven deadly sins, was collapsed together with concupiscence to form the basis for the character of the fat, comic man. This is, of course, part of the Renaissance version of the Western myth that reads moral decay on the body as much in the deformation of Richard III as in the decaying or decayed body of Falstaff. The disease is read on the body or, in the case of Ben Jonson, on his "rocky face" marked with the pox. But is it smallpox or the great pox, syphilis?

Shakespeare introduced Falstaff in *Henry IV, Part 1* (*1H4*) as a boon companion to Prince Hal, who by the end of *Henry IV, Part 2* (*2H4*) has become Henry V. The comic turns of Falstaff are here presented as destructive, the rule of law ultimately triumphing over the rule of carnival. Falstaff is the embodiment of male obesity and represents misrule in Shakespeare's world. He violates the norms of both masculine honor and health. He is, according to the prince, "Sir John Paunch," Mr. Gut, and a "coward" (*1H4* 2.2.65). He is "fat guts" (*1H4* 2.2.30) and a "fat-kidneyed rascal" (*1H4* 2.2.5). He is "ye fat paunch" (*1H4* 2.4.142). He is also, however, one of those "base contagious clouds of anarchy that the prince can use to discuise his own motivations" (*1H4* 1.2.192). He jests with Falstaff in terms of contagion and disease. Falstaff is a whoreson (*1H4* 2.4.225). When the prince accuses Falstaff of consorting with whores he evokes their "pox" (*1H4* 2.4.225). All of these comments refer to Falstaff's role in the body politic and also evoke the metaphor of disease as being quite appropriate for such potential and real disruption of the state.

Falstaff's illness is a reflex of his character. This "huge hill of flesh (*1H4* 2.4.241) is "sanguine" (*1H4* 2.4.239), not phlegmatic, at least according to the prince. Yet Falstaff sees his character as reflecting his development from a sanguine young rake to a phlegmatic old debauchee: "A man can no more separate age and covetous than 'a can part young limbs and lechery. But the gout galls the one and the pox pinches the other" (2H4 1.2.229-31). If the young Falstaff suffered in the past from the pox, the old one suffers from gout, traditionally seen as a disease of the gluttonous. Falstaff is presented within a discourse of pathology and corruption from his appearance at the very onset of the play. This marks him as potentially as disruptive in the court as those who rebelled against Henry IV. His baleful influence on the prince is seen to be infectious. The political and medical aspects of Falstaff are so closely linked that Prince Hal can judge them both when he finds a bill for what Falstaff has eaten: capons (not exactly partridges, but close enough), a food of expense and delicacy, and anchovies, likewise a luxurious dish. He drinks huge amounts of sack (1H4 2.4.529-34). The prince is appalled that he has eaten but a halfpenny's worth of bread for every two gallons of sack he has drunk (1H4 2.4.535). Falstaff's diet signifies a disruption of the natural order, in which man should live by the bread that he earns. Hal's dietetics are somewhat different from Christ's admonition that "man shall not live by bread alone, but by every word of God" (Luke 4:4). For Hal bread is the food of the masses, while sack and capons are the indulgences of those who would disrupt the health of the body politic with their sybaritic and useless lives.

The new state needs healthy new citizens whose allegiance is not to the disruption of order but to its lawful constitution. Thus, the new king dismisses Falstaff at the end of the play and demands that he remedy himself before he may ask for any benefits: "Make less thy body hence, and more thy grace. / Leave gormandizing. Know the grave doth gape / For thee thrice wider than for other men. . . . And, as we hear you do reform yourselves / We will, according to your strengths and qualities, / Give you advancement" (2H4 5.5.52-54, 68-70).

Falstaff's character, however, has been clearly delineated well before this. For if Hal's moral courage, which appears when he becomes king, is foreshadowed in the plays, it is in the battle scenes of the first part. Falstaff, too, appears in these battle scenes and reveals his character as very much the opposite of Hal's. He may appear to be a knight, but he is a cowardly one whose primary concern is for his own skin. Falstaff's anxiety about his body is central to his sense of its decay. No monologue better exemplifies a tragic and somber Falstaff than the following address, where he explains why risk in battle is a bad thing:

> 'Tis not due yet; I would be loath to pay him before his day. What need I be so forward with him that calls not on me? Well, 'tis no matter; honour pricks me on. Yea, but how if honour prick me off when I come on? how then? Can honour set to a leg? no: or an arm? no: or take away the grief of a wound? no. Honour hath no skill in surgery, then? no. What is honour? a word. What is in that word honour? What is that honour? air. A trim reckoning! Who hath it? he that died o' Wednesday. Doth he feel it? no. Doth he hear it? no. 'Tis insensible, then. Yea, to the dead. But will it not live with the living? no. Why? detraction will not suffer it. Therefore I'll none of it. Honour is a mere scutcheon: and so ends my catechism. (1H4 5.1.127–41)

Thus, as a "young" man, Falstaff dismisses honor as a quality that he feels necessary to his calling as a soldier, a knight, a member of the retinue about Hal. It is telling that he later claims authorship of a heroic deed that he has in no way actually done. It is clear, however, that the central metaphor for honor is that it is not a physician. It cannot cure the diseases of the mortal body. Still, as is unspoken in Falstaff's monologue, its violation can be the source of disease. One disease in particular would mark the infected as dishonorable: syphilis.[9]

Old men, according to the common knowledge of the age, were supposed to tend toward being "sadde" and "melancho-like," as Falstaff acknowledges (*1H4* 1.2.74).[10] Old age was the time, however, when "naturall complexion and temperature naturally and of its owne accord is euidently changed."[11] Melancholy was believed to be a potential cause, as well as symptom, of syphilis.[12] These two states were seen as meaningfully related. The passage of time, as well as the experience of youth, caused melancholy and obesity in old men. This is quite parallel to the fat Hamlet. "He's fat and scant of breath," complains Gertrude in the final scene (*Ham.* 5.2.287). He prays that his heart "hold" and his sinews "grow not instant old, / But bear him stiffly up" (*Ham.* 1.5.94–95). Hamlet is melancholy and in some controversial readings also seems to be suffering from syphilis. Indeed, it is even intimated that his melancholy is a product of his physical state. Yet it is his body as much as his character that reveals his diseased and unhappy nature, and this then causes his death.[13] Young fat men can also suffer from disease. Indeed, it was thought that even bad foods, such as "corrupted meats," might cause the disease.[14]

The notion that specific body types have specific psychic makeups is as old as the Babylonians and as recent as Ernst Kretschmer's claim of a corollary between his "pynkic" (short, rotund) physique and manic-depressive illness in the 1920s.[15] Old men, however, suffer in their own particular manner. In a 1636 translation of Leonard Lessius's autobiography, so much indebted to Cornaro, he wrote that "for one kinde of proportion belongs to Youth, when it is in its flower; another to Consistencie; a third to Old Age."[16] He noted that as a young man one can eat more extensively, but old age marks the decline of such excess. One should not eat more than one can in order that one is not "made unfit for the duties and offices belonging to the Minde" (30). A "Sober diet doth by little and little diminish this abundance of humours, and abates this ill moisture, and reduceth them to their due proportions" (34). Central to Lessius and his Jacobean translator is the avoidance of those foods that cause illness in the elderly male, those that "breed cataracts, clouds, dizzinesses, distillations and coughs; and in the stomack breed crudities, inflations, gripings, gnawings, frettings, and the like" (60). If one does not avoid these, one has no "plainer proof of his thraledom to gluttonie, than when he thus thrusts and poures in that which he knows is hurtfull unto him, onely to content his licorish appetite" (60–61). Such a sober diet is necessary, for it "drives away Wrath and Melancholie, and breaks the furie of Lust; in a word, replenisheth both soul and bodie with exceeding good things; so that it may well be termed the mother of Health" (202). Everard Maynwaringe noted somewhat later in the century that such indulgence does not solely impair the individual but also the entire future of the state. He writes: "We and our posterity shall degenerate yet still into a worse and sooner fading state of life. For, as the principles of our Nature are more infirm, tainted, and debauched from our parents and Progenitors, then those of former Ages, of more vigour, soundness and integrity; are likewise more propense, and liable worse to be depraved and degenerate, and consequently of shorter duration and continuance" (4). What might be lost can be lost not only by gluttony but also by concupiscence, by "indulging Venus too much, by immoderate and too frequent acts, thereby enervating all the faculties, dispiriting and wasting the body: by wearing and fretting the mind with various passions" (6). The result is that "the Body which was fat, or plump and fleshy, afterwards grows lean and thin; or if lean and spare bodies grow big and corpulent; here is just cause of suspition, that all is not right" (41). Fat bodies have their own problems, and they reflect the image of *acedia*: "Avoid day sleeps as a bad custom; chiefly fat and corpulent bodies" (92). Here the soul is itself perceived as fat when the body is in distress: "The Soul is languishing, heavy and inactive, altogether indisposed to the government and tuition of the body; and perhaps desirous to be discharged and shake it off, being weary of the burthen; taking no delight in their partnership and society, as in melancholy despair and grief" (133). In this the trope of the obese male body is extended to the metaphor of the body as a state.

Old men have a cold and dry temperament by definition; they are therefore melancholic. Falstaff is melancholic because of his aging body. Yet melancholy also can arise from syphilis, as Robert Burton notes in *The Anatomy of Melancholy*.[17] Melancholy, on the other hand, can also predispose one to syphilis, as Girolamo Fracastoro, who coined the word *syphilis*, notes: "For those whose veins are swollen with black bile and throb with thick blood there is in their case a greater struggle and the plague clings more tenaciously."[18] Youth (or Falstaff trying to look youthful) has a sanguine complexion: "A goodly portly man, I' faith, and a corpulent, of a cheerful look, a pleasing eye, and a most noble carriage" (*1H4* 2.4.422–24). What is happy corpulence in youth is inherently different from melancholic obesity in old age.[19]

Old fat is a sign of disease. La Fontaine observes that what one wishes to achieve in life is "embonpoint raisonnable."[20] One cannot be too thin, nor can one be grossly fat. Such fat on the stage was almost always "tinged with malice," as in the case of Montfleury, the Parisian actor who drew attention to his comic girth only to be skewered for it in public.[21] Being too fat was a sign — at least on the stage — of the male body being read as diseased, even freakish. Falstaff's body was a public sign of his character. And it is not a truly masculine one.

Shakespeare's continuation of the history of Falstaff in *The Merry Wives of Windsor* (*MWW*) provides a set of readings of a male body fallen into ruin. While Falstaff still appears to be the ideal knight, at least according to the middle-class women he is attempting to seduce, he is merely a simulacrum (*MWW* 2.1.51–60). His goal is not seduction but money to buy food and drink. His diet (and therefore his character) remain quite the same as they were in the *Henry* plays. After he is rescued from the Thames, where the women have thrown him, hidden in a clothes hamper, after discovering that he had approached all of them, he orders "a quart of sack" and "a toast in 't" for his meal (*MWW* 3.5.3). This is more or less the meal that Hal finds so appalling in its revelation of Falstaff's character. Falstaff, however, is not only a mock knight in this version; he has also been transformed into a mock woman. To escape again the husbands of the women of Windsor he disguises himself as "the fat woman of Brentford" (*MWW* 4.2.68). The disguised Falstaff has now been transformed into an "old woman" (*MWW* 4.2.158). In this guise the very women he sought to seduce again torment him. The worst of this is that the fat old man fears he might face a diet regimen. He is so mortified by his treatment at the hands of these good citizens that he is anxious that the news not reach the court, for the courtiers would "melt me out of my fat drop for drop and liquor fisherman's boots with me" (*MWW* 4.5.92–93). Fat Falstaff is "the image of the jest" (*MWW* 4.6.16–17); he is the fat fool in the court and an exile in the town. More than that, however, he is the comic representative of moral decay: St.

Augustine's "puffed man" (*MWW* 5.5.151). It is no accident that Shakespeare uses this phrase. Falstaff is full of his own role in the body politic even when that role has become a parody because of his character. Falstaff is "old, cold, withered, and of intolerable entrails . . . and given to fornications, and to taverns, and sack, and wine, and metheglins, and to drinkings and swearings and starings, pribbles and prabbles" (*MWW* 5.5.152–58). To all of this Falstaff accedes. He is a hollow man, an old man, a fat man, and thus not much of a man at all.

Sexual overindulgence in youth and the infections that result from it become written on the body of the old man. His danger then to the married women of Windsor, no matter how attracted they may be to his status as a knight, is clear. This inner anxiety is one that haunts the marriage bed throughout Shakespeare's comedies: the infidelity of one partner can spell the other partner's death. The syphilitic Jacques in *As You Like It* remains celibate and hermitlike at the close of the comedy, when all of the other "pure" couples are betrothed. Shakespeare's Falstaff is a danger to the order of the court, which is why he is banished, but he is also a danger to the social order exemplified by matrimony at Windsor. Falstaff's death, reported by the hostess (see *Henry V* 2.3.6–28), brings the danger he posed to a close.[22] His off-stage death is the act that caps his character, for it seems to reveal the decayed nature of his body and soul. He dies slowly from the extremities, as death proceeds "upwards and upwards and all was as cold as any stone." The report of his death absolves the king of any sense of guilt at having exiled Falstaff: "He's in Arthur's bosom, if ever man went to Arthur's bosom. A' made a finer end and went away an it had been any christom child." Yet the slow death described is not at all a "good" death, except in its presentation to the king. It remains the final commentary on the decay of Falstaff's body, now in its last stages of dissolution.

Falstaff's death is the fulfillment of the promise or curse made to Adam by Michael at the close of John Milton's *Paradise Lost* (1667):

> [I]f thou well observe
> The rule of not too much, by temperance taught
> In what thou eatst and drinkst, seeking from thence
> Due nourishment, not gluttonous delight,
> Till many years over thy head return:
> So maist thou live, till like ripe Fruit thou drop
> Into thy Mothers lap, or be with ease
> Gatherd, not harshly pluckt, for death mature:
> This is old age; but then thou must outlive
> Thy youth, thy strength, thy beauty, which will change
> To witherd weak & gray; thy Senses then
> Obtuse, all taste of pleasure must forgoe,
> To what thou hast, and for the Aire of youth
> Hopeful and cheerful, in thy blood will reigne
> A melancholly damp of cold and dry
> To waigh thy spirits down, and last consume
> The Balme of Life.
>
> *Paradise Lost* X: 528–43[23]

If Adam leads a moderate life he will die a good death; if not he will die in corruption and illness. Yet in Michael's eye even a good old age must end in "a melancholly damp of cold and dry," as indeed Falstaff's death "as cold as any stone" shows. The humoral state of old age marks the entry of mortality into human existence beyond the Garden of Eden. The exile from paradise, however, was also connected with human sexuality. Falstaff is indeed Adam at the end, cursed not only by death but also by his sexuality.

122

When Giuseppe Verdi began to write the opera *Falstaff* in the summer of 1889, his anxiety about the exhaustion of age was clear. He had had a major success with Arrigo Boito's version of *Otello* when it was premiered on 5 February 1887 at the Teatro alla Scala in Milan. What could follow this success? Boito, who composed the libretto, suggested a great, comic opera, which under Verdi's tutelage became the great opera of the happy fat man. Here Verdi's own understanding of old age must have played a role. According to Verdi's friend Italo Pizzi, Verdi believed the advice of the pamphleteer Mosso, who argued that old men were at risk of cerebral anemia if they overindulged in any area.[24] Thus, all old men were advised that they would live longer if they worked only two hours a day. After having worked two hours a day for two years, due to his anxiety that the expenditure of vital energy would lead to his own collapse, Verdi finished *Falstaff*. As a review in the daily newspaper *L'Italia del popolo* states, *Falstaff* was considered a work that presented the composer as an "example of a virtuous, severe, and serene life."[25] The opera, therefore, is the product of the aged but productive composer.

One must ask, however, whether in the late nineteenth century Verdi's *Falstaff* could have been read as more than a "comic opera." Indeed, when critics comment that this is the perfect opera of old age — Verdi's, that is — the question of what the "fat" of Falstaff means is open to interpretation. Are all striking men of middle age condemned to an old age of obesity and collapse? Would Verdi himself be condemned to such an end? Or is moderation the answer? Could Falstaff be read as a case study of a specific type of senescence?

Opera before Verdi is full of fat men. Certainly, there are enough fat male characters to warrant some type of supposition about the means by which composers of opera create the sound of the fat male character. Thus in the libretto by Gottlob Stephanie Jr. (based on a text by Christian Friedrich Bretzner) for Mozart's *The Abduction from the Serail* (1782), Osmin, the servant, is a comic figure, and his music is programmatically comic male music. In this opera his role is written as a bass with hints of a higher-pitched, or feminine, voice. He is comic because he only appears to be male. His bass voice sounds essentially masculine — basses are clearly not altos — but that sound deceives. The implication for Mozart and Stephanie's eighteenth-century audience would have been that Osmin had been castrated as he was supervising a harem. The comic turn results from the juxtaposition of the aggressive sexuality of the character, his deep, profoundly male voice, and his social role. Castrati were understood in both the medical and the musical literature of the time to be marked by a high, pure voice. The implied castration of Osmin, however, is as much a social as a physical castration, a distinction based on the impossibility of sexual contact with certain groups. He desires what he can never have, and this is reflected in the image of his "oriental" body. Osmin prefigures the type of comic character whose better-known manifestation is the black servant/guard Monostatos in Mozart's (and Emanuel Schikaneder's) *The Magic Flute.* Monostatos, however, is additionally marked by his black skin as "socially castrated," this status reflected in his high tenor voice, whose timbre directly evokes castration. Here again the character's "castration" functions as a mark of social castration, as any sexual contact between him and his object of desire is deemed impossible, not solely because of his social status but also because of his color. The fat boy is equally "castrated" in terms of both the popular image of the castrati's obese body and his social castration. Castration in this operatic context means a heightening of illicit or inappropriate sexual desire on the part of the male.

When we move to the late nineteenth century prior to Verdi and look at the appearance of a fat male character as the central figure of an operatic tradition, the very definition of "fat" changes. Osmin and Monostatos are representatives of clearly evoked and vocally represented failed masculinity. Osmin's bass voice reflects this fact as much as the tenor of Monostatos. Medical discussions of castration often evoke the obesity of the castrated male. Indeed, the obese male body is often read as the direct result of castration, after the model of the castrated animal, such as the capon. Castration, however, is also read as causing a diminished libido and impotence.[26] In opera this is exactly reversed. The marginal figures representing social castration are oversexed as well as physically ill proportioned.

The tradition of the ultimate fat man in opera, Falstaff, proceeded along nearly the same trajectory until the end of the nineteenth century. In the earlier operatic versions of Shakespeare's character he was sung as a comic basso. This was the means by which fat male characters could be differentiated vocally from all of the other set roles in operas. Falstaff, perhaps more than any other of Shakespeare's characters, seemed to lend himself toward operatic interpretation in the eighteenth and nineteenth centuries, at least as a buffo character. In Falstaff operas beginning (at least) with Antonio Salieri's opera buffa *Falstaff* (1798), with a libretto by Carlo Prospero Defranceschi, Falstaff is a comic figure, and his voice, like those of other comic bassos, marks his divergence from other masculine voices on stage. In 1824 Henry Rowley Bishop (the composer of "Home Sweet Home") and Frederic Reynolds staged their musical version of the play at Drury Lane. It reappeared on the London stage in different forms until the 1890s.

Larded with songs taken from many of Shakespeare's other plays set by Bishop, it was a success especially because of the exaggerated comic basso songs provided for Falstaff. Certainly, the high point of this tendency in the opera of the mid-nineteenth century was Otto Nicolai's comic opera *Die Lustige Weiber von Windsor* (The merry wives of Windsor; 1849). Coming after the great wave of German Shakespeare translations, beginning with Christoph Martin Wieland in the eighteenth century and continuing to the now standard Romantic translations by Friedrich Schlegel and Ludwig Tieck, Nicolai's opera sets S. H. Mosenthal's libretto. Mosenthal followed, in very rough form, a theatrical translation of Shakespeare's *Merry Wives of Windsor*. In this opera Falstaff, to no one's surprise, is a comic basso.

Giuseppe Verdi's Falstaff, too, seems to stand in this tradition, yet with a rather important difference. The figure, as drawn in Boito's libretto, presents a new twist on the idea of "fat" music. Central to this is that Verdi set Falstaff as a baritone. How then is the audience to understand the character and its musical representation? It is clear that on one level Verdi is reaching back to a comic tradition of Italian opera best represented by the work of Rossini and Donizetti. He also seems to be presenting an answer to the "fat music" and "fat singers" of Richard Wagner (perhaps especially the comic twists of *Die Meistersinger*). Yet it is clear that *Falstaff* is neither a traditional Italian opera buffa nor a post-Wagnerian *Gesamtkunstwerk*.[27]

What is Verdi's version of what becomes the new comic opera? Fundamental to this question is the ambiguous relationship among the voice, the body, the text, and the music representing Falstaff. These altogether present a comic, fat body, but with a powerful change. The power of Verdi's Falstaff is such that Edward Elgar's tone poem "Falstaff — A Symphonic Study in C Minor" (Op. 68, 1913), commissioned for the 1913 Leeds Festival, reflects the psychological complexity of Verdi's representation. For Elgar, too, the "comic" Falstaff is hidden within the texture of the composition, and he uses the bassoon to represent this quality. This is part of the quality of the symphonic poem, as Elgar notes in a written commentary published in the *Musical Times* on 1 September 1913, before the premiere of his text. Interestingly, Elgar also added a section that is not found in any of the Shakespearean (or indeed Verdi's) versions, a short dream interlude in which Falstaff recalls his time as a boy, when he was page to the Duke of Norfolk, and wonders how different his life might have been had he been given a greater sense of his own self. Influenced by the whimsical tone poem, Ralph Vaughan Williams wrote his own *Falstaff, Sir John in Love*, first performed at the Royal College of Music on 21 March 1929. Falstaff represented here is, of course, a baritone. This version of the character is more lyrical than Verdi's comic version. The baritone voice of Falstaff is not the comic basso, but neither is it the *Heldentenor*. Indeed, the vocal range of those who sang (and sing) Verdi's role often bridges both.

In operatic terms Verdi's Falstaff was a clear break from the fat, comic tradition of the Osmin figures, as well as the early Falstaffs, especially that of the widely popular Nicolai. Under the guidance of Verdi, Boito provided a textual break in the libretto that enabled the opera to present a rather different "comic" Falstaff to Verdi's late nineteenth-century audience. The result is a comic opera with seemingly profound overtones in which the fat of the central character is also to be read as the prime indicator of his character. The fat of the character, however, is not simply equated with the pseudomasculinity of the comic basso. Falstaff is a baritone. This baritone voice (and what Verdi chooses to do with it) seems to represent the decay of "real" manhood into the pathology of aging. The text and the voice mark the distinctions among the older buffo settings of Falstaff, as well as the difference between the body of Falstaff and all of the other "fat" male bodies on the stage. Verdi's Falstaff is different from the inherently pathological, represented by the comic basso, as well as from the merely "fat" males on the stage. The pathology represented by Falstaff is found in the sung voice of the character within the structure of the libretto.

Something else changes in the space between Boito's libretto and Verdi's musical interpretation of Falstaff. Boito and Verdi both employ the double image of Falstaff, using translations of *The Merry Wives of Windsor* as well as passages from the *Henry IV* plays as translated by Giulio Carcano (Italian) and Victor Hugo (French). Boito self-consciously interpolates some selected passages from the Henry plays into a text based on *The Merry Wives of Windsor*. These passages present the contrast between the early image of Falstaff as a knight in decay and the later comic image, found in *The Merry Wives of Windsor*, of the decayed knight. Yet in this process the libretto (and the music) undermines both images by merging them. Verdi and Boito present an amalgam of the first stage of Falstaff, that of the bragging soldier, and the second stage, that of the comic fop. To do this, the first aria given to Falstaff is an interpolation of Falstaff's monologue on the nature of honor, especially on the nature of the relationship between honor and the body. Boito's version of this monologue, which comes early in the first act of the opera, delineates Falstaff's "fat" character. He does not represent *all* old men but rather the pathological case, the old man in decay:

L'onore!

Honor!
Scoundrels! You dare talk of honor! You!
You swear of debasement tell me of honor.
Who can always live by honor? Not even I. I can't even.
Ever so often I must go in the fear of Heaven
When I am forced by want to veer from honor with hellish
   lies
And half-lies and stratagems: to juggle, to embellish.
And you, with rags and tatters, the look of half-dead owls,
And lice for comrades, who go through life surrounded by
   scornful howls,
Talk honor now! What honor? You swine! You filth!
How funny! What rubbish! Can this honor fill your
   paunch?
When you are hungry? No. Can this honor heal a leg
   that's broken?
No, so. A shoulder? No. A finger? No. Not a thumbnail?
   No.

Nè un piede? No, Nè un dito? No. Nè un capello? No!
L'onor non è chirurgo. Ch'è dunque? Una parola.
Che c'è in questa parola? C'è dell'aria che vola.
Bel construtto! L'onore lo può sentir chi è morto?
No. Vive sol coi vivi? Neppure: perchè a torto
Lo gonfian le lusinghe, lo corrompe l'orgoglio,
L'ammorban le calumnie; e per me non ne voglio!

For honor's not a surgeon. What is it then? A word.
What's in this word? There is a vapor that scatters.
What a structure! This honor, think you a dead man feels
   it?

No. Lives it with the living? Not either. Our lust conceals
   it.
Our vanities corrupt it, our enjoyment infects it.
And calumnies debase it; as for me I reject it! Yes!
Will I miss it? No! But to come back to you, you
   scoundrels!
Now I am full up and dismiss you![28]

Falstaff's monologue of the cowardly soldier on the risks run
in battle, risks to life and limb, becomes an aria that begins
with the pathetic gestural cry of "honor" and ends with anxiety about infections and collapse. As in Shakespeare, this signals anxiety about disease, now in the decaying, ineffectual
body of the old man. The audience (and the singer), however,
see this as an indicator of the ambivalence of the warrior figure, now aging and facing the inevitable decay of old age.
Verdi marks this "serious" decline with the increased speed of
Falstaff's aria. It begins with the opening "l'onore" marked as
"allegro sostenuto" (lively sustained) with a marking of 112 for
the quarter-note. It slows down to "poco meno mosso" (a little less agitated) at 100 and then to "poco più mosso" (a little
more agitated) at the line, "honor is not a surgeon." The or-
chestral line prior to that point, before the music becomes
"more agitated" when Falstaff announces that honor cannot
heal even a broken fingernail, includes two solo double
basses, whose mocking tone "profoundly" underlines the
irony of Falstaff's notion of the inviolate body. Verdi directs
one of the basses to use a "drop-D tuning" (lowering the E
string to a D) to enable it to hit the lowest note in the aria.
Here, and only here, do we have Verdi's signaling of the hidden and missing comic basso aspect of Falstaff's character.
The baritone voice of the warrior (in his comic version) is also
the voice of the "fat man" hidden within the character of Fal-

staff. Falstaff is not the comic bass in the opera; the soldier Pistole, his comic sidekick, is the true comic bass in the opera — he is a shadow of Falstaff. Yet Falstaff places in the music a key to understanding the complexity of Falstaff's character and his body. Comic yet not comic, diseased yet only aging, threatening yet ineffectual, Falstaff dominates the stage.

The drop-D tuning of the bass is the figurative shadow of Verdi's use of "fat" music, which only the attentive can note. As the aria steadily increases in tempo, Falstaff picks up a broom and flails it about to clear the stage (57)! What begins as a mock gesture of honor ends as a comic, feminized sign of anxiety about the body. It is a suspension of Shakespeare's opposition between "fat and effeminate Egypt [and] lean and virile Rome."[29] For Falstaff is not a woman, nor is he overtly feminized in the opera. He is a desexed male whose virility is in question (he desires the merry wives' money more than their love). He uses the broom as a weapon since drawing a sword would be impossible in his middle-class world. This defines an aspect of Falstaff's character, but one that is not dominant. This is why Verdi and Boito cut the scene in which Falstaff disguises himself as the old woman of Brentford and is beaten for his troubles.

No doctor can cure what honor causes. The hidden "fat" voice that haunts Falstaff is the voice of the infected, immoral character. It is the basso hidden within or below. Falstaff's baritone voice is thus an ambiguous sign of pathology and decay. It can be read as a sign of the *miles gloriosus*, the braggart soldier of the Henry plays, but also as a mask for the innate corruption of the "old" Falstaff. In the operas written during this period old men and sexless figures often were endowed with either extremely high voices (a sign of physiological castration either through castration, disease, or the aging process) or markedly low voices (a potential sign of social castration). Good examples of these voices would be the dwarf Mime's tenor in Richard Wagner's *Ring* (1853-71), Herodes in Richard Strauss's *Salome* (1905), Althoum in Giacomo Puccini's *Turandot* (1926), and Abdisu in Hans Pfitzner's *Palestrina* (1917) — all of which immediately precede or follow *Falstaff*. The comic basso is demonstrated by Osmin, by Wagner's Hagen, by Strauss and Hugo von Hofmannthal's fat Baron Ochs in *Der Rosenkavalier* (1911), and even by Arnold Schoenberg's *Moses und Aaron* (1932). These operatic traditions/conventions mark an indeterminacy or ambiguity in Verdi's choice of a baritone Falstaff. Unlike the castrated or comic men with their "marked" voices, Verdi's Falstaff is not an easy iconographic representation of difference or disease. Boito's borrowing from the Henry plays marks this ambiguity; the setting of the text by Verdi provides the clues to this ambiguity. For of course the ambiguity must be resolved for Falstaff to be a comic character. And it is never quite resolved. Verdi merely points at this with his musical puns. The musical quotation from his *Requiem*, in which the word "Domine" (God) is replaced by Falstaff's "abdomine" (stomach), points toward a number of musical and textual plays that reveal the coarseness of the character, rather than his descent into senescence.

This is not the old man on the stage, not the standard comic character of either the opera or the stage, but the immoral figure whose decaying body is captured in the words (*parole*) of the monologue. The sexual desire of Falstaff is pathological because the old man, unlike the healthy follower of Mosso who is promised a long and healthy sexual life, is now neutered. His fat is a mirror not of his character but of his old age. Vanity and lust cause some bodies to decay into fat and licentiousness. And Falstaff, in Verdi's aria, marks the new notion of a "fat" voice, a voice in decay because of the wasteful immorality of the life of the character. Thus there is never any chance that Falstaff could fool the female figures in the opera. They hear the "basso" under his baritone voice. His vocal body seems to reveal his character, and his dissipation seems to reflect his danger to the institutions of marriage, though his role as a braggart claims much more than he can actually deliver.

By the end of the nineteenth century Verdi and Boito were able to stage the ultimate comic opera: the opera of old age, in which the central comic character is not the representative figure of aging but the anomaly. Verdi's Falstaff is comic because his decay is evident to all as a pathological sign present in the aging of those old men who have dissipated their vital fluids. Thus the "happy" conclusion of the opera, when all conflicts are resolved, is fated to take place at the dinner table. Falstaff's dangerous private acts of seduction have been unsuccessful. No matter how the women of Windsor view him, it is not as a potential lover. In the audience we have seen the private (read: sexual) made public by Falstaff's humiliation when he is dumped in the river after the women of Windsor discover his hypocrisy (he sends them all the same letter of seduction promising love and adoration). Falstaff's need is not for sex but money, and this, the audience quickly realizes, makes him a comic figure. The opera, however, does not conclude with Falstaff being dumped into the Thames in a basket. It ends with the ultimate reconciliation of all the figures, including Falstaff, over food. The death of sexual desire is at last presented as a positive force in the reconstitution of social order. Sexual desire is replaced by the communal breaking of bread, a communion that now truly links God with the act of eating. We men in the audience (and here we are all the old Verdi's surrogate) find this comic because we know in our heart of hearts that we are different from Falstaff. Our sexuality will remain vital even into our old age. Our sins are not written upon our bodies. We are not to be bought off by a good meal. Or are we?

FAT AND DISEASE IN THE NINETEENTH AND TWENTIETH CENTURIES: MORE FALSTAFFS

Social castration is a central concept in late nineteenth-century European culture, the culture out of which Giuseppe Verdi's *Falstaff* (1893) arose. In Conrad Rieger's monograph on castration, the emphasis is on the social isolation of an individual rather than the actual biological results of the removal of the gonads and/or penis.[30] Falstaff, as a comic baritone who reveals his own anxiety about his body, reflects his castration from the society in which he lives. He has become an asexual being, as represented by his "fat" and its reading as a sign of disease and danger. The danger was clear to the late nineteenth-century eye. Verdi wrote his opera in light of this danger and provided an answer to it with the integration of Falstaff into the world through the sharing of food at the close of the opera. His comic sexuality may be the result of one who is "decrepit and whose sexual life has already become extinct. . . . [M]edical science recognizes the fact that such an impulse depends upon the morbid alterations of the brain which lead to senile dementia."[31] It is also clear, however, that Verdi needed to integrate Falstaff into middle-class society for this dangerous male to become domesticated. In sharing a meal Falstaff actually achieves what his seduction had initially intended, using the world of Windsor to fill his belly.

In this, is Falstaff obese because of the temperament with which he was born but that can change "naturally" over his lifetime, or is he melancholic because of the impact of illness, such as syphilis? This conundrum faced the nineteenth century as it did the seventeenth century. At the end of the nineteenth century, as in the Renaissance, obesity was tied to specific forms of illness that were associated with melancholy and old age. As in the Renaissance these were often sexually transmitted illnesses, which had obesity as one of their most salient symptoms.[32] This had not changed by the end of the nineteenth century, when Emil Kraepelin, in his standard handbook of psychiatry, noted obesity as one of the primary symptoms of *dementia paralytica*, tertiary syphilis.[33] In the nineteenth century such illnesses were considered psychiatric in nature; they were illnesses of the mind as well as of the body. General paralysis of the insane was the model mental illness of the day, and it was believed to have clearly defined symptoms, among which obesity and madness were two of the more frequently cited. Indeed, "gluttony" (*Eßlust*) was listed as a sign of the presence of this illness (393). This was closely connected to evident stupor and idiocy in Kraepelin's representation of the final stage of syphilis. Falstaff's "madness" in Verdi's opera is in imagining himself as attractive. The very form and shape of his "fat" body provide the comic distance needed in the opera. Verdi wants to domesticate this body. He wants to diminish its threat as a danger from disease (and madness) and emphasize that an asocial body can be socialized. That only works, however, when there are other readings of Falstaff's body already present in the culture.

The idea that "old men" suffer from such illnesses is not unique to the construction of sexually transmitted illness in the late nineteenth century. Verdi's folk belief in the limited amount of energy in a human being and the problems of dissipating such energy is one that had haunted the literature on fat from the eighteenth century. Certainly Honoré de Balzac subscribed to it. A century before Luigi Galvani's study of the effects of electricity on muscular motion had commented that certain illnesses of the brain "are particularly prevalent in old men, because in them a more abundant supply of contaminated animal electricity seems to accumulate, both on account of their intermitted labors and exercises, and because of the dryness of the parts induced by old age."[34] The dryness of the parts was explained by Albrecht von Haller, who notes that the fat in men is collected in other places, specifically "under the pulp of the glans penis," where the fat, "by mixing with many of the humours, abates their acrimony." But too much fat is deleterious to the health of the male: "It proves injurious by compressing the veins; and, by causing too great a resistance to the heart, it makes a person short-breathed, and liable to an apoplexy or dropsy."[35] The old man collects bad fat and then collapses and dies of it. Falstaff is described in *Henry IV, Part 2* as having "a moist eye, a dry hand, a yellow cheek, a white beard, a decreasing leg, an increasing belly. . . . Is not your voice broken, your wind short, your chin double, your wit single, and every part about you blasted with antiquity?" (*2H4* 1.2.180–84). Such "bad fat" at the end of the nineteenth century was read as a result of amoral behavior and the resultant infections unto death. Thus, not *all* old men die of fat, only immoral old men. Such a death is foreshadowed by a period of collapse that is the direct result of a life misspent.

The social castration of the syphilitic in the culture of the late nineteenth century also led to a type of feminization wherein a neutered man was understood as a variety of woman. "Feminization" is here to be understood both in its general, cultural sense and in its very specifically medical sense. "Feminization," or the existence of the "feminized man," is a form of "external pseudo-hermaphrodism."[36] The feminized male was perceived as sharing with women external, secondary sexual characteristics, such as the shape of the body or the tone of the voice. This concept first appeared in the middle of the nineteenth century with the introduction of the term *infemminsce* — to feminize — to describe the supposed results of the castration of the male.[37] In the 1870s the term was used to describe the "feminisme" of the male, who through the effects of other diseases, such as tuberculosis, was thought to take on feminine traits.[38] Henry Meige, at the Salpêtrière, saw this feminization as a form of atavism, in which the male returns to the level of the "sexless" child.[39] "Feminization" was the direct result of actual castration or its physiological equivalent, such as intensely debilitating illness. It reshaped the body. Thus, disease and age were understood as having the ability to shape the male body and, in so doing, to reveal its underlining pathologies. This set of assumptions meant that the medical literature of the time sought to find an exemplary patient who would illustrate the life course of the old, fat man. To no one's surprise that patient turned out to be Falstaff.

Between Otto Nicolai's *Merry Wives of Windsor* (1846) and Verdi/Boito's *Falstaff* (1893), the reading of Falstaff as a medical case came into general usage. By the time Verdi set Boito's version of Falstaff, the eponymous character had become a model for a specific model of "corpulence" in the medical literature. This is in part what the opera works against. As noted above, the model defined in the opera is based on a reading of a composite illustration of "Falstaff" that took qualities from both aspects of the character. This is echoed in Wilhelm Ebstein's classic study of corpulence, a study that went through some twenty editions from the 1870s to the 1920s, in which he describes the portrait of "fatty degeneration."[40] This terminology, still used today, is presented as a specific model of illness. According to Ebstein, fatty degeneration presents itself in three stages. In the first the individual is a "person to be envied": "We admire his stoutness, his embonpoint, the body grows fatter, the outlines become rounded off, the muscular system still keeps pace with the increase of fat" (10). This is the young Falstaff, whose memories of his earlier life (and body size) haunt the Henry plays.

In the second stage of fatty degeneration the progression moves to a comic figure: "The corpulent becomes ridiculous." Falstaff here is the example: "The ancients jeered at the . . . capacious Falstaff who is the popular embodiment of low comedy. The works of the poets are so full of drastic descriptions of the various aspects of corpulency, that pathologists might learn many a lesson from them. In the first period of this stage the corpulent bear with a certain dignity the inconveniences entailed on them by their increasing bulk, and greater bodily weight" (10). Here is the figure of Falstaff at the very beginning of the Henry plays, but the progressive expansion of his figure ultimately leads to his physical collapse: "Such people of the Falstaff type with bellies of a hundred pounds are subject to many discomforts. Falstaff bemoans his own fate: 'A man of my kidney . . . That am as subject to heat as butter; a man of continual dissolution and thaw' " (11). Falstaff has, at this moment, become a classification for morbid obesity. He is the "Falstaff type."

It is at this last state of gross size that Falstaff's body and mind fail, according to Ebstein: "In this third stage the corpulent become seriously ailing and pitiable objects of commiseration" (12). And this is Falstaff in *The Merry Wives of Windsor*. By examining the sequence of Shakespeare's plays, a very real degenerative pattern emerges, which struck a chord with medical practitioners of the nineteenth century. Thus, Falstaff was already a case study of fatty degeneration by the time Boito sat down to write his libretto. Unlike Verdi, working to preserve his mind and body, Falstaff has lost his mental acuity. Ebstein quotes Dr. Cantini of Naples: "Fat quenches the divine flame of the mind even before old age has deprived it of the oil of cerebral nourishment" (13). Falstaff's sexual exploits and dissipation of vital bodily fluids marked him as the sort of individual who would decay into a type of sexuality — asexuality — and he is granted comic, hypersexual gestures. This view was a mainstay of the sexology of the late nineteenth century and persisted well into the twentieth century. Max von Gruber, in his standard study of the hygiene of sex, argues that the retention and reabsorption of seminal fluid heighten its functioning capacity; its dissipation leads to decay and collapse.[41] Like the figures of Osmin and Monostatos, Falstaff acts as if he will seduce or rape but does not have the ability to act. For Ebstein also places much of the "etiology of corpulency" as the result of the "derangements of the sexual functions. . . . In the male sex, also individual cases of obesity are on record, which at the time of puberty somewhat suddenly set in, associated with a defective development of the penis and the testes" (18). Sexual dysfunction is either the cause or the result of morbid obesity.

With Ebstein's taxonomy Falstaff becomes the exemplary patient in studies of obesity. His figure is culturally available in ways that few fat men are. Hilde Bruch, perhaps best known for her public championing of anorexia nervosa in the 1950s, returned to Falstaff in a seminal 1943 article on obesity in children.[42] Her essay argues that obesity is a psychiatric illness rather than a purely metabolic or inherited one, which was the dominant position by the 1940s.[43] She answers the more superficial argument that obesity is an illness of will that begins in early childhood: "The obese adult owes his plight either to the juvenile philosophy of 'eats' as the paramount interest in life, or maladjustment to the multitudinous worries and tensions of existence. . . . Seeking this outlet habitually despite increasing weight, the tensive individual becomes the calm, jolly, rolypoly 'fatty.' Yet, he worries over his obesity."[44] While Bruch acknowledges the social stigma of the "tragicomic appearance, conspicuous size and slow-moving clumsiness" (752) of the obese child, she sees obesity as inherently a symptom of children deprived of emotional security. It is specifically the "overindulgent and possessive attitude of the mother" (756) that is at the heart of this syndrome. This reading is not at all unusual in an age that sought familial causation (such as the schizophrenigenic mother) for a range of mental illnesses. Later, in her monograph on obesity, Bruch cites approvingly Ebstein's three stages of obesity.[45]

Bruch, however, concludes her essay with an evocation of Falstaff. The Falstaff she draws on is that of *Henry IV*, who has claimed that he has killed Hotspur. She comments: "Though only pretense it gives him an inkling of what it would be like to be a real hero. He leaves the scene, carrying the body of Hotspur, with these words: 'If I do grow great, I'll grow less.' It seems to me that this line expressed the essence of the obesity problem" (756). Bruch's view is that Falstaff incorporates the very essence of the psychological nature of the etiology of obesity, the insecurity of the smothering mother. Bruch's reading parallels the symphonic 1913 poem of Edward Elgar, where he adds a dream interlude to represent Falstaff's desire for a different childhood. Even though Bruch's and Elgar's readings of the play seem to corroborate their own conclusions, the play itself provides no sense of this. These cases demonstrate, however, that by the 1940s Falstaff is the exemplary fat man in medical culture.

Following Bruch there was a concerted effort in the medical literature to examine the "medical history" of Falstaff, which provides the title for John Sullivan's essay of 1986.[46] This type of retrospective diagnosis is not unusual for literary figures.

Some physicians have a propensity to take their classifications and see how well or poorly they match up with the illnesses of literary characters. Falstaff, however, seems to cry out for such analysis. John Sullivan provides a line-by-line reading of all of Falstaff's ailments and sees them as in some way related to his "horrible obesity." Obesity is for Sullivan the result of Falstaff's life choices, which are then a reflection of his character. Each aspect of the physical description of Falstaff's pathological body is defined by specific, contemporary medical diagnosis. Sullivan reads Falstaff's alcoholism as possibly leading to rhinophyma and Cushing's syndrome. Alvin Rodin and Jack Key add cirrhosis and diabetes to this list of Falstaff's ailments while noting that about 20 percent of United States teenagers are overweight.[47] Falstaff seems to stand as an example of early onset obesity. Abraham Verghese picks up a thread in John Sullivan's argument that Falstaff died of an epidemic illness rather than his fat.[48] His choice is typhoid. Herbert S. Donow stresses Falstaff as the model for anomalous aging. Falstaff is a "sinner and an old man . . . the old man has failed to adapt successfully."[49] Henry Buchwald and Mary E. Knatteraud present Falstaff as a "treatise on identifying the co-morbid diseases of morbid obesity."[50] In all of these analyses Falstaff is "Patient Zero." He is the exemplary fat male whose diseases must be understood as reflecting the state of the medical art as physicians practice it today. Falstaff continues to haunt the imagination of physicians when they think about obese males in terms of their own medical specialty. It is of note that there is no "psychology" in these analyses, only the results of various forms of overindulgence or the exposure to infection. And their authors give their imagination form by projecting their understanding of the meaning of this state back into the historical moment.

One illuminating thread that defines the function of Falstaff as a medical case study (rather than a literary character reflecting the ideas of medicine in Shakespeare's age) can be picked up in 1983. Jack J. Adler wrote a letter to the *New England Journal of Medicine* asking whether Falstaff had sleep apnea syndrome.[51] Obstructive sleep apnea syndrome is a condition in which people stop breathing for very short intervals of time during their normal sleep periods. This results in the patient having a marked loss of oxygen in the blood system and lethargy while awake. In Shakespeare's work Falstaff is described by one of Hal's courtiers as "snorting like a horse," and Hal remarks, "Hark, how hard he fetches breath" (*1H4* 2.4.25–26). Sleep apnea syndrome was by the 1980s commonly called "Pickwick syndrome," a name coined by C. Sidney Burwell and his colleagues at Harvard in 1956.[52] As John Sullivan's essay of 1986 notes, Falstaff's "inappropriate somnolence and intermittently confused mental status might be considered signs of Pickwickian syndrome" (398). Sullivan suggests, following Adler, that this terminology be replaced with "Falstaff snore." Burwell's paper presents a single case study of the "association of obesity, somnolence, polycythemia and excessive appetite" and defines a new syndrome. Despite the syndrome's name, the eponymous figure is not Charles Dickens's Mr. Samuel Pickwick from *The Pickwick Papers* (1836–37) but rather one of the servants in the book, Mr. Wardle's fat boy, Joe.[53] Juliet McMaster argues convincingly that Dickens presents two kinds of fat boys. The first is Mr. Pickwick, who is, to use her words, "fat-cheery" instead of "fat-bloated."[54] Joe is the latter. Pickwick is the plump man "charged with energy, solar or otherwise. He bursts, he beams, he bulges. . . . His fatness . . . is scarcely even heavy." This is quite the opposite of Joe, whose fat seems to have "its customary association with inertia."

Mr. Pickwick is one of many such comic "plump" men of the time. Thomas Love Peacock (1785–1866), in his *Crotchet Castle* (1831), presents the reader with Dr. Folliet, who, while quoting Greek poetry to a nightingale, is attacked by two armed robbers and drives them off with his walking stick. He is able to do so in a rage because he imagines them thinking that he is an easy target, since he appears to be a fat, old man:

> One of them drew a pistol, which went off in the very act of being struck aside by the bamboo, and lodged a bullet in the brain of the other. There was then only one enemy, who vainly struggled to rise, every effort being attended with a new and more signal prostration. The fellow roared for mercy. "Mercy, rascal!" cried the divine; "what mercy were you going to show me, villain? What! I warrant me, you thought it would be an easy matter, and no sin, to rob and murder a parson on his way home from dinner. You said to yourselves, doubtless, 'We'll waylay the fat parson (you irreverent knave) as he waddles home (you disparaging ruffian), half-seas-over (you calumnious vagabond).'" And with every dyslogistic term, which he supposed had been applied to himself, he inflicted a new bruise on his rolling and roaring antagonist. "Ah, rogue!" he proceeded; "you can roar now, marauder; you were silent enough when you devoted my brains to dispersion under your cudgel. But seeing that I cannot bind you, and that I intend you not to escape, and that it would be dangerous to let you rise, I will disable you in all your members."[55]

His fat only appears to be unmasculine; in reality he is "plump," not fat — and dangerous too.

Such active stout men are the antithesis of Joe, whose fat seems to have "its customary association with inertia," according to Juliet McMaster (88). It is read as an example of the obesity of youth. As Edward Jukes noted in 1833, "Fat, when moderately diffused over the body, indicates a sound state of health, and an easy disposition, gives a symmetry to the figure, and (which by many is valued more than all these) it contributes much to the beauty of the countenance; but on the contrary, where it accumulates to excess, it becomes an absolute disease, and is frequently the cause of death, particularly in habits where some chronic disorder has preceded it, or where acute attacks of disease have been aggravated by its presence."[56] The causes of fat, according to Dickens's contemporary, are occasioned either "by indulging in the use of highly nutritious foods" or, as in the case of the fat boy, by "a peculiarity of constitution predisposing to this state" (289–90). Fat boys can be a separate class, born to be fat.

Joe, the comic parallel to Pickwick's clever servant Sam Weller, is defined in the novel by his blank expression, huge appetite, and ability to avoid work by falling asleep instantaneously. He is a version of Sancho Panza except that all of the Quixotes in this novel are "fat-cheery" except him. He is regularly described as snoring "in a low and monotonous sound." Joe is comic because of his girth and what it implies:

> "Come along, Sir. Pray, come up," said the stout gentleman. "Joe! — damn that boy, he's gone to sleep again. — Joe, let down the steps." The fat boy rolled slowly off the box, let down the steps, and held the carriage door invitingly open. Mr. Snodgrass and Mr. Winkle came up at the moment. "Room for you all, gentlemen," said the

stout man. "Two inside, and one out. Joe, make room for one of these gentlemen on the box. Now, Sir, come along," and the stout gentleman extended his arm, and pulled first Mr. Pickwick, and then Mr. Snodgrass, into the barouche by main force. Mr. Winkle mounted to the box, the fat boy waddled to the same perch, and fell fast asleep instantly.[57]

In this description we are presented with the stereotype that fat boys like Joe move their buttocks comically (like an animal) and are lazy, falling asleep whenever they cease moving as a sign of their almost medieval sinful sloth and stupidity. At the beginning of the nineteenth century the Surgeon-Extraordinary to the Prince-Regent William Wadd stated that "if the Goddess of Wisdom were to grow fat, even she would become stupid. . . . Fat and stupidity, says the accomplished Lord Chesterfield, are looked upon as such inseparable companions that they are used as synonymous terms."[58]

Joe is primal in his appetite and his body. Fat children were indeed so seen. They were considered throwbacks to the world of the primitive. They lacked a specific sense of "masculinity" that was inherent to Victorian ideas of manliness.[59] Louis Robinson, in an essay in *Nineteenth Century*, asked: "Why should babies be so fat, when the children of their pithecoid ancestors must have been lean? . . . The suicidal swallowing capacity of the modern baby is an inheritance from the habits of the crawling cave-dweller."[60] An anonymous wag in *Punch* replied:

Baby boy, whose visage chubby
    Doting mother marvels at,
Full of health, albeit grubby —
    Why are you so fat?

How unlike your rude forefather —
  Prehistoric, pithecoid!
  Who with nuts he chanced to gather
  Filled his aching void . . .

No! but later generations
  Come, in which the infant staves
  Hunger off by dint of rations
  Picked up in the caves.

Holding future meals in question,
  Grasping all with eager fist, —
  To the mill of his digestion
  Everything is grist.

Consequently, you, who follow
  Him in lack of self-control,
  With atavic impulse swallow
  Dirt, and pins and coal.[61]

Fat is the product of an evolutionary development that gave purpose to actions in the past that have become atavistic today.

Such a view is little different from that proposed in the seminal 1994 paper on the fat gene (*ob gen*) in mice that concludes with the evolutionary biological explanation that the gene's intent was to "provide a selective advantage in human populations subjected to caloric deprivation."[62] The fat mouse was "discovered" at the Jackson Laboratory in Bar Harbor, Maine, in the early 1950s. This mutant mouse was so huge that it was assumed to be pregnant, until the discovery that it was male. Jeffrey Friedman, now head of the Laboratory of Molecular Genetics at Rockefeller University, discovered the genetic factor for this in the early 1990s. He was inspired by the work of Ethan Allen Sims, a physician at the University of

Vermont College of Medicine who had been exploring the link between obesity and diabetes using male inmates at the Vermont state prison. Sims had found that only very few inmates could easily put on weight, and these found it the most difficult to lose. At this point the meanings associated with childhood obesity shifted radically from psychological to genetic explanations. However, the genetic explanations were given an evolutionary meaning to explain their "function."[63] Fat had to have purpose if it were an inherent part of the genome.

Fat had a true function, at least in our distant past, but today fat boys are primeval throwbacks, unable to function in contemporary society. Joe's body is different from that of Pickwick and all of the other plump, middle-class adventurers in Dickens's novel. His body is read not merely as a symptom of his class (Sam Weller's body is the body of the healthy and wily servant) but as an example of the physiognomy of the primitive that haunts this world of work. It is the worker who has a lack of will because of his ancestry and background. At the extreme it is the worker as alcoholic and criminal. Here it is the worker as fat boy, condemned to live out his desires because of his physical inheritance. But Joe is not sick.

Indicative of this concern about the association between childhood obesity and its existent amoralistic characteristics, there was some anxiety in the medical literature of the early nineteenth century regarding the overfeeding of infants in the nursery.[64] However, fat babies in general were seen as healthy babies. Indeed, one of the decisive works on pediatric illness, Johannes Joachim Becher's posthumous *Medicinische Schatz-Kammer* of 1700, lists the entire range of diseases that were seen to befall children (including syphilis), but obesity is never mentioned.[65] In the eighteenth century Christoph Wilhelm Hufeland (see chapter 1) argued that if children are fat it is the fault of their upbringing, but they are the exception to the rule. Even at the beginning of the twentieth century the public health concern about children's bodies focused on malnutrition and the diseases associated with it in children — not obesity.[66] To be sure, the beautiful (fat) baby contests became part of the eugenics movement to assure a healthy breeding stock of human beings who delighted in the fat baby.[67] However, through the 1930s and 1940s fat babies became more and more pathologized as they were seen as the origin of fat (and sick) adults. In this there was a decisive shift from moral degeneracy as the cause of obesity. By the 1940s the universal argument that fat babies suffered from illness — either endocrine imbalance or neurosis — provided the means of defining them as ill.[68] More important, fat drew an absolute line between sick and healthy children and was seen to have predictive force.

In William Golding's *Lord of the Flies* (1954) the character of Piggy is described as a "bag of fat."[69] He is introduced to us as a fat boy defined by his pathologies: " 'I was the only boy in our school what had asthma,' said the fat boy with a touch of pride. 'And I've been wearing specs since I was three' " (8). Suffering from asthma, from shortness of breath, he becomes the representative of the rational trapped in the body of the fat boy. Thus, he is eventually the human sacrifice that signals the final breakdown of all civilization among the children on the island: "Piggy fell forty feet and landed on his back across the square red rock in the sea. His head opened and stuff came out and turned red. Piggy's arms and legs twitched a bit, like a pig's after it has been killed. Then the sea breathed again in a long, slow sigh, the water boiled white and pink over the rock; and when it went, sucking back again, the body of Piggy was gone" (181). He is the most degenerate of the children in terms of his dependence on civilization (such as for his glasses) and at the same time the most civilized. Once his tenuous ties to civilization are destroyed, he is unable to function in the "natural" world of childhood thinness and cruelty. His "asthma" marks his body as much as does his corpulence. By the 1970s obesity had become a "peril" for children.[70] Indeed, in the case of three-year-old Anamarie Regino, when her weight topped 130 pounds, she was taken in 2001 from her "abusive" family (which fed her) and placed in foster care.[71] In literature this was also clearly the case.

Instead of considering the societal ramifications of obesity as demonstrated in the character of Piggy, Burwell sees Joe in terms of his pathophysiology and not in terms of the morality read into his body as a throwback in this model for his syndrome. Joe is the fat boy, the young man who, unlike Sam Weller, will never be able to accomplish anything because of his girth. He is a curiosity, kept by Mr. Wardle precisely because of this fat. Burwell strengthens his argument that Joe is a case study by citing William Wadd's early nineteenth-century medical account of "corpulence." Indeed, there have been claims of a greater antiquity for this syndrome.[72] Wadd's account concerns the case of "a country tradesman aged about thirty, of a short stature and naturally of a fresh, sanguine complexion and very fat," who was suffering from the combination of symptoms that Burwell finds in Joe. The Burwell article presents a *single* case study of a man, fifty-one years old, five feet five inches tall, who weighed 263 pounds. The salient incident in this patient's life that brought him to the hospital was the fact that he had fallen asleep during a poker game while holding three aces and two kings! In a completely phenomenological description of the case Burwell and his colleagues see excessive eating as both cause and symptom but avoid any discussion of the etiology of the patient's (and Joe's) illness. Burwell cannot use a child, a real fat boy, for his case, as these cases were the stuff of the debate about the etiology of obesity, not its phenomenology.

Hilde Bruch counters this rather mechanistic reading of the fat boy. She too cites Dickens, employing a passage where Joe awakens abruptly when he is offered food. She continues: "During the 1930's and the 1940's, Joe's behavior was often cited as evidence of the sleepiness of the pituitary type of obesity. During the 1950's the eponym 'Pickwickian Syndrome' was given to the clinical picture of extreme obesity associated with alveolar hypoventilation and hypoxic somnolence. Yet I doubt Joe suffered from it. I have never seen an organically determined somnolence in which one word had such a vitalizing influence."[73] She then provides a further case study of a four-and-a-half-year-old child weighing ninety pounds. The child had been accidentally conceived during the war and was initially rejected by the mother (138). For the mother "feeding showed love and expiation of guilt" (140) for rejecting the very idea of bearing the child. Bruch thus provides Joe with a childhood of rejection that explains his obesity.

Joe as a case study trapped between purely physiological and psychological explanations of obesity is, in this sense, the medical offspring of Falstaff. He is the fat boy who will become the fat man, or, as in the case of the patient described by Burwell, has already become him! What is striking is how the definitions of masculinity in Falstaff (as soldier, knight, courier, and lover) are compromised due to his obesity. So too with the case of the "wonderfully fat boy" in Dickens, and with the case material that Burwell and Bruch assembled for their argument.

Despite these readings, the idea that Falstaff suffered from Fat Joe's "illness" was elegantly rebutted by R. P. Junghans, again in the *New England Journal of Medicine*. Junghans notes that Falstaff is drunk in the scene that Adler (and later

Sullivan) quote. He ironically counters: "I have it on some authority that even a skinny man, when sufficiently perfused with spirits, will so snort in his stuporous repose as to disturb another's slumber. Cure is effected by an intervening day of sobriety. . . . 'Falstaff's syndrome,' indeed. Fie!"[74] This is perhaps the best possible answer to the transformation of Falstaff into a modern medical case.

From Shakespeare to Bruch, Falstaff functions as a character whose internal life is written on his fat male body. Shakespeare's Falstaffs (and there are more than one) represent the dangers of masculine sexuality, which in excess are a sign of bad character. Like Milton's Satan, we may find him the most interesting character on the stage, as did many of Shakespeare's contemporaries, but only because of the moral lesson that his fat and disease clearly intended. Where Verdi wished to rescue Falstaff and recuperate him, Ebstein and Bruch endeavored to heal him. Physician-critics see him as a classic example of their ability to diagnose. When the British National Audit Office published its first official assessment of the weight of the British population, it placed a smiling but clearly obese Falstaff on the cover of its 2001 report, *Tackling Obesity in England*. Falstaff had long become Patient Zero and had already created a medical offspring in Dickens's fat boy.

How Fat Detectives Think (And Fat Villains Act)

If there is a moment when fat seemed to become a positive quality in shaping the image of the "fat man," it was at the close of the nineteenth century. The body of the fat detective aids his mental processes, as his body size and shape seem to account for his different way of thinking. Steven Shapin, a short, rather rotund scholar of the history of science, has written a striking essay on the eating habits of skinny philosopher-scientists throughout the past.[1] His argument is that, at least in the West, there is a powerful myth as early as Marsilio Ficino's Renaissance book on the health of the scholar about the need for such men to have a "lean and hungry look."[2] That all of Shapin's examples are of men is not incidental. Our collective fantasy of the appropriate body of the male thinker stands at the center of his work. I want here to ask a corollary question: What happens to the image of the "thinking male" when the male body is fat, even obese? Shapin's point, of course, is that Sir Isaac Newton, that proverbial thinker who is reputed to have forgotten whether he had eaten his chicken or not, actually died hugely bloated. Shapin addresses the great disparity between the way we imagine how bodies should look and function and our myth making about them. In complicated ways the fat detective is the antithesis of the lean philosopher and his fat analogue.

The model of the fat detective reflects in complex ways how general as well as medical culture shifted its image of the thinking body in the late nineteenth and early twentieth centuries. What is there about the representation of a fat, thinking body that puts the fat detective into a different category than the thin philosopher? This tale is rooted in a certain notion of the body and its relationship to thought. The image of the fat detective can be found well before the nineteenth century and has continued through the twentieth. One example in modern media is the overweight title character in the recent BBC detective series *Cracker*, Dr. Eddie "Cracker" Fitzgerald (played by Robbie Coltrane, whose Falstaff in Kenneth Branagh's 1989 version of *Henry V* was more comic than conflicted). Dr. Eddie Fitzgerald is an out-of-work forensic psychologist who occasionally helps the Manchester police "crack" hard to solve cases by interrogating or "cracking" suspects and witnesses. The central quality of this character, however, is his own nervousness, his own sense of himself as a misfit, his own marginal status as a professional. His oversized body seems to symbolically represent this. But it also evokes his mode of inquiry. Fitzgerald's approach seems to be empathetic rather than analytic, as he feels with and for the victims, and even the criminals, rather than being a "pure intellect" whose forte is unmasking the perpetrators or logistics of a crime. One can note, however, that when ABC unsuccessfully remade *Cracker* (1998) for American television (the protagonist now called Gerry Fitzgerald and acted by Robert Pastorelli) and moved its setting to diet-conscious Los Angeles, Cracker became svelte. The character was essentially the same; only the body was different. The viewers' response was equally different. Somehow, with the diminished body mass, the character of Cracker lost a vital element that appeared to be in direct correlation with his size and the marginality implied by it. His intuitive effectiveness was relationally compromised and thus translated poorly in a new, thinner body.

The fat detective's body is of a different sort than that of the skinny philosopher. Huge, ungainly, sedentary, it houses the brain of a detective. It is a different sort of detective, however, than the strong hard-boiled or the thin ratiocinating one. It is a body out of all moderation. It is not a "modern" body, if by modern we imagine the body as trained, lithesome, strong, active, and thus supremely masculine. Such an obese body seems more feminine, but certainly not female; it is expressive of the nature of the way the detective seems to "think." His thought processes strike us as intuitive and emotional rather than analytic and objective. In other words, the fat detective's body is read as feminine. The ratiocinating detective, such as Edgar Allan Poe's C. Auguste Dupin, thinks with his brain. The hard-boiled detective (such as Dashiell Hammett's Sam Spade, at least in Humphrey Bogart's rail-thin depiction) thinks with his fists. Our fat detective seems to think with his gut.[3] For it is the visible body fat that marks his body. This seems to be a quite different version from the ratiocinating detective such as Sherlock Holmes, whose "kingdom is his study" and whose "weapons are intellectual — logic, memory, concentration. He traps criminals in the corridors of his own mind rather than in a back alley at midnight. He is a cultivated gentleman, whose recreation is the library."[4] The fat detective seems to be a countertype to this actively rational or hard-boiled detective. He seems to be primarily intuitive and empathetic; he seems to need his fat as a shield from the world. His physical immoderation seems to become a means of showing both his vulnerability and his strength. He is sedentary rather than active; his intellectual gifts seem to feed his intuition rather than his rationality. The reality, however, is actually quite different.

Michel Foucault, in *The Uses of Pleasure*, wrote that there has always been a contrast between pleasure and the rational in the West: "The relationship of the logos to the practice of pleasures was described by Greek philosophy of the fourth century. . . . Moderation implied that the logos be placed in a position of supremacy in the human being and that it be able to subdue the desires and regulate behavior. Whereas in the immoderate individual, the force that desires usurps the highest place and rules tyrannically, in the individual who is *sophron*, it is reason that commands and prescribes."[5] What happens when desire becomes a means of thinking, an alternative mode of intelligence? The immoderate, according to the Greeks, could never think rationally. Contrary to this, our fat detectives seem to do well in this department, for their job, always well done, is to solve the case. And that they do with elegance and grace — not in spite of but because of their bulk.

FICTIONS OF FAT DETECTIVES

In 1891 Wilhelm Raabe, best known as one of the foremost regional colorists in late nineteenth-century German letters, published his novel *Stopfkuchen*, subtitled "A Murder and Sea" tale.[6] Translated into English as *Tubby Schaumann*, a rough approximation of the nickname of the protagonist, it is the exemplary and, perhaps, first account of the mental process of the fat detective. Here we have an amateur sleuth whose primary qualities seem to be his huge body and his insatiable appetite. Heinrich "Stopfkuchen" Schaumann's bulk and his fleshly desires make it seemingly impossible for him to leave the world of the small village where he was raised. He lives for cakes and pies; his primary position is lying prone under the hedges looking for people who come down the paths. He is the prototypical fat man, "so lazy and so fat and so decent and so loveable."[7] His body is "seen" as different. Indeed, his name, Schaumann, means one who sees or is seen.

The antithetical body in this murder mystery is that of his youthful friend Edward, whose narrative frames the novel. He returns from making a new life in South Africa in order to visit his hometown. There, he discovers that his old friend Schaumann has married the daughter of Quakatz, the owner of the isolated and infamous Red Bank Farm. Decades before, the farmer Kienbaum was found dead and Quakatz was immediately accused of the murder, as he had often quarreled with the deceased. Quakatz was not prosecuted for the crime due to lack of evidence, but his guilt was evident to everyone in the town. Nevertheless, he had spent all of his waking hours trying to prove his innocence. Into this home, and infamy, came the young Tubby Schaumann to marry Quakatz's vivacious, red-haired daughter: "How a man with Tubby Schaumann's physical constitution managed to have her fall in love with him so quickly I don't know, but he did" (186). Told through the perspective of someone who has arrived after the fact, the novel goes on to reveal how Schaumann uncovered the identity of the real murderer. In his investigation the physical nature of the sleuth was his greatest asset. No one imagined that this passive, overweight farmer would be able to unravel any mystery, especially one that the community had believed long solved.

In the process of unraveling the mystery Tubby's fat body is his most powerful ally. He is invisible in his bulk, and he is tenacious in his powers of observation. He is the scientist-observer that the late nineteenth-century detective story used to great effect. He is an amateur paleontologist whose discovery of a mammoth skeleton makes his reputation in scientific circles. His contemporaries, however, see him in much the same terms in which he sees his discovery — as a huge, unwieldy, primitive object. This double vision frames his scientific gaze. Tubby's body is a primitive body, which should infer a primitive consciousness.[8] His school biology teacher had compared him to the bradypus: "Look at him, all of you, Schaumann, the sloth. There he sits again on the dullard's bench, like the bradypus, the sloth. Has hair the color of withered leaves and with four molars. Crawls slowly up onto another class — I mean, climbs up a tree and stays there until he has eaten the last leaf" (215). Even his friend sees his preoccupation with food as a sign that he should be "let to crawl sloth-like into his tree" (225). But this slothlike demeanor hides a "cold-bloodedness which had something uncanny about it" (225). Of course the fat body of the detective here is not the body of the sloth. What appears to be slothfulness is, in fact, introspection. Tubby's hobby, collecting fossils, is a closer clue to his relationship to the "primitive" body of the sloth. He is the observer whose passivity masks the rational mind at work. He is pure intellect encased in an immobile body.

Schaumann proves, at least to himself, that he has solved the crime when, in good detective style, he deduces the murderer at the grave of his accused father-in-law. Evoking the means by which Hamlet captured the conscience of the king, Tubby watches the postman Störzer as he listens to the preacher's eulogy at Quakatz's grave. Tubby Schaumann knows that Störzer is the murderer by observing him silently;

his trick is to place his bulk in one place and look at the world, whether at the landscape of Quakatz's Red Bank Farm or the world of the murderer. He sees Störzer's discomfort in confronting the corpse and perceives his guilt. He knows because of his bulk, and his bulk seems almost an extension of the farm. Schaumann later unveils the crime to Edward, revealing to him that Störzer, whose friend and disciple Edward was, committed the crime, dying just before Edward's return. The perpetrator, however, is unknown to everyone else.

The "model," if we need to ask for a model at all, for Raabe's fat man is Falstaff's heir, Charles Dickens's fat boy from *The Pickwick Papers* (1836).[9] Raabe was a fanatical reader of Dickens and saw in his work the best type of narrative presentation for complex and contradictory characters. There is one odd but effective moment in *The Pickwick Papers* where Mr. Wardel's "boy," Joe, accidentally sees an attempted seduction take place in the garden. He is seen, and the seducer observes him "perfectly motionless, with his large circular eyes staring into the arbour, but without the slightest expression on his face that the most expert physiognomist could have referred to astonishment, curiosity, or any other known passion that agitates the human breast. Mr. Tupman gazed on the fat boy, and the fat boy stared at him; and the longer Mr. Tupman observed the utter vacancy of the fat boy's countenance, the more convinced he became that he either did not know, or did not understand, anything that had been going forward" (89). But of course he understands all too well. As Tupman walks off "there was a sound behind them, as of an imperfectly suppressed chuckle. Mr. Tupman turned sharply round. No; it could not have been the fat boy; there was not a gleam of mirth, or anything but feeding in his whole visage." His fat physiognomy is unreadable, but he knows! Later he turns to his employer's aged aunt, to whom he wishes to reveal all. She is initially frightened at his desire to speak, because he has been marked by a silence that reflects his girth, and protests that she has always treated him well and given him enough to eat. He responds with the ambiguous statement: "I wants to make your flesh creep." In revealing what he has seen in all of its detail, he shows that not only did he recognize its significance but he can also tell the story for his own betterment.

Raabe's protagonist does precisely the same. Schaumann is able to observe because in his girth he is invisible. His physiognomy is unreadable, like that of Joe. In Wilhelm Ebstein's study of obesity, already a standard when Raabe published his novel, Ebstein quotes the eighteenth-century German essayist Georg Lichtenberg, who says that "there be people with such plump faces that they may laugh under their fat, so that the greatest physiognomist shall fail to notice it, while we poor slender creatures with our souls seated immediately beneath the epidermis, ever speak a language which can tell no lies" (11). Tubby is inscrutable in his obesity, but the tale he tells will make all notice him. He tells stories that will indeed "make your flesh creep," but at his own pace and in his own time — only when the murderer is dead and, by chance, his youthful companion has returned to town for a visit. He suddenly has his audience and his time. James Joyce knows the power of this moment: in the Scylla and Charybdis chapter of *Ulysses* he has John Eglinton say that Stephen Dedalus "will have it that Hamlet is a ghost story. . . . Like the fat boy in Pickwick he wants to make our flesh creep."[10] And our flesh does creep at these ghost stories.

Tubby Schaumann's childhood friend, in spite all of his peregrinations, knows much less of the world than the fat man who remains at home. He is a German in the sense that Raabe evokes national identity in representing the fat boy's body. As discussed in the introduction, obesity is often seen as a quality of a nation to which one does not belong. Here Tubby's fat is a sign of a German quite happy with his national identity as a fat boy. That is also true of Hamlet, however, as an anonymous English commentator in 1830 observed of him: "He is by birth a German; and from indulging in the inactive habits of that deep-thinking nation, he has become 'fat and scant of breath' as the Queen says."[11] By 1844 "Hamlet is Germany," as the revolutionary poet Ferdinand Freilingrath states at the opening of his poem on Germany before the revolution of 1848. Germany is unable to act, is poised to seek revenge but cannot. Germany is trapped in Hamlet's fat, immobile body:

Having done that, he was too immobile.
He stayed and read too long in bed.
He was, because his blood was thick,
Short of breath and too fat.[12]

Germany is Hamlet for Freilingrath, but Raabe in Imperial Germany has Tubby Schaumann take over the national, fat body and use it to his advantage. Edward's lean and fit look is appropriate to the explorer, but his exploration cannot uncover the basic truths of the world, which Schaumann's sedentary life of observation can. He comments to his friend: "We licked our plates and we licked the world, poor creatures that we were. For the many things that I had to keep to myself down there in the town and in that school of yours I had all the outlet in the world up here. And this is where I developed the lyrical and epical qualities buried within my genial corpulence, as you used to call it down there. Of course, my sense of the dramatic I gladly left lying dormant there in what you termed my paunch" (241). It is only at the end of the novel that Tubby discloses to Edward the name of the real murderer in the town pub so that all will know his father-in-law's innocence. This is the dramatic moment that he uses to reveal to the world not only the identity of the real murderer but also his insight into the workings of the human mind. His gut knows and reveals the truth.

The gut truth of the fat detective is not to be found in the world of the intellect but in his body. Tubby's doctor warns him to avoid the "strain of the mind." This is ironic, as the life of the mind is and has been Tubby's hallmark. The doctor, however, believes that too much mental activity might be harmful. At the pub Tubby is invited formally to expose Störzer to the public prosecutor so as to clear the name of his father-in-law: " 'I'd love to, if it were possible and my doctor hadn't forbidden it,' laughed Schaumann. 'Oh, if you had any idea, Schellbaum, how emphatically that man Oberwasser has forbidden me intellectual stimulus of any kind, you would leave me lying under my hedge as in other and better days' " (301). He leaves with his friend, having solved the murder and without claiming the laurels of the detective but with the truth revealed to all who would overhear.

The fat detective in Raabe's novel is able to solve the case of Kienbaum's murder over the course of decades simply because of the passive, sedentary nature of his body. His body, which appears to be bloated and obese, is the perfect vehicle for this sort of emotional — not intellectual — exploration of the inner souls of those about him. He is not an "intellectual" but a keen observer. His ability, like Cracker's, to place the real murderer into circumstances in which he reveals his crime is the reflex of the fat that forms his body and that reflects the empathetic nature of his soul. He does not track the murderer down but waits until he comes to him and confesses. This is another form of intelligence, an intelligence seemingly contradicted by the visible form of Tubby's "slothful" body. Schaumann is more than corpulent; he is fat incarnate. His fat is not only the sign of the successful farmer, as his friend notes when he first sees him sitting at the farmhouse, having not seen him for decades; it is also a sign of the type of archeology of the soul that the detective undertakes. Tubby's girth seems to be an impediment to his role as a scientist; indeed, however, it becomes the sign of his success, as a farmer, a paleontologist, and a sleuth.

Tubby's body seems indeed to be a return to the primitive, prerational (and preindustrial) world. However, it only masks his inner nature. In that sense it is a truly "modern" body. During World War I Gottfried Benn in his "Gesänge" conjures, like many of the moderns, the return to the primitive as desirable:

> O that we were our ancestors' ancestors.
> A lump of slime in a warm moor.[13]

This desire to return to the primitive state before the rational seems to be a result of the war and its destruction of the value of the rational. As Theodor Adorno notes about this poem, the "repulsive nature of the state to which the poet pretends he wishes to return, but to which no return is possible, reinforces his protest against a suffering which has historical causes."[14] Still, it is only the intellectual (a designation that Benn comes to detest) who can write about this return to the primal state. The return to the primordial fat body can be accomplished while the return to the slime cannot. This modern body, with fat masking the internal processes of civilization, is that of the fat detective. The fat detective represents a reaction (or at least half a reaction) against the claims of science and objectivity, of the world of the intellect. This is a world against which the modern (even in the form of Raabe's world) reacts.

The clear antithesis of Tubby Schaumann is the most important detective of the 1890s, Arthur Conan Doyle's Sherlock Holmes.[15] Created in 1887, whip-thin, addicted to cocaine rather than food, always ready to head off on a chase at the drop of a clue, Holmes remains the exemplary rational detective.[16] (Remember Joshua Duke's 1885 suggestion that the new drug "cuca" could be used as an aid for dieting. Perhaps Holmes knew how to keep his body so thin?)[17] His regular feats of observation stun his rather dull-witted companion Dr. John Watson, but all rely on the ability causally to link "facts" following the model of analytic thinking he learned in medical school.[18] Again it is the scientist, but here the scientist as activist, who makes the perfect intellectual detective. He often sinks into a contemplative stupor, aided by his tobacco and cocaine. But this detective also goes out into the world gathering facts. Holmes roams the length of Europe — all the way to Tibet — for knowledge. His is the explorer's body, Sir Henry Morton Stanley's body, as well as that of the detective.

There is another Holmes in these tales, however. Holmes's older and wiser brother, Mycroft, is introduced in 1892 in the *Strand Magazine*'s publication of "The Case of the Greek Interpreter."[19] Like Tubby Schaumann he is huge and sedentary: "Mycroft Holmes was a much larger and stouter man than Sherlock. His body was absolutely corpulent, but his face, though massive, had preserved something of the sharpness of expression which was so remarkable in that of his brother."[20] Mycroft's intelligence, glimmering in his eyes (the mirrors of the soul), seems overburdened by his primitive body. There is something quite archaic about him; he has "a broad fat hand, like the flipper of a seal" (295). He is not quite a sloth, but close enough.

Mycroft is the better brother, as his younger sibling grudgingly admits. Holmes states, "He was my superior in observation and deduction. If the art of the detective began and ended in the reasoning from an arm-chair, my brother would be the greatest criminal agent that ever lived" (293). What makes Holmes the better detective is that he is willing to use his powers in the world. Mycroft, like Tubby Schaumann, in the end is merely an amateur sleuth, not really a professional one, unlike the pompous fat detective whom Sherlock Holmes bests in *The Sign of the Four* (1890). And the amateur nature of his undertaking is seemingly tied to his lack of desire to pursue truth to its bitter end: "What is to me a means of livelihood is to him the merest hobby of a dilettante" (294). Here the quality of the amateur, in Tubby's case the amateur paleontologist as detective, is central. These are not professional detectives whose world is the world of action, but amateurs whose interests include other models of the world besides that of rational detection. This is the model that eventually evolves into a string of fat detectives, culminating in *Cracker*. Such detectives of the 1890s and the turn of the century are imagined as thinking differently. They are related to the figure of Sherlock Holmes but are represented as thinking in a different manner. They appear to think through their bodies, but this is deceptive. Their bodies provide an image of obesity that masks their sharp powers of observation and deduction.

FAT VILLAINS

If the fat detective is different from the thin one, so too is the fat criminal different from his slim confederates. Heta Pyrönen notes in her theory of the detective novel that the criminal is often a projection in the mind of the detective.[21] Vance Thompson stated in 1914 that "there is a strange kinship between obesity and financial crime — almost all embezzlers are fat."[22] White-collar crime, the crime of the intellect, is what the fat boy undertakes when he goes bad. There is an inherent symmetry between the detective and the criminal. Thus the intellectual and physical attributes of Sherlock Holmes match exactly those of his antithesis, Professor Moriarty.

An examination of two obese villains of very different stripe reveals a pattern found in the Victorian and early modern fat detective. The first modern British detective fiction, Wilkie Collins's *The Woman in White* (1860), introduces the "immensely fat" villain Count Fosco.[23] The ally of the novel's nemesis, Sir Perceval Glyde, Fosco is indelibly imprinted on the mind of the narrator, who had "always especially disliked corpulent humanity" (220). There had always been the assumption that "either no people but amiable people ever get fat, or that the accidental addition of so many pounds of flesh has a directly favourable influence on the disposition of the person on whose body they accumulate" (220). Fosco's physiognomy is dominated by his fat making his skin "smoother and freer from all marks and wrinkles than mine, though . . . he is close of sixty years of age." Here we have an answer to Charles Dickens's unreadable Fat Joe or Brillat-Savarin's classic statement that "obesity fills up those hollows which nature formed to add highlights and shadows; thus nothing is commoner than to see faces which once were very interesting and which fatness has made almost insignificant."[24] Fosco's fat is exactly what makes his face fascinating. While it is only in Collins's *The Moonstone* (1868) that the first unofficial detective (like Tubby Schaumann and Mycroft Holmes) in English fiction appears, the narrator Walter Hartright, in all of his slim daring, serves this purpose in *The Woman in White*. (He is a private detective, an echo of the official police inspector Buckett in Charles Dickens's *Bleak House* [1852–53].) He is unable to completely see through the count. Fosco is fat and old, yet "his movements are astonishingly light and easy." Brilliant, "with a daring independence of thought, a knowledge of books in every language, and an experience of society in half the capitals of Europe" (223), this fat villain has but one major flaw, and it is neurological. "This fat, indolent, elderly man" has "nerves that are so finely strung that he starts at chance noises, and winces when he sees a house-spaniel get a whipping" (223). It is his nerves that betray his sensitivity, even as the plot is posthumously revealed in a letter he penned to the hero. Fosco's fat does not quite shield his inner secret.

In the figure of Michaelis in *The Secret Agent* (1907) Joseph Conrad presents a huge, bloated conspirator that is a caricature of the anarchist that haunted the imagination of Europe for decades.[25] (This fear permeated even the fiction of Arthur Conan Doyle, who has a character in "Adventure of the Six Napoleons" [1904] complain of a "Nihilist plot," for "no one but an anarchist would go about breaking statues. Red republicans — that's what I call 'em.")[26] Yet of course this farce turns into a tragedy, quite the opposite of Karl Marx's claim about history. Michaelis, perhaps a parodic version of the obese anarchist Mikhail Bakunin, had become fat during twenty years in prison: "He had come out of a highly hygienic prison round like a tub, with an enormous stomach and distended cheeks of a pale, transparent complexion, as though for fifteen years the servants of an outraged society had made a point of stuffing him with fattening foods in a damp and lightless cellar" (73). His fat is a mark of his role as a true believer, which is why he served the term in prison. After being released he tried to cure his obesity at Marienbad, where an admirer had sent him, but the police expelled him immediately. His body is read as criminal because of its fat, yet Conrad is quick to dismiss any reading of it as "degenerate." When one of the conspirators attempts to evoke Cesare Lombroso's theory of degeneration in another context, another dismisses it with an expletive: "Lombroso is an ass" (77). Michaelis's body bears its weight as a sign of its conviction (in both senses of the word).

For Michaelis is the only one in the band who is a true believer: "His ideas were not in the nature of convictions. They were inaccessible to reasoning. . . . He confessed rather than preached . . . pathetic in his grotesque and incurable obesity" (121). His is a failure of judgment in the face of pure belief. He believes in a radical and uncompromising way. All of the others in the conspiracy have personal reasons for joining it and are, in that sense, much less dangerous than he is. Yet in his obesity Michaelis is seen as "not dangerous," as "no longer in a position to take care of himself," as "recommended to follow a treatment of some sort," and as " 'quite startling,' 'monstrous,' 'most painful to see,' [and] 'grotesque' " by the do-gooders who wish to intervene in his case (121). Yet Conrad knows better, as do we. What is fascinating is that the "detective," or at least the secret agent, Veloc, who infiltrates this band, is "very corpulent" (56). He is described by one of his employers as "fat — the animal" (57). He is "burly in a fat-pig style." Veloc has become fat because he has easily adapted to the soft life of a spy without undertaking any great risks. (Conrad based the character on his own brother-in-law, who both edited an anarchist paper and was a police agent. His body is very different from those of other police figures in the novel, such as the assistant commissioner.) Thus, criminal and agent are both defined by their corpulence. Their visibility makes the very notion of a hidden conspiracy into a joke — one with, sadly, deadly results. Based on a real case, the so-called Greenwich Bomb Outrage in 1894, when an anarchist was killed by a bomb he was transporting, his characters' obesity was a substantial part of Conrad's invention, designed to present an answer to newly emerging notions of what forms danger could take. The danger was seen to lie in the faculty of judgment, for neither Veloc nor Michaelis judges the world in ways that are adequate to their own sense of identity. These figures are the antecedents of criminals such as "The Fat Man" in Dashiell Hammett's *The Maltese Falcon* (1930), who is "flabbily fat with bulbous pink cheeks and lips and chin and neck, with a great soft egg of a belly that was all his torso, and pendant cones for arms and legs."[27] It is no surprise that the master of the hard-boiled detective story calls him Casper Gutman, Esquire.

THE SCIENCE OF THINKING WITH YOUR GUT

To understand the notion of the fat detective, it is necessary to examine the perceptions regarding the faculties of thinking and judgment in relation to the body during the long turn of the century, from 1880 to 1914. During the course of the nineteenth century the relationship between the brain and the nervous system came to be relatively well established. The notion of "thought," which had been a component of the "soul," was transmuted with the introduction of a medical materialism by scientists such as Johannes Müller into a model of thinking by way of the body. The nervous system was seen as the place where thought and therefore judgment took place. The central discoveries were in the realm of the nature of the nerves themselves, and one of the most important developments through the course of the nineteenth century was the discovery that nerves consisted of two types of fiber. One fiber carried electrical impulses, and the other, in the terms of the model of electricity dominant in representing the nervous system during this period, served as insulation. The substance surrounding the nerve was a fat, which came by midcentury to be called *myelin*. It was understood as absolutely necessary to the correct functioning of the nervous system in that it increased the speed of the transmission of nerve impulses.[28] One can think of this model of the nerve as insulation wrapped around energy: the inert shielding the active, or thought clothed in fat. It was seen as the sign of the evolutionary development that had enabled human beings to become human. And that leap was defined in their new ability to think, but most specifically to make judgments.

It is clear, as a number of contemporary scholars have shown, that the concept of the body as a thinking mass is ancient. It is tied to notions of brain localization, which have their modern formulation in the phrenological work of Franz Joseph Gall and Johannes Spurzheim but their roots in ancient physiognomic theory.[29] Fat bodies were imagined to "think" differently, as "fat" came to be a physiognomic characteristic. Permanent features of the body (like bone structure) rather than mobile qualities (like expression) were used to define character. The idea that the fat body thinks intuitively is an inherent aspect of Talmudic discourse. Indeed, in *Baba Metzia* 83b–85a, so ably explicated by Daniel Boyarin, the tale of Rabbi El'azar, the son of Shim'on, reveals that El'azar intuitively knows the truth because of his fat body. As a Roman "quisling" he makes judgments that seem destructive, arbitrary, or foolish, but because he knows the truth intuitively, he is always right. He is a fat sleuth, whose solutions turn out always to be accurate, even if at first glance they appear to be false. One day he has a "certain laundry man" who has insulted him arrested. Before he can come to his senses, the man is hung. As he stands below the body and weeps for his error, he is told that the man had violated a number of *mitzvoth* (laws) that would have condemned him to death anyway. When his judgment is so affirmed, "he placed his hands on his guts and said: 'Be joyful, O my guts, be joyful! If it is thus when you are doubtful, when you are certain even more so. I am confident that rot and worms cannot prevail over you.' " In spite of this, however, he remains unconvinced of his inherent fat facility. He is drugged, and "baskets of fat" are ripped from his gut and placed in the July sun: "And it did not stink. But no fat stinks. It does if it has red blood vessels in it, and this even though it had red blood vessels in it, did not stink."[30] It is the belly, now separate from the body, that has a life of its own. It represents the intuitive ability of this otherwise suspect figure to judge truth from falsity; it is a gut feeling, quite literally.

The ancient trope of the fat body thinking differently foregrounds, through the course of the nineteenth century, the question of how the body thinks. What had been assumed to be the emotional, intuitive response of the body to the world was shown to be a form of rationality. The notion of the brain as the site for ratiocination provided an odd Cartesian moment. In thinking the brain separates itself from the body, but if the brain is part of the neural network, even if it is a central and vital aspect, then the body itself, through the nerves, thinks. This thought may be different from, or more primitive than, the thought of the brain. As the "layers" of critical action and localization are explored, even the brain is seen to have a history, an ontogeny, inscribed on its anatomical structure. Fat around nerves becomes the sign of the development of "higher" powers of thought. Thought becomes possible only with the increased speed of neural transmission. Thus it is, of course, neurologists who become the caretakers of the thinking body. The loss of fat in the nervous system becomes a means of measuring the efficacy of healthy nerves.

Historically, fat has had a central role in constituting the neurological body. It was Robert Remak who, in 1836, demonstrated that the "nerve" has differentiated "parts," identified as myelinated and unmyelinated fibers (*myelin* being the term for the fatty sheath around a conduit of pure energy).[31] He thus discovered that white-matter tracts are really attached to cell bodies. This took place as Justus von Liebig at Giessen University was uncovering how fat was formed in the animal body and how this was connected to the animal's nutrition. Liebig as a chemist spent his career studying the energy-producing function of food through careful measurement. He saw carbon-containing fats as a type of fuel that was absolutely necessary for the maintenance of the healthy body. He labeled carbohydrates and fats as "respiratory foods." From this came his view that when such foods are eaten to an excessive amount fat accumulates on the body. Diet was for Liebig the cause and control of morbid obesity, but fat was recognized as essential for the proper functioning of the body. Liebig's work, initially published in 1840, paralleled and influenced the work of those interested in the functioning of the nervous system.[32] For if fat was necessary for the well-being of the entire body, should it not also be for the function of the nerves?

While Remak never actually used the word *myelin*, he recognized the difference between fat and nerve tissue, building upon Albrecht von Haller's eighteenth-century notion of the irritability of nerve tissue. It is not simple coincidence that the discovery of the "fat" of the nerves as the key to their function paralleled the discovery of the meaning of fat in the metabolic process. There had been older views that collapsed the image of body fat with the fat imagined around the nerves, following Haller's view of the irritability of the nerves. In 1811 Thomas Jameson wrote in his tractate about obesity that it "also diminishes the irritability of the system, since fat people are remarked for good humour, and for bearing cold better that those who are lean, on account of the defensive coat of fat surrounding their nerves."[33] Here is a basic assumption of the nature of fat men and their fat nerves, which is made universal by

Remak. All of our nerves are covered with fat, and that is what enables them to function. Yet the new neurology continued to carry hidden assumptions about masculinity and character. Based on Remak's observations in the 1830s, new theories of human development and the way we ascertain it evolved, but they carried with them older ideas of the meaning of fat.

Remak, a Polish Jew, was always marginalized in the science of his day. As with many Eastern European Jews who followed the Enlightenment's promise of science as the true universal, Remak rejected any form of religion and its demand for a metaphysic of the soul separate from the physical body. Thus, Remak followed the materialism of scientists such as Johannes Müller. Like Müller he desired to understand the material basis of the "soul" in its physical manifestation as nerves. In 1836 he provisionally described the difference in the nerve between "the primitive band" (the band of Remak), which was myelinated fiber, and the "organic fiber" (the fiber of Remak) but also suggested that the nerve cell and the nerve fiber were in direct communication with one another. Vital to Remak's distinction was the image that would later dominate research on the nature of the nerve: the fat/myelinated fiber developed earlier on both ontological as well as phylogenic levels.

Louis Ranvier (1872), continuing Remak's work, showed that there are nodes in the myelin and that these "adipose cells" (endoneurium) are part of the connective tissue of the nerves.[34] Unlike Remak, who used a microscope to make his distinction between the two types of fiber, Ranvier used a new silver impregnation stain, which provided the first detailed "look" at the nature of the myelin sheath and the "node of Ranvier" in the nerve. While this was an obvious anatomical structure when it was stained, it was not so to the unaided eye. The ability to "see" fat made it real. "Seeing" fat in the body was as important to the neurologists as acknowledging its presence. A complete nerve was a nerve with a myelin sheath, and the discovery of demylenating diseases, such as multiple sclerosis, which afflicted major personages from K. F. W. Marx at the beginning of the nineteenth century to Jean-Martin Charcot at its close, demonstrated the pathological effect of the loss of "fat."[35] Nerves worked only with the presence of the sheath of fat, and they ceased to work once it was lost. If the loss could be seen, as in the muscle's inability to operate, could not the loss also impact those qualities that defined the human being even more directly, thought and the thought processes?

As with most aspects of nineteenth-century science, it was the ability to "see" the fat around the nerves that made it concrete for neurologists. Fat could be seen and therefore could be distinguished from other aspects of the nerve. The stain used by Ranvier, while a specific stain for myelin itself, replaced providing a means to distinguish myelin from other nerve fibers. Carl Weigert (1882) developed a special staining technique to make myelin visible with a bright red dye.[36] Suddenly, the striking visualization of this fat made it even more "real." From 1878 Weigert had studied topical issues of pathology, such as coagulation necrosis and pathogenesis of tuberculosis. But his primary contributions to the visualization of the nerves were his studies into histological staining techniques and his development of the principle of elective staining, including staining of myelin sheaths. Once the specificity of seeing myelin was possible, then a complicated theory of its nature and history evolved.

After the job of identifying and making myelin visible for inspection was completed, it was Paul Emil Flechsig who returned to the earlier premise of Remak and in 1900 theorized how myelin developed.[37] (Yes, it was *that* Flechsig, Daniel Paul Schreber's doctor and the subject of his most intense fantasies. The vocabulary of Flechsig's scientific studies of the brain and the nerves finds its way into Schreber's text in grotesque and complex ways.)[38] Flechsig built on the localization work of Freud's teacher, Theodor Meynert, who first related regional structural differences in the cerebral cortex to the specific functions. Flechsig was able to identify groups of fibers and the thirty-six specific and constant regions of the cortex with which they are associated. Most important, he showed how these cortical areas developed in a chronological sequence. Fibers in various parts of the nervous system acquire myelin sheaths at different stages of development. Thus, a study not of where "fat" appears but when provided a clue to an archeology of the human nervous system. Fat was the key to the history of human judgment. It provided the benchmarks by which one could distinguish between "primitive" and "higher" stages of development. Myelin was the sign of the potential for human intelligence. With its appearance, according to Flechsig's theory, there was a leap in the possibility for thought.

Flechsig's theoretical work mapping neural development began in 1893 and was based on the discovery of myelinization in the subcortical white matter of the fetus and infant. He observed that there seemed to be three zones and periods of development of the nerves based on the nature of the myelin: first, the motor and sensory areas, which matured earlier — the primordial zones; then, the intermediate zones; and finally, the regions of late development, the terminal zones. Flechsig notes that his project of myelogenetic localization seemed to be "falling back to the phrenology of Gall." Like the eighteenth-century phrenologist Franz Gall, he attempted to see in the structure of the brain and nervous system reflections of the higher or lower "nature" of human responses. Flechsig's work came after that of Raabe's fat sleuth. He postulated a developmental scheme that would have seen "fat" (now understood as myelin) as the means by which the nerve functioned and thus made thought possible. It was a measure of the course of the development of the nervous system from the most primitive, uninsulated nerves through to the highest cortical function. To extrapolate, fat detectives think with their guts, but only because of the heavy myelinization of their nervous system.

In 1920 Flechsig published his last work on the topic of the anatomy of the brain and its development. In this atlas of brain function he repeats his thesis on the stages of human development as mirrored in the myelinization of the brain. As an anatomist he returned to the problems of pathology to point out the functions of such levels. By noting the deficits in the living patient, Flechsig correlated them (he believed) with the deficiencies of the myelin in the postmortem. His map of human development thus relies on pathological manifestations for its empirical underpinning. For Flechsig the history of the brain focuses on the development from the elemental processes to those provided by higher neural activities. The "projection centers" are the earliest and thus the most primitive areas of the brain. They provide "bodily sensation, visual, auditory, olfactory and taste." The sense of the body is provided by the nerves sheathed in their fat; the more primitive the nerves, the more rudimentary the reactions. The sensorium is the earliest and most basic level of bodily awareness. Fat is the essence of this layer, defining its place in the body's history. (Needless to say, Flechsig's views were hotly contested, to no little degree by the neurologist Luigi Bianchi.) Thus, the "fat" that protected the nerves was necessary for

176

higher thought processes but also for the basic physical structure of the senses, which provide information to the brain.

It was another neurologist of the time, Sigmund Freud, who closely connected the idea of myelin to the ability to produce judgments. Clearly, in Flechsig's model the increased intelligence ascribed to the presence of myelin implied the ability to judge, but Freud made this explicit. Freud's early, unpublished project for a scientific psychology of 1895 proposes a neurological model of the body, and this model was really never lost in his conception of the biological "space" for the psyche. It postulates a basic or primitive neural network that underlies all consciousness. Freud makes a distinction between the permeable and the impermeable neurons. The former offer no resistance and are the transmitters of perception; the latter are the place of memory and are "loaded with resistance."[39] Freud makes an analogous distinction (in the same essay) between remembering and judging (1:330–31). Perception has implanted memory on the impermeable neurons, and judgment occurs when there is a disparity between new perception and stored perceptions. Thus, for Freud judgment is "not a primary function but presupposes the cathexis from the ego of the disparate non-comparable portions of the perception" (1:332). Judgment is an unconscious process that is, as Freud notes, a "method of proceeding from the perceptual situation that is given in reality to the situation that is wished-for" (1:332). All judgment resides in the nerve's ability to retain mimetic images of actual perceptions and recall them on an unconscious level. Judgment occurs through the body's memory.

The image of where judgment takes place is also central to much of Freud's later work, such as *Beyond the Pleasure Principle* (1920). In part 4, Freud postulates a model of the nervous system in which the unconscious dominates because of inherent limitations in the evolution of the nervous system. Consciousness, in this account, is notable in not being a medium where memory can be stored. Rather, the aspects of the psyche engaged in the "excitatory process" are provided with a literal shield against these stimuli of perception (28:27). This shield envelops the cortical layer and shields it from external stimuli, but not from internal ones. Freud theorizes that this is a higher or later level of embryological, and therefore evolutionary, development. The most simplified organism is, for Freud, "an undifferentiated vesicle of a substance that is susceptible to stimulation" (28:26). Such exposed organisms can exist only if they develop some form of protection against unmediated exposure to the world. And that is accomplished through evolutionary change: "Indeed embryology, in its capacity as a recapitulation of developmental history, actually shows us that the central nervous system originates from the ectoderm; the grey matter of the cortex remains a derivative of the primitive superficial layer of the organism and may have inherited some of its essential properties" (28:26). This external level, the primitive level, becomes "permanently modified" by acquiring a crust in order to limit and channel the reception of stimuli. The nervous system wants to limit such excitation, and this external, procrustean layer begins to serve as insulation. It permits internal stimulation from the unconscious while limiting and structuring access from the external world. Freud is speaking of the psyche in this context, but his model (and his structure) is of the nervous system with its layer of insulation.

Fat thinks; fat judges. Or at least the fat around the nerves provides the most elemental level of response to the world. The fat detective, all nerves and sensations, seems to think with the most primitive part of the nervous system, with his fat. This primitive response, the response of the body, seems on the surface to be intuitive. Therefore, in a world that doubts rationality as the sole answer, the fat detective solves the case. The rereading of this at the close of the nineteenth century, however, actually posits the thought of the fat detective as the model for all human judgment.

The key to Freud's differentiation between internal processes and their dependence on the evolutionary structure of the brain is keyed to the meaning of fat as a sign of health, rather than pathology. If myelin is the sign of the ability of the nervous system to work more efficiently and thus to permit the detective's judgment, body fat in the nineteenth century becomes the analogous "public" sign of this health. To be simple: fat is good for the neurologists, including Freud. It is a sign of that quality that makes the human being human. That quality is thought and judgment.

This positive evaluation of fat is no different when we turn to the therapeutics of the period and look at those places where fat comes to be understood as curative. S. Weir Mitchell, in his *Fat and Blood and How to Make Them* (1877), ties the lack of "visible" body fat to the notion of an insufficiency of the nerves. Hysteria can result when the body becomes too thin: "I think the first thing which strikes an American in England is the number of inordinately fat people, and especially fat women. . . . [T]his excess of flesh we usually associate in idea with slothfulness."[40] In fact, Mitchell proceeds to state, such fat is a prophylaxis against disease: "This must make . . . some difference in their relation liability to certain forms of disease" (15). It is primarily women who suffer from this loss of fat and the resulting nervousness — "a large group of women, especially said to have nervous exhaustion, or . . . described as having spinal irritation. . . . They have a tender spine, and sooner or later enact the whole varied drama of hysteria" (25–26). They are "lacking in color and . . . had not lost flesh" (27). Even men, however, can suffer from such a debility of the nerves, specifically through traumatic experiences: "Nor is this less true of men, and I have many a time seen soldiers who had ridden boldly with Sheridan or fought gallantly with Grant, become, under the influence of painful nerve wounds, as irritable and hysterically emotional as the veriest girl," undergoing "moral degradation" (28). Fat men and women are mentally healthy; thin men and women suffer. The result, of course, is the "rest cure," made popular in our own day in the readings of Charlotte Perkins Gilman's 1892 tale *The Yellow Wallpaper*, which is the account of Gilman's own treatment by S. Weir Mitchell.[41] The neurological basis of Mitchell's understanding of the definition of fat, however, has not been explored, nor has the notion that fat impacts a specific type of thinking, the intuitive. For S. Weir Mitchell a certain amount of fat was necessary to protect the nervous system and thus the psyche from distress. He argued that "blood thins with the decrease of tissues and enriches as they increase" (15). And the more blood, the more psychic energy. It is a sign of "nutritive prosperity" (16). Such prosperity is signaled by the social station of the individual. Thus, he proposes that the "upper classes gain weight in the summer" (and intelligence) while the working classes lose it. This prescription, however, is also determined by the individual's gender. Fat men are all in all healthier than fat women.

Body fat is the visible equivalent of the myelin around the nerves. Fat makes the body healthy since it prevents the exposure of the nerves. It is thus the sign of the possibility of higher thought (as in the fat sheath around the nerves) and the preservation of mental health (bodily fat).

This model, of the thinking and judging body as it is found from 1891 to the mid–twentieth century, is embodied in the fat sleuth. His body is a thinking and judging body, unlike the "fat" body of the female of the time, which is a reproductive body. S. Weir Mitchell differentiates between the soldierly and reproductive functions of the healthy, fat bodies of men and women. The male body thinks with its visible fat. It is empathetic and responsive. His body is a healthy body because of its fat. The fat detective only functions in his role as an intuitive solver of problems when he responds to his "gut" feelings. His body thinks and judges. It is a basic form of rationality. Here Freud's model in *Beyond the Pleasure Principle* has its appropriate place, for limitations on the experience of the world provide a barrier to other, external experience. Such experience must be highly structured and controlled. Thus the passivity of Tubby Schaumann and Mycroft Holmes becomes a means, in their own narratives, of limiting the world's access to them, rather than their access to the world. The internal processes of remembering the forgotten, of sensing that which cannot be experienced, shape their ability to discover hidden or forgotten truths. This ability seems to be primitive (like a sloth or walrus), but it is indeed the hallmark of the most sophisticated and highly developed male body. It is the body that thinks. Here our contemporary notion of the "enteric nervous system that is pharmacologically more complex than the sympathetic or parasympathetic systems, involving many neuropeptide and other transmitters (such as 5-hydroxytryptamine [a.k.a. serotonin]) often described as a collection of 'little brains,' " can be evoked.[42] The body itself is understood as the place of thinking. The parallel nature of the nineteenth-century understanding of fat and thinking is that the cultural assumptions that shape the language of neurology simultaneously shape the language of popular fiction. It is a language that sees the need for "fat" as part of a cultural discourse of appropriate, if slightly quirky, masculinity.

The model of the primitive body that thinks, and thinks in what seems to be an intuitive way, became one of the models for the detective in the course of the twentieth century. The rationality of the fat detective is hidden within the unreadability of his fat body, for who would assume that such a body could contain a rational mind? Other versions of the fat amateur sleuth followed Raabe's and Conan Doyle's. In 1911 G. K. Chesterton began the publication of his Father Brown tales.[43] Here the question of belief and the body of the fat amateur detective are again linked. The priest's body is represented as chubby; his response to the murders he investigates is rational rather than intuitive. Indeed, Chesterton saw the Father Brown stories as a means of furthering his Anglo-Catholicism, seen in England as a form of the irrational. The squat body of Father Brown represents the innate seeking for truth beyond logic. He is the embodiment of the idea of thought and faith being aspects of one truth. It is a truth to be found by those who are able to see it, not necessarily by those ordained by the state to seek it.

By 1934 and the publication of Rex Stout's first Nero Wolfe mysteries, the tradition of the fat detective as a countertype had been well established.[44] By 1929 there was Duddington Pell Chalmers, the obese detective hero of John T. McIntyre's *The Museum Murder*, as well as Gerald Verner's Superintendent Budd, "the stout detective," "who is fat, lazy, graceful on his feet," "prone to shut his eyes while thinking," and "not susceptible to feminine beauty."[45] Like Father Brown's celibate by definition, Nero Wolfe's body is not a sexualized one — any more than is that of Mycroft Holmes. Yet this feminizing quality of the male body masks a life of passion. In the course of the Nero Wolfe mysteries we learn of his earlier romantic attachments. All of these took place at a point before his bulk both inhibited and freed the detective from the power of physical passion.

In Rex Stout's first novel, *Fer-de-Lance* (1934), Wolfe's hard-boiled associate Archie Goodwin notes the almost archaic form of Wolfe's body as similar to early twentieth-century fantasies of Neolithic man: "Wolfe lifted his head. I mention that, because his head was so big that lifting it struck you as being quite a job. It was probably really bigger than it looked, for the rest of him was so huge that any head on top of it but his own would have escaped your notice entirely."[46] Wolfe's body is not only fat; it is huge and archaic in its form.

Wolfe's fat is the fat that protects: "I said to him something I had said before more than once, that beer slowed up a man's head and with him running like a brook, six quarts a day, I never would understand how he could make his brain work so fast and deep that no other man in the country could touch him. He replied, also as he had before, that it wasn't his brain that worked, it was his lower nerve centers."[47] Wolfe, unlike Archie, thinks with his guts, and invoking the popular beliefs of his day regarding fat, he states, "I am too sensitive to strangers, that is why I keep these layers over my nerves."[48] His fat isolates his nerves: "I carry this fat to insulate my feelings. They got too strong for me once or twice and I had that idea. If I had stayed lean and kept moving around I would have been dead long ago."[49] One of the best commentators on the Wolfe novels observed that "upholders of order are our romantic heroes, and Wolfe qualifies under that category. His daily schedule is as much an insistence on order as a tribute to it: similarly, Wolfe's fat, his gruffness, and his seclusion betray his struggle to insulate himself from emotions, to harness them, to grant them a place, but a smaller one than they claim. Reason then is a goal; it is also a process, a struggle. The Wolfe novels value it as both."[50] The archaic body struggles with its basic emotional nature. And fat is the weapon that enables Wolfe to succeed as a detective.

In this sense Wolfe is "modern." Franz Kafka, at almost six feet tall and 133 pounds, the exemplary "thin man" among the moderns, feared a body without fat.[51] Not only in his tale "The Hunger Artist" (1922), in which he presents the idea that starvation shows the body to be merely determined by drives, not desire, but in his own life he looked at the thinness of his body as an embodiment of his ill and diseased spirit. Kafka's body was long and thin, a statement in a world where pulchritude was a sign of success, of substance:

> It is certain that a major obstacle to my progress is my physical condition. Nothing can be accomplished with such a body. . . . My body is too long for its weakness, it hasn't the least bit of fat to engender a blessed warmth, to preserve an inner fire, no fat on which the spirit could occasionally nourish itself beyond its daily need without damage to the whole. How shall the weak heart that lately has troubled me so often be able to pound the blood through the length of these legs. It would be labor enough to the knees, and from there it can only spill with a senile strength into the cold lower parts of my legs. But now it is already needed up above again, it is being waited for, while it is wasting itself below. Everything is pulled apart throughout the length of my body. What could it accomplish then, when it perhaps wouldn't have enough strength for what I want to achieve even if it were shorter and more compact.[52]

However, Kafka's equation of thinness with a lack of "inner fire," of spirit, his reading of his outer body as a sign of his soul, are part of the common wisdom about the fat boys of the nineteenth century. They are smart and not nervous; they are in control of their bodies.

The very act of thinking for Wolfe is thinking with his body: "Wolfe looked up again, and his big thick lips pushed out a little, tight together, just a small movement, and back again, and then out and back again. How I loved to watch him doing that! That was about the only time I ever got excited, when Wolfe's lips were moving like that. . . . I knew what was going on, something was happening so fast inside of him and so much ground was being covered."[53] The pursed lips are the organ of eating but also the organ of thought. Here the parallel to Tubby Schaumann (and the rest of the lineage of fat detectives) is clear. The body has its own life and its own rules. It compliments or contradicts the rational mind and provides the means by which fat detectives set themselves off from all other scientific observers.

When in 1942 Wolfe decides to diet, the result is a shambles. In the novella "Not Quite Dead Enough" Rex Stout's own major commitment to the war effort is emulated by his character, who also decides to get into shape. The thin man within him desires to reappear. Wolfe was thin before he gained weight so as to protect his nerves because of unpleasantness with a certain woman in Montenegro. But the effect of a thin Wolfe is ludicrous, as Archie comments: "He didn't look smaller, he merely looked deflated. The pants were his own, an old pair of blue serge. The shoes were strangers, rough army style. The sweater was mine, a heavy maroon number that I had bought once for a camping trip, and in spite of his reduction of circumference it was stretched so tight that his yellow shirt showed though the holes."[54] Wolfe simply looks ridiculous. He moves, he acts, and he believes that he is thin, but it is only a simulacrum of thinness. Running up and down the stairs, short of breath, he is simply the fat man within the thinner one. Most important, according to Archie, Wolfe's intelligence has lost its edge. His fat self conquers when he is confronted with a fascinating case that demands his attention. He leans back "comfortably in his chair, his arms folded, with his eyes closed, and I had a suspicion that he was about two-thirds asleep. He had finished two bottles of beer, after going without for over a month, and he was back in the only chair in the world he liked, and his insane project of going outdoors and walking fast twice a day was only a hideous memory."[55] Wolfe returns to that state of obese equilibrium in which thought and body seem to be one. When he later tries to lose weight as part of a case in which he has to disguise himself, in the novel *In the Best of Families* (1950), he seems shrunken and ill proportioned: "With more skin supplied for his face than was needed, it had taken up the slack in his pleats and wrinkles, and that may have accounted for his sporting a pointed brown beard, since it must be hard to shave pleats."[56] The natural Wolfe is not the thin man of his youth, but the fat boy of his old age. Wolfe's thin body is similar to the fantasy of Falstaff's vanishing weight. Falstaff says to Bardolph that he is fading away when he is out of the prince's favor: "Do I not bate? Do I not dwindle? Why, my skin hangs about me like an old lady's loose gown; I am withered like an old applejohn" (*1H4* 3.3.2–5). Unlike the fantasy of the thin man trapped within a fat body that we find in Cornaro, here the very loss of weight compromises the essence of these fat men. They are their fat.

The fat detective Nero Wolfe took to the screen in *Meet Nero Wolfe* in 1936, with Edward Arnold as the protagonist. Edward Arnold was one of the very few clearly portly leading men of the age who could do Nero Wolfe and in the same season play a romantic lead, as he did in *Come and Get It* (1936). The popularity of Nero Wolfe continued with a rather long series of spin-offs of fat detectives in the mass media, beginning with Dashiell Hammett's *Brad Runyon*, which aired from 1946 to 1950 on ABC radio. The announcer opened the show with the following observation: "He's walking into that drugstore . . . he's stepping onto the scales . . . (SNICK! CLICK!) Weight: 237 pounds. . . . Fortune: Danger! Whoooo is it? The . . . Fat Man!" The oversized actor J. Scott Smart, who actually outweighed his character by thirty pounds, played him on the radio. World-weary, Runyon was a cross between Wolfe and Sam Spade. The first episode, written by Hammett, was "The Black Angel," broadcast on 26 November 1946. The body of the fat detective on the radio could only be evoked by the image in the listener's mind. As such, his bulk became part of the fantasy of the obese body as heard rather than seen. Rex Stout's Nero Wolfe himself became part of the invisible world of the fat detective on the radio. In 1982 the Canadian Broadcasting Corporation tried their hand at bringing back old-time radio with thirteen one-hour episodes of Nero Wolfe, all based on novellas or short stories written by Stout. The svelte Mavor Moore played the bulky Nero Wolfe, but all the listener heard was the voice of the fat detective.

In 1956 Orson Welles turned Whit Master's novel *Badge of Evil* into the stunning study of corruption *Touch of Evil*, starring Charlton Heston. Welles played a malevolent private detective of gargantuan proportions. He also directed the film, and his camera seems fascinated by his own corporality. Welles moved from the figure of the fat detective to his *Chimes at Midnight/Falstaff* (1965), in which the obscene body of the Shakespearean knight serves as a metaphor of innocence doomed by failure to come to terms with the real world. Welles's Falstaff, however, has a malevolent quality, although this is tempered by the pathetic sight of the fat man acting like a spoiled child. Starring Welles, Walter Chiari, Marina Vlady,

Jeanne Moreau, and Sir John Gielgud, the film was an attempt to compile all of the Falstaffs that Shakespeare offered in *Richard II*, *Henry IV Parts 1 and 2*, *Henry V*, and *The Merry Wives of Windsor*. Welles's own ever-expanding male body served as the rationale for such films, but the detective in *Touch of Evil* and the protagonist in *Falstaff* serve as readable and oddly related versions of the male obese body. In *Touch of Evil* Welles's Detective Quinlan remarks, "My game leg, it's talking to me." His body speaks to him, as Falstaff's does in Welles's version of the story. And it speaks to him in a doubly autobiographical manner. "The truth of Falstaff," he would later observe, "is that Shakespeare understood him better than the other great characters he created, because Falstaff was obliged to sing for his supper."[57] It is the association with this type of professional identity that permeates the fat male body in Welles's representation.

A more visible world of the fat detective played itself out on television.[58] William Conrad, whose voice was well-known from his role as the lanky sheriff on radio's version of *Gunsmoke*, went on to play Frank Cannon in *Cannon* as a tough, expensive, overweight private detective — a sort of hybrid of Sam Spade and Nero Wolfe.[59] Directed by George McCowan, *Cannon* began a highly successful run in 1971 that concluded only in 1976. According to the plot the key to Cannon's character lies in the fact that his wife and infant son died in an automobile accident, after which he placed all his energy and considerable weight into his new profession of private detective. In 1981 NBC aired a TV series based on novellas and short stories by Rex Stout that starred Conrad as Nero Wolfe. Then in 1987 Conrad continued a version of the Nero Wolfe character in *Jake and the Fatman*, produced by Ron Satlof and Fred McKnight, in which his role as J. L. "Fatman" McCabe is much more sedentary. He has been transformed into a slovenly former Hawaiian cop turned Honolulu district attorney. From the "Fatman" to "Cracker," the space of the fat detective comes again to be one filled with the emotional, elemental, intuitive, and empathetic. Yet all of these qualities are shown to be a form of judgment, oftentimes more compelling than "pure" rationality. And all of this began on a German farm with Tubby Schaumann's careful observations of those around him as the key to solving the murder that haunted his world.

No modern fat detective has been more purposely immobile than Raymond Burr as Ironside. Burr, already quite portly in his successful *Perry Mason* television series, began this new role with a made-for-TV movie in 1967. While as Perry Mason Burr played Nero Wolfe to his detective, Paul Drake, in *Ironside* (1967–75) he undertook the role of Robert Ironside, chief of detectives at the San Francisco police department. Shot by a gunman, Ironside was paralyzed from the waist down, wheelchair bound in the initial movie. Ever-large Burr returned in 1993 for a last time with another made-for-TV film. Ironside's limitations seem to be those of the thinking detective. As a private detective Ironside is able to function because his staff serves as his "legs." He is also transported in a specially fitted van to pursue the villains. The coupling of the portly actor and his sedentary role provides a further rationale for the immobility of the fat detective.

Certainly, the most notable figure in the contemporary representation of the "fat detective" is to be found on ABC's long-running television drama *NYPD Blue*. He is Detective Andy Sipowicz, played by Dennis Franz. Since premiering in 1993, the show has centered around this character. Cocreators Steven Bochco and David Milch, along with executive producers Mark Tinker and Michael Robin, continued Franz's character from one who had appeared in Bochco and Milch's earlier success, *Hill Street Blues*. Franz had played Lieutenant Norman Buntz on that show from 1985 to 1987, but Buntz was merely a "tough cop." With Sipowicz, the darkness and complexity of the figure are clearly related to his sense of himself as a detective. Sipowicz is portrayed as a recovered alcoholic, the father of a son whom he has neglected (and who is killed in the course of the show), a man of open emotions and clear prejudices. He is a muscular man gone to fat. It is because rather than in spite of these "flaws" that he is able to be empathetic with his colleagues and generally have insight into his own character. The flaws in his character, represented by his overweight body, make him into a better detective. Franz had acted in two short-lived detective series (*Beverly Hills Buntz* [1987] and *NYPD Mounted* [1991]) in which the complexity of the "fat" character was lacking. In *NYPD Blue* he was at last able to develop his role as a detective, self-consciously using his fat body as the outward projection of his flawed character. Bochco and Milch use this quite self-consciously in the series. The body size of the character was literally exposed in a nude scene — one of the first on commercial television — in which Franz was filmed from the rear. In addition to this overt pointing to the size of the character, an ongoing theme of the early seasons was a new official mandate for all overweight police officers to lose weight, and the subsequent diets and exercise that they undertook. All but Sipowicz. Dennis Franz's body became the key for the figure of the fat detective. His mode of approach is that of the hard-boiled detective, the muscular detective gone to seed, but his fat body is also seen as an external sign of his empathetic nature.[60]

Certainly, the image of the powerful male gone to seed is nowhere better illustrated than in James Mangold's 1997 film *Copland*. Sylvester Stallone (as sheriff Freddy Helfin), Robert DeNiro (as IAB investigator Moe Tilden), and Harvey Keitel (as officer Ray Donlan) all play overweight, older policemen in a world in which power seems to be receding from the grasp of the white male policeman. Stallone's "belly bulges beneath his shirt; his pants, which are too short and tight, accentuate the curves of his rear and his shambling gait."[61] His "stomach appears even larger." For Stallone, the star of innumerable *Rocky* films, playing the role of the fat, aging cop meant that he was working very much against type. His body is self-consciously depicted as aging. His character suffers from increasing deafness that shapes his sense of a decaying fat body, not unlike that of Banting. Stallone had to "train" to gain weight: "It was heaven at first, Stallone said. But he soon learned that the road to stardom tastes like the road to hell. . . . In time, he had to force himself to choke down an entire pizza."[62] It is Stallone's obese body that is now on display. Nevertheless, the power of the character lies in the contemplative way that he sees but does not act on the corruption about him. Only at the very conclusion of the film is he moved to action. His "heroism does not involve feats of extreme strength or agility, but rather patience, endurance, and, in the end a touch of stupidity."[63] Yet this "stupidity" is infused with a sense of moral superiority, coming from what had appeared to be a decaying, fat body. Stallone's figure triumphs in his obesity.

The image of the giant, hulking, primitive body, which responds seemingly intuitively to a stimulus more basic than rational thought, remains a powerful cultural commonplace. It is only the appearance of the fat detective that leads us to assume his "primitive" state. In a cartoon drawn by Scott Adams, the creator of *Dilbert*, a baby dinosaur comments to Dogbert: "My Dad says that good is what you know in your heart. He says evil is a bad gut feeling." Dogbert replies, "Well, of course, your dad's brain is so tiny that his other organs have to pitch in like that." The baby dinosaur says, "Maybe I shouldn't learn about life from a guy who counts with his toes." And Dogbert concludes: "And thinks with his guts."[64] This is the way that fat detectives seem to think — but of course we know better.

Fat Ballplayers and the Bodies of Fat Men

Hippocrates warned professional athletes who competed in the Olympic games about the dangers of reforming their fat bodies (*Aphorisms* I, III). He stated that professional athletes, much more than amateurs, ran the risk of never being able to regain their thin and youthful bodies once they began to age and get fat. For Hippocrates — and since Hippocrates — the world of sports represented that realm in which "health, harmony, and beauty" have reigned.[1] The sportsman's (and more lately the sportswoman's) body is the ideal body type. But how are these qualities to be perfected or even maintained with bodies that seem constantly out of control? They grow fat in the off-season, they become ill, they age. Still, the myth remains that an athlete is born, not made.

Central to the history of the body in the world of sport is

diet; it is tied to body size. You are, as is said over and over again, what you eat. In the 1820s William Wadd told of a "sportsman . . . in excellent health whose size interfered with his plans — 'he could not get through the woods so easily as he used to' and 'it was not so easy as formerly to find a horse to carry him.' "[2] He asked Wadd for a pill "to counteract the effects of a dose of strong ale, two gallons a day being his moderate allowance" (48). Athletes, to quote one twentieth-century authority, are especially sensitive to the "vogue for bizarre diets," which, in his estimation, include "the exaggerated importance of fillet steak."[3] Diet and weight are linked in the discourse of sports medicine, almost always because of the anxiety of weight reduction — fat people don't make good athletes. Sumo wrestlers represent the exception to the rule in the imagination of the West. Sumo becomes a means of recuperating the obese male. Lenard Fritz Krawinkel's 2000 film *Sumo Bruno* illustrates how a grossly overweight, unemployable former East German (played by Hakan Orbeyi) regains dignity and his manhood by winning the qualifying sumo championship in Riesa, a depressing factory town. Through this he "gets the girl" and becomes a valuable member of the new German society even though he loses his final match in the national competition.

But in general in the West "at the beginning of the season," if the athlete "is overweight, he must reduce, and this is best accomplished by lowering the caloric intake."[4] Lose weight and you can accomplish your sport goals, which are in point of fact a form of exercise. So athletes, from the time of Hippocrates, strain to perfect their bodies, to strip the fat from them so that the body will conquer. "An athlete," states a late nineteenth-century handbook, "should not have four ounces of fat on his whole body."[5] So they diet or they fast or they dehydrate themselves, all, as sports physicians well know, paths to a weaker, less competitive body, not a beautiful, healthy, harmonious one.[6]

Indeed, athletics today are touted as one of the prime means for the control of obesity.[7] Diet to become an athlete, and do athletics to reduce. No fat boys wanted in either case. Thus, when Jan Jarvis frames her newspaper story on what has come to be called the contemporary "epidemic of childhood obesity," she tells of a certain "Richard Olivas who was two days away from finally trading his baggy wrinkle-free, Catholic schoolboy blue slacks for a pair that fits. To get there, the 13-year-old gave up pepperoni pizza and chicken wings. He said no to Nintendo. And he joined a baseball team."[8] In this case sports, but more specifically baseball, are part of the cure for obesity. The history and culture of baseball itself, however, are part of the history of the medicalization of exercise.[9] Yet in baseball, the American national game, there is the exemplary figure of the fat ballplayer George Herman "Babe" Ruth, whose beer belly and odd waddle seem to define his superhuman nature.

Born in 1895 in urban poverty in Baltimore, he was, according to Donald Honig, "big, big, big, from the statistics to the personality to the impact. He was Moby Dick in a gold fish bowl."[10] According to the sportswriters of the time Ruth was the Bambino, the Sultan of Swat, the Behemoth of Bust, the Maharajah of Mash, the Wazir of Wham, the Rajah of Rap, and the Caliph of Clout. Alliteration and exoticization aside, all monikers pointed toward his extraordinary body. When he moved, the poet Marianne Moore commented, "his pigeon-toed stubbed little trot lacked beauty."[11] Others disagreed. One writer claimed that he may have been "shaped like a barrel, but he moved gracefully."[12] Ty Cobb, his rival on and off the field, spoke of him as an "amazing graceful fellow for one so huge."[13] Is this not always the assumption — that the fat boy cannot move well and when he does it is startling?

Ruth's odd physical presence defined and continues to define baseball and the countertype to the rail-thin athlete. He was, according to the sportswriter turned novelist Paul Gallico, "one of the ugliest men . . . a figurine that might have been made by a savage."[14] The intense photo coverage of baseball helped to turn his body into a recognizable and reproducible textual image, as a contemporary biographer noted: "*Everyone* knew and recognized Ruth's huge, round, flat-nosed, wide-mouthed face, his hulking body, his beaming grin, his unhappy pout."[15] He was seen to be "misshapen." In a world defined as a microcosm of the Darwinian universe baseball saw the male bodies of the players as tools in a struggle for survival. "Baseball is a red-blooded sport for red-blooded men," Cobb said. "It's a contest and everything that implies a struggle for supremacy, a survival of the fittest."[16] Real men play baseball. Can a fat ugly man be a real baseball player (or, to take the case of Socrates, a philosopher)?

Babe Ruth was seen as a glutton, but this was reported with a sense of awe. It was reported that for dinner he could eat an entire capon, potatoes, spinach, corn, peas, beans, butter, bread, pie, ice cream, and three or four cups of coffee. He was known to have eaten a huge omelet made of eighteen eggs and three big slices of ham, plus a dozen slices of buttered toast and several cups of coffee. Ty Cobb said: "I've seen him at midnight, propped up in bed, order six club sandwiches, a platter of pigs' knuckles and a pitcher of beer. . . . Next day, if he hit a homer, he'd trot around the bases complaining about gas pains and a bellyache."[17] "Lord, he ate too much," recalled Harry Hooper, a teammate of Ruth's with the Red Sox. "He'd stop along the road when we were traveling and order half a dozen hot dogs and as many bottles of soda pop, stuff them in, one after another, give a few belches and then roar, 'OK boys, let's go.' "[18] Ruth's capacity for food was extraordinary, but not out of order in an age when the consumption of food was a marker of male society.

Another aspect of Ruth's masculine identity was his sexuality. Even though he was married twice (his first wife died in a fire), he was a notorious womanizer. His sexual prowess was admired by his teammates. One told of sharing a suite with him when he returned with a young woman. After every bout of very loud lovemaking Ruth would come into the parlor to smoke a cigar. When asked at dawn how many times he had made love to the woman, Ruth pointed at the ashtray, where there were eight cigar stubs. Indeed, as a result of his stamina there was much speculation about the size of Ruth's penis. His teammates, who had seen him in the shower room, stated that he was of normal size but that "what was extraordinary was his ability to keep doing it all the time. He was continually with women, morning and night. I don't know how he kept going." Lou Gehrig told of an incident when Ruth appeared in their suite with two women; Gehrig was awakened late in the night when one of the women came to him to ask him to comfort Ruth. Ruth sat weeping on the edge of the bed, in tears because he had been unable to service both of the women.[19] This sexual appetite defined Ruth the man as much as his appetite for food.

Ruth's weight increased over his career. When he signed with the minor league Baltimore Orioles on 27 February 1914, at the age of nineteen, he weighed about 185 pounds. Well over six feet tall, he was at his slimmest then. A colleague from that time, when asked whether he had a huge appetite in 1914, answered, "Oh, my God. Oh, lord-a-mighty!"[20] He made his debut as a major leaguer in Fenway Park with the Boston Red

Sox on 11 July 1914, after only four months in the minors. In December 1919 Babe's contract was sold to the New York Yankees. After 1919 he seldom weighed under 220 pounds. It was said that before he stepped to the plate he often ate ten hot dogs and drank a few bottles of soda to bolster his strength. When something seemed to help him once, it became a superstition for him, repeated for every game. His compulsive actions reflected his need to have some control, even though his ritual eating before games certainly resulted in his weight gain.[21] In 1921 Ruth was invited to the Laboratory of Psychology at Columbia University to undergo tests to discover the basis of his phenomenal batting skill.[22] Weighing 220 pounds, he was at the peak of his game. His breathing was measured, reaction time judged, memory and learning ability checked, and attention span determined. Further tests measured coordination, steadiness, and "tapping speed." The conclusion was that Ruth had "supernormal reflexes, much nearer to perfection than the normal man."[23] Superman, however, soon gives way to the fat, mortal man.

In the spring of 1925, shortly before he collapsed and almost died in Asheville, North Carolina, he weighed 256 pounds.[24] He felt that weight was hampering his game, and he went on a crash diet. While Ruth later attributed his collapse to his weight, the fact that he had lost 21 pounds in twenty days may well have played a role. At 235 pounds he collapsed, running a high fever and showing all of the symptoms of a major intestinal disorder. His wife assumed that it was an attack of influenza. When he was shipped home to New York, his late arrival caused a report to circulate that he had died on the way. He was taken from the train on a stretcher because he had fainted and hit his head; the impression was that he was deathly ill. He then went into convulsions.[25] This experience, whatever its cause, altered Ruth's sense of the fragility of his body.

This fragility became part of his image. In the spring of 1926 the *New York Times* published Ruth's weight and the diet he was putatively using to reduce it.[26] The transformation of Ruth's body became the site for speculation and rejoicing. It was necessary to show that "George Herman had shoulders like Atlas, biceps like Thor, a chest like Hercules and a waist of which Achilles would not have been ashamed. . . . Contrast this picture with the vivid memory of that day last April when Ruth, a few minutes after he fainted and brought his head into smart contact with the floor of a Pullman car, was lifted on a stretcher through the car window and bundled off to the hospital. Contrast this picture also with that of the portly but feeble individual who could barely carry his own weight at the Yankee Stadium in June and July."[27] The classical beauty of the Greeks was clearly an idealization when applied to Ruth. What is seen is a reformed and healthy body, which is by definition a beautiful one.

In 1928 Ruth penned his (ghosted) autobiography, in which he comments on his fat and aging body: "Very frequently, ball players are broken down physically before they waken to the fact. That's tragedy. I came near falling into that kind of tragedy myself."[28] Ruth believed that his illness was the result of his overindulgence and resultant fat. Many older players (as both Ruth and Hippocrates warned) "run to surplus flesh. I'm one of that sort" (276). For Ruth, and medical practitioners, this surplus is dangerous as it makes players unable to play the game due to the illnesses that result from their fat. But not all players. There are some who are "slim and wiry, who are always underweight rather than overweight" (276). Ruth, however, "naturally runs to surplus flesh." He was born with the desire for food (and women) but with a body that was marked by his consumption. The reason for his fat, ill body was his overwhelming natural desire for food: "I used to have quite an appetite myself. I was cursed with an iron constitution. And I really mean cursed. For my constitution was so strong that I could commit those excesses of eating without apparent harm for several years. When I did begin to have trouble, I had it in bunches and job lots. I eat a little fruit juice and toast and coffee for breakfast. I seldom eat lunch at all, and when I do I have only a vegetable salad of some sort. I eat one good meal a day and that's dinner. At that meal I have meat — but always plenty of vegetables and green stuff" (277–78). Why does he undertake this type of reform (at least within the pages of his autobiography)? Because if he does not, he will "eat himself out of the league" (278). He will be without his occupation as a ballplayer.

By 1931, with strenuous workouts at McGovern's Gym, his weight was at 235 pounds.[29] He stayed with the Yankees until 1934, when he was brought back to Boston to play with the Braves. His last game was in May 1935. He was diagnosed with throat cancer in 1946, and his emaciated body, thin to the point of death, appeared on 27 April 1947 at Yankee Stadium for "Babe Ruth Day" one last time. Ruth had spent months in the hospital, where he had lost more than 80 pounds. The photograph of him that day has become a classic.

The reality, however, was not captured at all in the photograph of the emaciated ballplayer. Ruth would become a medical subject when his case was presented to the fourth annual Internal Cancer Research Congress in St. Louis that September. He had been treated with the new chemotherapeutic agent teropterin, which slowed the cancer and enabled him to eat for the first time. Still, the course of his illness progressed inexorably, and he died of lobar pneumonia caused by his metastatic nasopharyngeal cancer on 16 August 1948.[30] The autopsy revealed that the cancer he had developed was not associated with the more typical ones seemingly caused by smoking and drinking. The therapy had therefore been wrong for the type of cancer. Yet the faulty assumption of the day was that Ruth's lifestyle, specifically his overindulgence in alcohol and tobacco, especially snuff, had caused his disease.

After Ruth's death a "biopic" was made of his life, directed by Roy Del Ruth and written by George Callahan. *The Babe Ruth Story* (1948) starred William Bendix, whose body type was broad and whose face bore a slight resemblance to the Babe Ruth of the caricatures. The story is saccharine sweet, showing Ruth overcoming his early abandonment to become a great baseball player. In 1992 Arthur Hiller made a crueler version of Ruth's life. *The Babe* starred a gargantuan John Goodman. Roger Ebert observed that "John Fusco's screenplay doesn't seem to like Babe very much. It shows him as an overgrown, recalcitrant kid who had one skill. He could hit the ball. And then it shows him growing up into a human pig who wenched and cheated on those who loved him, who was drunk during many of his games, who was small-minded and jealous, who wasn't much of a team player, who lost his temper and screamed at the fans, and whose little trot around the bases looked like the gait of a constipated alderman."[31] Again it is the gigantic body of the ballplayer that takes center stage. His body and his soul, at least in the representation by John Goodman (and the eye of Roger Ebert), mesh but are inappropriate for a film about the mythic world of baseball, where everyone, including dead ballplayers, is supposed to look like Kevin Costner in Phil Alden Robinson's *Field of Dreams* (1989).

If there was an antithetical body to Babe Ruth's in his time it was Lou Gehrig's. Born Henry Louis Gehrig in 1903 in

Yorkville, the German section of Manhattan, he was huge, weighing fourteen pounds at birth. He was the only child of four siblings who survived childhood and was a "chubby-faced, fat-bodied boy who plugged doggedly away at his school work, and refused to stay home even when he was sick."[32] When Gehrig attended the High School of Commerce, he was a "fat, round boy with curly black hair and soft, sensitive blue eyes." He was laughed at because he wore "knee pants, which exaggerated the size of his body." He was the "little fat boy" (19) who transformed himself into a high school football and baseball player of some repute (18), the fat boy who through training with his father at the local gym became an athlete but still remained fat. When he attended Columbia to play football and baseball as well as study engineering, his friend Mike Sesit observed, "Lou was about 158 pounds then, mostly belly and ass."[33] He trimmed his body, fought with the clumsiness that he sensed in his fat frame, and transformed himself into the slugger who rivaled Ruth. He was a serious power hitter.

The Iron Horse, as Gehrig was known, was renowned for his stamina and health. He had vowed never to miss a game, and from 1 June 1925 to 2 May 1939, Gehrig never did. His consecutive-games-played streak of 2,130 shattered the old record of 1,307 and often required Gehrig to play in great pain. He was second only to Ruth as his era's greatest batting star. Gehrig drove in one hundred runs for thirteen consecutive years and hit at least thirty home runs for nine straight years. Unlike Ruth there is no litany of exaggerated appetite, of passions, of illnesses. Gehrig was in many ways the exemplary player and therefore much less the media darling than Ruth.

During the period from 1936 to 1939, however, Gehrig's game clearly deteriorated. In retrospect it is clear that his physical condition had begun to decay. What appeared to be the trained and hardened body of the perfect baseball player was betraying itself (at least retrospectively). Even his appearance in a film (*Rawhide* [1938]) revealed anomalies of movement.[34] In June 1939 Gehrig went to the Mayo Clinic. There the physicians diagnosed him with amyotrophic lateral sclerosis (ALS), which spelled the end of his career as a player. This disease affects the motor neurons and thus causes progressive muscle weakness, atrophy, and spasticity. Eventually, denervation of the respiratory muscles and diaphragm causes death. Gehrig was thirty-six years old when he was diagnosed. Expecting the support of the Yankees, he was told by the owner that he should "get himself another job." On 4 July 1939 Lou Gehrig Appreciation Day took place at Yankee Stadium. Among those present was Babe Ruth. Gehrig spoke about being "the luckiest man on the face of the earth" because of his time in baseball. He closed by saying, "I might have had a tough break; but I have an awful lot to live for."[35] Gehrig died on 2 June 1941, and his name became eponymous with his disease: ALS came to be known as "Lou Gehrig's disease" — as one commentator notes, "a macabre form of immorality."[36] When Hollywood imagined Lou Gehrig's body, however, it was Gary Cooper who loped across a baseball diamond in the movie *Pride of the Yankees* (1942). Cooper's exaggeratedly thin and healthy body was a marked contrast with the public perception and reality of Babe Ruth.

The irony is that in 2002 Mark Mattson at the National Institutes of Health's Institute on Aging claimed that the spinal cords of victims of Lou Gehrig's disease show an abnormal buildup of fatlike substances in the cells targeted by the disease.[37] Here "bad" fat seems to mark the progress of the disease. There is little substance to the corollary assumption that decreasing fat intake would ameliorate or prevent this (or any other neurological illness). Clearly an aging metabolism uses lipids differently than does a youthful one. Fat seems to be implicated in the illness — at least the sort of fat that neurologists worry about (see chapter 4).

It may well turn out, however, that ALS is a disease of slim athletes as well — even of formerly fat athletes who become thin and wiry. The slim Lou Gehrig's illness, ALS, seems now to be keyed to his "vigorous physical athletics (heavy labor or athletics)." Recent work argues that having this type of body is a clear risk factor for the disease.[38] Ruth's cancer was attributed to his lifestyle; Gehrig's illness was seen as an unlucky coincidence. Yet quite the opposite may well be true.

Fat baseball players remain as stigmatized as ill players. The same is true for other participants in professional sports. When the major league umpire John McSherry died at Cincinnati's Riverfront Stadium of coronary occlusion on 1 April 1996, obesity was seen as the sole cause. He reportedly weighed 328 pounds at his death, although later reports placed the number as high as 380 pounds. As a result, ESPN's *SportsCenter* aired a segment addressing the health and conditioning of major league umpires. There were calls for umpires to be "put on a diet" or be required to exercise. Yet a recent study of the correlation between weight and batting performance argues, to no one's surprise, that "baseball has become a big man's game," as the Yankees' owner George Steinbrenner puts it.[39] Looking at the 1997 baseball season it seemed that there was a significant correlation between a batter's weight and the number of home runs he hit.[40]

Exercise has come to be a standard component of the treatment of obesity. Tobias Venner in the 1620s devoted a chapter to "rest and exercise" (211–19). But with the rise of the science of obesity at the end of the nineteenth century exercise and athletics seemed to merge as concomitant ways of controlling the body. Thus Albert Reibmeyer, one of the most often cited specialists on obesity, suggested in 1890 a series of exercises for the obese.[41] He provided a series of images of twenty-seven exercises, all the images of men but one. All of the men (and the one woman) are depicted as very slim, indeed athletic. Fat boys have to do exercises but are not portrayed as doing them. Perhaps they are not graceful enough?

IMAGINING THE FAT BALLPLAYER

Many readers consider Mark Harris's *Bang the Drum Slowly* (1956) the ultimate American baseball novel.[42] It is actually the second of four novels that chronicle the career of a pitcher named Henry Whittier Wiggen. This novel seems to outrank any of the others because of the tension it creates between healthy team spirit and individual friendship, as well as the claim that while set in the world of baseball it is not about baseball. The novel is written in the first person, and its title page states that its author is "Henry W. Wiggen Certain of His Enthusiasms Restrained by Mark Harris," the conversational first-person voice echoing that of Babe Ruth's autobiography. Indeed, Wiggen turns out to be a fat boy. When he goes to weigh in he is told, "What you need is a truck scale." He weighs in at 211½ pounds, and so he "threw his banana away" (96). Ten pages later he is down to 210½ pounds (107), and by page 136 his weight has dropped further, to 205½. He sees himself as "fatter than a pig" (57). One of his teammates (Ugly Jones) sees this as an advantage as it makes the management nervous: " 'Good,' he said. 'That is the way to convince them, for it worries them more than it worries you. It might not even be a bad idea to show yourself around. Leave the brass see how fat you are' " (57). Getting into shape is part of becoming a ballplayer, especially when you are negotiating a contract: "You are looking over your weight. . . . It will no doubt take you many weeks to get in shape" (57). "He looks 10 pounds over his weight at least," opines the owner about Wiggen (64). But another pitcher, Paul Richard Byrd, known as Horse, weighs 240 pounds. When asked why he is called Horse, he replies, "I am a little large" (141). He is on the same team as Wiggen but confirms and validates his bulk by naming it. Unlike Wiggen, Horse is not seen to lose weight. In varying ways these fat boys can and do tame their bodies.

However, the other protagonist in the novel, a second-rate catcher named Bruce Pearson, cannot tame his body. He has been diagnosed with Hodgkin's disease, which threatens not only his life but also his role as a baseball player. We meet him when Wiggen visits him in Rochester, Minnesota, at the unnamed Mayo Clinic. He does not appear to be ill, and indeed, when Wiggen asks him his weight and is told that it is 185, he is reassured. But he is indeed "doomeded [*sic*]," as he says (12). Wiggen befriends him and forces the team to keep him on, and through this Pearson becomes, at least for one stellar moment, a true athlete. He literally dies in harness, collapsing while catching a last game. No one from the club shows up at his funeral except Wiggen, who is one of his pallbearers. Here we have the tension between the image of Ruth, who represented a type that could through willpower tame his body, and that of Gehrig, whose body became the prison that robbed him of any control.

In 1973 the film version of Harris's *Bang the Drum Slowly* presented Robert DeNiro as the doomed catcher Bruce Pearson (complete with Georgia accent), and his work is unexpectedly gentle and touching. John Hancock directed from Mark Harris's screen adaptation of his own novel, and Michael Moriarty delivered an almost perfect performance as Henry Wiggen. The film made the National Board of Review's list of the year's ten best films. Harris's novel had been dramatized once before, for TV, in 1956, when it was directed by Daniel Petrie. In this adaptation Paul Newman played Wiggen with Albert Salmi as Pearson. In none of these cases does the ballplayer appear either fat or truly ill. After the model of *Love Story*, illness does not waste the body. One simply dies with one's body intact. No fat pitchers here. Neither Moriarty nor Newman attempts to present an image of a Babe Ruth.

The split in the novel between the fat player and the ill player is one means of providing the fat baseball player with a healthy, reformed, able body. The fantasy about the transmutation of the player's body is worked out in the most detail in the exemplary novel of the fat baseball player, Douglass Wallop's *The Year the Yankees Lost the Pennant* (1954), better known as *Damn Yankees* in its musical and film incarnations.[43] The musical, with music and lyrics written by Richard Adler and Jerry Ross, a script by George Abbott and Douglass Wallop, and choreography by Bob Fosse, opened at the Forty-sixth Street Theatre on 5 May 1955 and ran for 1,019 performances. George Abbott directed the much less successful film version, which premiered in 1958.

In the original novel (and its adaptations) an aged, overweight Washington Senators fan named Joe Boyd (played in the film by Robert Shafer) is approached by the devil in the form of Mr. Applegate (Ray Walston). This version of the Faust legend, like Goethe's *Faust I*, also plays on the physical rejuvenation and transformation of the aging body. The "middle-aged real estate salesman" (7) is tempted by Applegate, who urges him to run: "His body felt light; indeed it felt thin. Thin and hard and wiry. In mid-flight he thumped his stomach. It was flat as a board, and as hard. It was not his own stomach, he thought headily, but all the better" (22). As he runs back he suddenly has his own, aged body, which moves "slowly, sluggishly, with heavy legs. After only a few steps he was breathing hard. His temples pounded. His stomach quivered out ahead of him" (22). When he returns home he looks in the mirror, "appraising his body closely for the first time in years, sharply aware of its spent tissue, its gray, grizzled appearance" (26). In your present life you are not much of a man, says the Devil: "The closest you ever got to any kind of he-man adventure was cutting your finger opening a bottle of salad dressing" (31). As with Faust's transformation, it is a sudden shift in the nature of his body that marks his new life. He is dressed by Applegate in new clothes — "slacks . . . tight in the waist and seat, and the jacket too large in the shoulders" — but suddenly everything fits (36). He is now transformed into Joe Hardy (played by — who else — Tab Hunter), a name that "sounded rather athletic" (36).

Unlike Faust, Joe Hardy is only seduced by the notion of helping his beloved Senators win a pennant against the perennial favorites, the New York Yankees. The seduction is not one of sexuality; indeed the grounds for his salvation come because he does not succumb to the wiles of his assistant, Lola (played in the musical and the film by Gwen Verdon), but desires only the athlete's body and prowess. His body replaces, in an odd way, the dwarflike body of the comic pitcher Roscoe Ent, who had been hired to draw a crowd (much like Bill Veeck's 1951 hiring of Eddie Gaedel, who, at three feet seven inches and sixty-five pounds, was the smallest player in the history of baseball). Ent is "five feet tall; certainly no more, and yet the little body was stocky and well proportioned" (81). He quits as Hardy becomes a star and is his alter ego in the novel. (He succumbs to seduction, a point that moves the plot at the novel's close.)

Hardy's feats as a hitter are compared to those of Ruth, Gehrig, and Mickey Mantle (88). When he learns, however, that Applegate will betray him, that the Yankees will win the pennant, and that he will be traded to them, he rebels. With Lola's help he thwarts the Devil, who turns him back into Joe Boyd in the middle of his game-winning run for home plate: "His temples pounded and his stomach quivered out ahead of him and his breath was coming in short, dry, harsh sobs, and the uniform was too tight, and his legs felt like wood" (232). Despite these odds, Joe Boyd touches home with the umpire's call of "safe!" The Senators win the pennant, and Joe Boyd returns to his middle-class life with his wife, to whom he has been consistently true.

Old men are fat men, but they can become youthful without falling into the seduction that success brings with it. Likewise, ethnic bodies can be transformed through baseball, at least in the eyes of ethnics. As Jews were entering baseball in the 1930s in larger numbers, the prominent view, as stated in 1935, was that "the Jew did not possess the background of sport, which was the heritage of the Irish. For centuries, the Jew, in his individual business, had to fight against heavy odds for his success. It sharpened his wit and made him quick with his hands. Therefore, he became an individualist in the sport, and skillful boxer and ring strategist, but he did not have the background to stand out in a sport which is so essentially a team game as baseball."[44] Jews do not good ballplayers make.

This view is rebutted in John R. Tunis's novel *Keystone Kids* (1943), which features a catcher named Jocko Klein whom everybody calls "Buglenose."[45] The other players talk about how he won't make it in the big leagues: "Those Jewish boys can't take it. . . . Everyone knows it" (104); "Jew-boys can't last in the big time" (143). Alongside the sentiment that disqualifies Jews from "making it" in the big leagues is the belief that the Jew somehow taints "America's pastime." Jocko is thus accused of not being American (146): " 'Whaddya mean he ain't an American? He was born in K.C. and raised there, went to school there, same as you were raised in Charlotte.' Bob became irritatingly disagreeable. 'Aw, well . . . anyhow, it's different' " (146). The characters believe that "Jews aren't athletes; they never were. They can't take it, they're gonna crack, they always crack" (147). Why is it that the "Jews" are "gonna crack"?

The fault lies in long-held assumptions about the "oriental" nature of the Jewish body (see chapter 2). Jews were seen (and often saw themselves) as being unable to compete physically with non-Jews because of the impact of "two thousand years in the ghetto," as one nineteenth-century French commentator notes, or the belief that they could not physically compete in the modern world because of their racial makeup.[46] They were seen as physically incompetent even if they appeared sportsmanlike. The Jewish body, even if it were in reality an ideal sportsman's body, as in the case of the eighteenth-century English boxer Daniel Mendoza, would at some point betray the Jew and turn to fat, revealing its inherent weakness. It was seen as an inauthentic body, merely mimicking the body of the sportsman, not the real body of a ballplayer. Thus there were movements in the nineteenth century to settle urban Eastern European Jews in farming communities in lands as disparate as Argentina and Palestine. Modern Zionism at the beginning of the twentieth century called for a "new muscle Jew" to replace the weak body of the ghetto inhabitant. The stereotype of the "fat Jew" as well as the "weak Jew" was a powerful one in the twentieth century. The South African Jewish artist William Kentridge juxtaposes images of the weak, passive body of the Jewish intellectual Felix Teitelbaum and the obese, acquisitive body of Soho Eckstein. In a series of short films beginning with *Johannesburg: Second Greatest City after Paris* (1989) and concluding with *Sobriety,*

Obesity, and Growing Old (1991), his protagonists represent the stereotypes of the Jew's body acting out the conflicts of apartheid South Africa. In this context the only "healthy" bodies are those of the Black miners exploited and destroyed by the political system.

Imagining the Jewish body in baseball means dealing with such stereotypical notions of hidden Jewish inferiority. In Irwin Shaw's *Voices of a Summer Day* (1965) the college athlete Benjamin Federer, a baseball and football player, applies for a job teaching public school.[47] Benjamin anticipates that his weigh-in, a requirement for job applicants in New Jersey public schools, will go smoothly as he is an athlete with a trained body. However, the doctor dismisses him as "obese" when the scale registers that he weighs 187 pounds: "He looked down at his powerful hard arms, his tucked-in, narrow waist, at the long, granite half-back's legs" (69). He "could tear telephone books in half with his bare hands. Obese . . . there isn't an ounce of fat on me." But the chart does not lie. At his height and age he should not weigh more than 165 pounds. All the while he is observed by a classmate, Levy, "a short, narrow-shouldered boy with sickly oysterish skin marked by the livid scars of years of carbuncles. His chest was concave, he was knock-kneed, his legs and arms were like sticks." Levy passes. He is found to be "perfectly normal" (71), while Benjamin, "officially obese," is told to lose 22 pounds if he wants to be a public school teacher. Both of the characters are Jewish, echoing the American fantasy of the Jewish athlete, an image that included Hank Greenberg.[48]

Philip Roth, in his *American Pastoral* (1997), reflects on the meaning attached to "looking American" in the 1940s and 1950s.[49] For men this meant looking like a sports figure. The protagonist of Roth's novel is the "Swede," Levov, whose "steep-jawed, insentient Viking mask of this blue-eyed blond born to our tribe" marks him culturally as among the first generation of Jews to be truly American and therefore as "happy" (3). A third-generation American Jew who played varsity football, basketball, and baseball, he appears to the somewhat younger narrator, Nathan Zuckerman, as the personification of the happiness that comes with Jewish acculturation. He is a "real" American and seemingly the antithesis of his model, Ernest Hemingway's Robert Cohn in *The Sun Also Rises* (1926), who came "out of Princeton with painful self-consciousness and a flattened nose," the result of boxing to prove that even a Jew could do sports.[50] For Roth the mask of acculturation hides the decay of the Levov family. It obscures the Swede's desperation concerning his daughter, who is lost in, and to, America after perpetrating a bombing during the Vietnam War demonstrations: "I remember when Jewish kids were home doing their homework. What happened? What the hell happened to our smart Jewish kids? If, God forbid, their parents are no longer oppressed for a while, they run where they think they can find oppression. Can't live without it. Once Jews ran away from oppression; now they run away from non-oppression" (255). This tension between the struggle to free oneself from stigma and heavy identification with the stigmatized became a leitmotif of the transformation of the Jewish body in the 1980s. Physical transformation into a baseball player is shown to be a form of false or at best superficial acculturation. What looks like a healthy American body only obscures the Jew within. Whether accomplished through intermarriage, identification with American goals, or aesthetic surgery, the ideology of progress and improvement is shown to be unobtainable. Roth's work carefully responds to the desire to change Jewish difference present among some American Jews in the 1940s and 1950s.

Yet in Roth's fantasy of the game fat players also exist and are defined by their fat. They are clearly not "Jewish." Thus Big John Baal in Philip Roth's grand parody of the first-person baseball novel, *The Great American Novel* (1973), has "ten fat fingers."[51] Early on in the novel he is introduced as "John Baal, the big bad first-basemen the sentimentalists used to try and dignify by calling him 'Rabelaisian'" (32). His weight, however, is part of his greatness: "Now, every ballplayer has his weakness, and that was Big John's. If he didn't drink, if he didn't gamble, if he didn't whore and cheat and curse, if he wasn't a roughneck, a glutton and a brawler, why he just wasn't himself, and his whole damn game went to pot, hitting and fielding. But when he had fifteen drinks under his belt, there was nobody like him on first base. Giant that he was, he could still bounce around that infield like a kangaroo when he was good and drunk" (104). Roth's parody of novels such as Mark Harris's (itself a parody of the Ruthian autobiography) sees the fat boys in the game as its essence and not as an anomaly to be reformed. The counterimage is also present in baseball fiction: the clumsy walk that is read as that of a fat man. In John R. Tunis's *Keystone Kids* a relief pitcher called Fat Stuff becomes Old Fat Stuff by the middle of the novel: "The veteran in the bullpen, pretending as usual not to hear the call, threw in a few extra warm-up pitches and then waddled across to the box where Spike and Klein were waiting. It was the first time Klein had caught the old-timer" (131). Old Fat Stuff is the myth of the clumsy Babe Ruth as opposed to the gluttonous but elegant Ruth.

The image of the fat ballplayer as the sign of corruption does turn up in the work of another major contemporary American-Jewish novelist. Of the Jewish-American writers who turned, as did many non-Jews of the mid–twentieth century, to baseball as the space to examine and excoriate the American soul, none is more successful than Bernard Malamud in his 1952 novel *The Natural*.[52] This novel centers around the life and times of the baseball wunderkind Roy Hobbs, from Middle America, discovered by an old, washed-up scout who thinks he has finally found his meal ticket. Like Babe Ruth, Hobbs had bounced around orphanages after his grandmother died. Also like Ruth, his father wants little to do with him. At the beginning of the novel Hobbs and the scout are traveling by train to Chicago for a tryout. On board is the Whammer, the big home-run baseball king "who looked . . . like an overgrown side of beef wrapped in gabardine" (15). Also on board is Harriet, a dark-haired woman who initially takes to Whammer but then attaches herself to Roy after Roy strikes Whammer out during an impromptu bet match set up by the scout. During this match the scout takes one of the pitches in the chest and, despite the washboard he wears for protection, dies of injuries sustained by the force of the pitch. Death and sexuality enter into the novel, linked to the idea of the game and the athlete's body.

Roy makes it to Chicago, and Harriet, the dark-haired woman on the train, calls him and offers to "welcome" him to Chicago. He goes to her hotel room, where she surprises him by shooting him in the gut. She reveals herself as the "femme fatale" who's been killing off the best and brightest sports athletes. Indeed, she seems to be the fate that awaits the perfect athlete who relies too much on his body and its natural gifts. The badly wounded Roy vanishes from the scene for fifteen years.

He reappears at the age of thirty-five as a new player for the New York Knights: "His face was strong-boned, if a trifle meaty. . . . [F]or his bulk he looked lithe" (39). No longer slim, he has become the older, fat ballplayer. He goes head to head with the star hitter, Bump, who makes his life exceedingly miserable when Bump realizes that Roy is a better player than he is. Roy's presence, even though the manager refuses to play him, inspires this bottom-of-the-league team to push themselves further, and they begin to play better. Bump is still the star of the team, until, caught up with this new zeal, he runs headlong into the wall attempting a flashy catch. Bump, a big man, dies from his injuries. Roy gets his chance and with his bat, Wonderboy, leads the underdog team in the rankings. No one even guesses at his story, even the "Sports Snoop" Max Mercy, who was on the train with the Whammer fifteen years before.

Roy becomes infatuated with Memo, the niece of the manager of the Knights and also the widow of Bump. She is bad business, however, and Roy loses himself in his longing for her. He goes into a slump and does not hit for a month. Finally, when the team travels to play against Chicago, he goes up to bat and a woman in red stands up for him in the bleachers. Deeply moved by this unprecedented show of support, he hits one out of the park, ending the streak of bad luck. He tracks the woman down and learns that her name is Iris. He falls in love with her but leaves abruptly when he finds out she's thirty-three and already a grandmother. But not until after they have consummated their affair.

Roy tries to forget about Iris and concentrates instead on the seductive Memo. Despite her apparent allure and the promise of an "ideal" life together, he feels a deep, empty gnawing inside. He begins to eat and eat, but nothing will fill him up. He is

the King of Klouters. . . . Yet no matter how many bangs he collected, he was ravenously hungry for more and for all he could eat besides. The Knights had boarded the train at dinner time but he had stopped off at the station to devour half a dozen franks smothered in sauerkraut and he guzzled down six bottles of pop before his meal on the train, which consisted of two oversize sirloins, at least a dozen rolls, four orders of mashed, and three (some said five) slabs of apple pie. Still that didn't do the trick, for while they were all at cards that evening, he sneaked off the train as it was being hosed and oiled and hustled up another three wieners, and later secretly arranged with the steward for a midnight snack of a long T-bone with trimmings, although that did not keep him from waking several times during the night with pangs of hunger. (151)

Roy is both consumed with desire ("he was sure that once he got an armlock on her things would go better" [152]) and consumes it in the shape of food. Again it is the image of the gluttonous Babe Ruth, now with a "disease of the will," that Malamud employs in this description.

Approaching the climax of the novel, the Knights are tied for first with the Pirates for the league championship, and only one series for each team remains to be played before the World Series. When one final game is left, Memo arranges a celebratory feast for the team supplied by a friend of hers, a bookie. Memo also tells Roy that she will finally sleep with him that night. Roy goes to the feast but cannot stop thinking about her and the possibilities of the evening. He eats and eats. She piles "corned beef, pastrami, turkey, potato salad, cheese and pickles" (169) on his plate. He eats what she gives to him but still feels empty, as if he were devouring paper. She tries to get him to eat more, but he excuses himself so that his teammates, who do not want to leave before he does, do not have to wait. He then goes down to the bar of the hotel and proceeds to consume six hamburgers and six sodas: "He thought he oughtn't eat any more, but then he thought I am hungry. No, I am not hungry, whatever that means . . . what must I do not to be hungry? He considered fasting but he hadn't fasted since he was a kid. Besides, it made him hungry" (172). In a food-induced stupor, he goes up to Memo's room, where she is in bed, naked, "chewing on a turkey drumstick" (174), waiting for him. Suddenly, he experiences agonizing pain in his belly and collapses: "Inside him they were tearing up a street" (175). His having been shot in the gut fifteen years before is now paralleled by the gluttony of his middle age.

He is rushed to the hospital where Bump died, and the doctors attempt to take out his appendix, only to find that he does not have one because of the earlier operation following the shooting. Instead, they pump his stomach "and dredged up unbelievable quantities of bilge" (176). He awakes from his fever to find that the Knights have lost the game. The Pirates lose as well, which means that a playoff game will determine who goes to the World Series. A doctor tells him that he will be able to play in this one game but that then he should retire from the sport. He has extremely high blood pressure, and that, coupled with "his athlete's heart" (178), means that he is a walking time bomb. He vows to play the game. Memo comes in and tries to convince him that he needs money if he wants to be with her. It begins to dawn on him that the Judge, the team's comanager, who is trying to buy out the other manager's shares, has put Memo up to asking Roy to throw the game in return for a huge payoff. He rebukes her, but the Judge himself goes in to see Roy, who finally agrees to throw the game in light of the life he could then give Memo.

Roy has mixed feelings about throwing the game and after much internal reflection decides not to bat, as he is also feeling extremely weak. However, he does at last go to the plate, hitting mostly fouls at a heckler in the stands. Suddenly, a woman in white stands up right behind the heckler. Roy misses the heckler but hits the woman in the eye. It is, of course, Iris, whom Roy takes to the clubhouse to be seen by the doctor. She tells him that she is pregnant and that he should win for his unborn son. He is filled with wild love for her and the child. He returns to bat but in the process breaks Wonderboy and, as a result, swears never to bat again. In the bottom of the ninth inning the Knights are down by one with a man on third. Roy is their last hope, and with a new bat resembling Wonderboy, he goes to the plate. Roy takes ball after ball. Finally, the pitcher is replaced by a young kid with the meanest fastball this side of the Mississippi. Roy sees himself in the boy. The young pitcher pulls two strikes off of Roy, who, determined to win and damn the Judge and Memo, swings at the last ball, which is bad. The game is over, and Roy has lost.

Amid speculation that Roy threw the game, he returns the money to the Judge, who pulls a gun on him. Roy wrestles it away, but Memo, who is also there, retrieves it and shoots him, grazing his shoulder. She holds the gun on Roy, vowing to kill the man who she says killed her husband, Bump. When Roy talks with her, she turns the gun on herself; he takes it away, and she leaves crying. As he walks away from the stadium, he sees a newspaper being sold on the street with a photograph of his wounded body from decades before and a claim by the commissioner that he will never play ball again. The novel ends with a young boy asking Roy to "say it ain't true," the line that was addressed to Shoeless Joe Jackson after the Black Sox scandals almost destroyed baseball. (How very different is Barry Levinson's 1984 film version with Robert Redford, which resolves everything in a happy ending.)[53] The fat boy, depicted as being out of control in all aspects of his life, thus cannot do anything but "fall" due to his self-indulgence. His health and strength fail him in the end, and the "immortal" aspect of sports is shown to be all too mortal.

By the 1950s display of male fat is already unpalatable. The middle-aged athlete can be transformed or condemned; his gut is the stuff of the observer's horror. By the 1990s the sports hero as fat man has become a joke rather than a sign of moral corruption. Garrison Keillor's fat ballplayer is a football player, gone to fat after a game in which he has shattered his knees.[54] At 165 pounds, he is persuaded by his female coach to go for the winning touchdown; she will marry him, she says, and have his babies: "I'm a wonderful lover. . . . And I bake" (216). He makes the goal by destroying his knee. Thirty years and multiple operations later he has become huge. Now he weighs 490 pounds and has become an icon for the lost glory of the ballplayer, winning an award from the Disabled American Football Foundation (217). He continues to put on weight, until he is up to 911 pounds. His surgeon urges him to diet, but instead he joins the carnival, with a sign saying that he was "once a 165-pound halfback, fleet of foot, darting lightly and avoiding tackles" (221). "How does he make love? Don't be silly," states the sign made by his wife. His children are put through college by his exposure, and he understands that people come to see him as much because he was once a thin athlete as because he is a huge fat man. When asked whether he would like to have a photograph of himself now he responds, "I would rather remember me as I was" (223). This is the mantra of all sports novels that deal with the fat boy, here as parody. Indeed it is the echo of Hippocrates' admonition about the bodies of professional athletes. The representation of the fat boy's body in the world of sports, however, is not merely the stuff of biography and fiction; it is also the stuff of "science": a science of the sportsman's body that seems even today to ring true.

From the time of Hippocrates, the physician as scientist as well as therapist has defined the athlete's body. In the early twentieth century, the age of Babe Ruth and Lou Gehrig, there was a demand for body classification that defined in rigid terms the limits of the acceptable athlete's body. If Hippocrates warned about the shift in the form and nature of the athlete's body over time, then the desire in the twentieth century was to see the athlete's body as beyond the effects of nurture (except in the case of pathology). The sportsman's body was born, not merely made. (Thus the Jew's body as a ballplayer was inherently inauthentic because it could only be made, not born.) Anti-Darwinian notions of body (and psychological) types reappeared with a vengeance in the early twentieth century. The first of these classification systems that resonated internationally was that of Ernst Kretschmer in 1921. He created three categories of body types: the asthenic (weak), sthenic (strong), and pyknic (compact). Of these the sthenic was the "strong and athletic in physique," the body of the athlete.[55] Kretschmer's body types were actually not new at all.[56] They were merely the reappearance in twentieth-century science of various body classifications that had been around since texts of classical Greek physiognomy, including Hippocrates' two pathological body types, the *habitus apoplecticus* (short and thick) and the *habitus phthiscus* (long and thin). Parallel to the history of the obese body, there has not been a period of Western culture in which such classifications within medicine were lacking. In an age when the external qualities of the body were the major source of information about all aspects of pathology, the desire to see in the fixed attributes of the body (shape, color, size, physiognomy) a means of predicting illness was overwhelming. Even with the development of means of "seeing" into the living body (such as auscultation and then x-rays), this desire remained with us. There was still a strong association between seeing the visible body and imagining that you could see the invisible psyche, soul, unconscious, or mind. Thus the Columbia-based psychologist William Sheldon argued that fragile but aesthetically superior physiques, not mesomorphoric (superior) ones, were more given to heroism in battle. As W. H. Auden mocked: "It is the pink-and-white, / Fastidious, slightly girlish, in the night / When the proud-arsed broad-shouldered break and run / Who covers their retreat, dies at his gun."[57] In ancient (and more modern) views these body types were inherently related to state of mind and emotion. In Kretschmer's categories the fat boy's body — the pyknic — was depressive, while the sthenic body was vigorous and aggressive.

Sheldon rethought the relationship between mind and body in the 1940s, moving from Kretschmer's emphasis on body size to body shape. Like Kretschmer's, Sheldon's work is a throwback to the world before evolution and bacteriology, a world in which the body, preformed, has all of its qualities already present at birth. In his 1926 University of Chicago dissertation, which attempted to correlate physical characteristics with intelligence and sociability, Sheldon elaborated upon the work of Sante Naccarati in correlating intelligence and temperament.[58] Sheldon's constitutionalism had, however, even greater reaches than did his prototype's.[59] His fascination throughout his career was with attempting to separate (radically) the positive body types from those that were less valuable. Trained also as a physician (a pediatrician), Sheldon, who never practiced, always had his eye on the pathological, the anomalous. In his dissertation he proves, by examining hundreds of undergraduates at the University of Chicago, that "fat or 'heavy set' men are more sociable than thin men," if only marginally.[60] His goal (among others) was to see whether the "common prejudice" that "fat men are . . . generally sociable and good-natured" (11) held. In creating body types Sheldon felt that he was working against the general consensus of his field in the United States since his "results rather contradict the common notion among psychologists that no such relations whatever can be shown to exist" (104). American academic psychology had come out strongly against the types of arguments presented by Naccarati about the relationship between body type and intelligence. It followed Edward Bradford Titchener's powerful rebuttal of racial differences in intelligence and the attempt to move psychology into a Wundtian model of laboratory experiments. In a very conservative move Sheldon intended to show that body types truly mattered.

Twenty years later, at Columbia, Sheldon had developed a full-fledged classification of body types and temperaments.[61] His categories of the endomorph (the fat boy), the mesomorph (the athlete), and the ectomorph (tall boy) still resonate in our popular idea of definite boundaries among body (and psychological) types. These quickly became the concrete manner of delineating body types in sports medicine.[62] Sheldon's categories were established for men — indeed, for white men. Neither Native nor African Americans were included, and only 10 percent of the subjects were Jews. (This was a substantially better demographic than his dissertation, which relied only on white fraternity boys, and was considerably higher than the ceiling for the admission of Jews to Sheldon's Columbia. Neither Chicago nor Columbia nor any of the other institutions with which Sheldon was associated gave him a formal appointment. Sheldon would rail against Jews and Italians as undermining the moral and physical qualities of Americans in his later study *Varieties of Delinquent Youth*.) In keeping with Sheldon's rather concentrated approach, women are literally placed as an appendix to his initial study; a decade later he published a specific atlas on masculinity.[63]

The fat boy, the endomorph, has a "relative predominance of soft roundness throughout the various regions of the body. When endomorphy is dominant the digestive viscera are massive and tend relatively to dominate the bodily economy" (5). His is the most primitive body, as the digestive processes arise embryologically from the endoderm, "the innermost of the original three embryonic layers" (34). Here the debate about the primitive body that was so present in the history of neurology (see chapter 4) echoes in the history of types. Fat boys are throwbacks, beginning at the most primitive level of embryological development and maintaining that association their entire lives. (One can add that Sheldon devoted an entire second volume to the psychological states implied by his somatotypes.)

The ectomorph is the most highly evolved as it stems from the outermost and most recent layer. Ectomorphy is the "relative predominance of linearity and fragility" (5). The ectomorph also has the "largest brain and nervous system" (5). Sports became one of the litmus tests for Sheldon's classifications. Thus his type "435" ectomorph "develops a magnificent 'bay window' later in life . . . while in 154 this physique could no more develop a 'potbelly' than a 117 could win a boxing tournament" (165). (These types are all composites. The first number is the mesomorphic index, the second the ectomorphic index, the third the endomorphic index. Each individual tends toward one fixed type or the other, yet all have qualities of each.) Another ectomorph, "162," includes the "professional athletes who tend to grow fat and heavy during their postathletic years, although they do not, of course, take on endomorphic proportions" (188). Type "362" "is ideally adapted for professional athletics but tends to put on weight

too fast and is always bothered with the problem of 'training' "
(200). At least one of his types, "532," seems to be Babe Ruth:
the "head is large and round, with a large face having a heavi-
ness or coarseness of feature. The eyes tend to be large and the
nose broad. The mouth has extremely full lips, often projecting or sucking lips, and it is a large, shapeless mouth. . . . The
532's are prone to eat gluttonously and to grow enormously
heavy. Frequently they are heavy smokers. . . . There is no
doubt that this serves in a measure to keep their weight down"
(197–98). Needless to say, these are not beautiful bodies. Sheldon's aesthetic is one of the age of fascism but is rooted in the
history of the fat boy. As George L. Mosse notes, the "longing
for a set standard of beauty was deeply ingrained in the European middle classes, and the definition of the beautiful as the
'good, the true, and the holy' was an important background to
the fascist cult that . . . annexed this as its own."[64] Its roots, as
Mosse is at pains to show, return to the eighteenth-century re-
appropriation of the ideal Greek body. Here too the brave are
not the fat: the beautiful are not the obese.

Somatotypes are inherent, and there is no sense in trying to
reform the body of the fat boy: "Tragedy could be prevented
in the lives of young boys if we gave up trying to make athletes
of nonathletic somatotypes. One of the most common causes
of frustration in the life of the male is this custom of expos-
ing boys promiscuously to the influence of athletic ambition"
(226–27). Thus the line between the types and their subtypes
is absolute, and transgressing it means that you are condemned to a life of neurosis.

Sheldon's three types and their multitudinous subtypes
were paralleled to temperaments in a later study.[65] In *The Varieties of Temperament* Sheldon presents three types that are
analogous to the physical types. His viceratonic type shows
"relaxation in posture and movement, love of eating, social-

ization of eating, greed for affection and approval, orientation to people, tolerance, evenness of emotional flow, complacency, deep and easy sleep" (33). These are his fat boys, with all of the qualities we would expect. His somatotonic type shows "assertiveness, love of physical adventure, energy, lust for power, love of risk and danger, physical courage, competitive aggressiveness, psychological callousness, Spartan indifference to pain, orientation toward the goals and activities of youth" (33). This is his endomorphic athlete. His intellectual type, the cerebrotonic, shows "restraint, a physiological overresponse, overly fast reactions, sociophobia, resistance to habit, unpredictability of attitude and feeling, hypersensitivity to pain, poor sleep habits, orientation toward later period of life" (33). The juxtapositions limit the fat boy's inclusion in the world of the physical and the intellect.

Sheldon's types echo the fascination in midcentury America with the body of the athlete as mirrored in the American baseball player. His science of types mirrors the anxiety about bodies out of their appropriate spaces. He provides a grid on which to predict the growing obesity of the athletic body and, therefore, the need for such athletes (or their owners) to tame their bodies or dismiss them before they become noncompetitive. Here the representations found in the sports novels of the obese and aging ballplayer's body have their place in the world of the pseudoscience of body classification. Transformation there is possible but unlikely. The types are fixed, and they bear no relationship to the necessary changes that all bodies undergo over time. In sports medicine the mantra became the tautology that the "athletic" type is an "athletic" type. It is a predictor of success. The reality lies more in the bodies (and the fantasies about the bodies) of "real" people such as Ruth and Gehrig. Our fantasies about their bodies seem to have little or no relationship to the natural history of the bodies themselves. We see them in moral or aesthetic terms that may (or may not) mirror their own lives. The fat boy who is supposed to die of his indulgences does not. The fat boy who tames his body dies of a disease that comes to be known by his name and that may (or may not) be a disease of athletic bodies.

Conclusion *Cutting into the Future of Fat Boys*

The future of the fat boy is just as complex as his past. The fat boy is more present today at the beginning of the twenty-first century than he was in the twentieth century. We have seen how obesity, a conceptual strategy, enables us to speak about male bodies in varied performative roles: as "soldier" (Falstaff), "servant" (Fat Joe), "detective" (Tubby Schaumann), or "athlete" (Babe Ruth). What is evident from these case studies is how criteria shift. From the Greek humors to those forces such as the obesity gene we now imagine shaping our bodies and minds, a certain progression in perceptions of the fat body becomes apparent. These perceptions evoke recognizable patterns that often are put to very different uses. The fat boy, however, continues to haunt the halls of medical science as well as popular culture. One major aspect in the struggle to understand shifts in meanings attached to obesity is

227

based on who is understood as competent to treat this pathology. In the late nineteenth century there began a struggle over who could treat "dysmorphophobia," now called body dysmorphic disorder. Fat boys turned up in competing fields of medicine as the object of treatment: aesthetic surgeons offered to remove the fat; neurologists, who became psychoanalysts, claimed to deal with the underlying psychological causes; psychiatrists wanted to deal with fat boys' anxieties about their bodies; and endocrinologists saw obesity purely as a metabolic disorder. All claimed the fat boy as their own.

Today body dysmorphic disorder has reappeared as a conventional means of labeling men's obesity as a problem of obsession in the clinical sense — an obsessive-compulsive disorder — rather than a failure of will.[1] Aesthetic surgery with liposuction and apronectomies (tummy tucks) still competes with psychiatry and various forms of twelve-step programs to "cure" obesity.[2] Recently, however, another type of surgical procedure has emerged as the most radical way of reshaping and thus controlling the male body. Surgery has often been the court of last resort for male obesity. Pliny the Elder describes in ancient Rome a "heroic cure for obesity" in an operation on the son of the Consul L. Apronius, and at the end of the twelfth century a surgeon cut open the belly of Count Dedo II of Groig to remove excessive fat.[3] In 1718 Rhotonet, a surgeon in Paris, removed nine pounds of fat from the abdomen of a patient.[4] The modern tradition of the surgical removal of fat began with Howard A. Kelly of Baltimore, who on 15 May 1899 removed the "pendulous abdomen," weighing 14.9 pounds, from a 285-pound Jewish woman.[5] Obesity surgery for men followed in 1908, undertaken by C. Schulz.[6]

By the late twentieth century discourse on the meaning of the male "gut," so important in the history of male obesity, had also become increasingly present. Today "body fat distribution is a better predictor of cardiovascular morbidity and mortality than is weight, total body fat, or BMI. Persons whose fat is confined primarily to the upper body (more common in males) are at greater risk of type II diabetes and cardiovascular morbidity and mortality than are persons whose adiposity is carried primarily in the lower body."[7] The gut, the beer belly, continues to define greater risk for the male, something that we have seen has a very long history.[8] Does the surgically happy thin boy without his gut have a different character? Or is he merely an unhappy fat boy in disguise? Has the surgeon merely stripped away the fat, leaving an obese personality behind? Over the past three decades there has been an explosion in the alternative surgical "cure" for obesity. In these procedures it is not the body fat that is mechanically removed but the metabolism that is altered through surgery.

Recently, there has been a spate of firsthand accounts by men in the public sphere about their newly reshaped bodies, bodies reshaped not from the outside but from within by bariatric surgery, such as gastric stapling, which decreases the size of the stomach. The actual number of these procedures has doubled, from forty thousand to eighty thousand in the United States from 2000 to the present. It is also a global phenomenon. An American Society for Bariatric Surgery was founded in 1983, but associations of bariatric surgeons can be found from the Obesity Surgery Society of Australia and New Zealand to the Yugoslav Obesity Surgery Society and virtually everywhere else. Such societies are not limited to the United States but are active in nations from Argentina to Kuwait and beyond. Obesity is a global concern. What these newly founded organizations demonstrate is that not only is there a global recognition of obesity as requiring intervention, but there is also a global wave in defining obesity through a means of intervention.

In the 1970s animal experiments were undertaken to reduce the size of the stomach in order to mechanically inhibit food intake. By the late 1970s stomach stapling had become a more widely used experimental procedure to deal with extreme obesity in people who had not been able to lose weight through any other means. This surgery is usually performed if the patient is at least one hundred pounds overweight (or has a BMI of forty) or has a serious condition assumed to be caused by the weight, such as diabetes or sleep apnea. The patients must have failed earlier psychological attempts at changing behavior, such as Weight Watchers or Jenny Craig. There can be no uncorrected metabolic diseases that may be responsible for the obesity, such as low thyroid function. Most important, patients are screened (most are eliminated) for any psychological imbalance or unrealistic expectations of surgery and weight loss (as should be the case in body-sculpting surgery also). As most surgeons admit, however, central to this "magic bullet" is the change in eating behavior after the surgery!

In a complex way this surgery is a type of placebo or behavior modification through a radical procedure. Such procedures are well-known in the history of aesthetic surgery. Thus when this patient population was given the standard Minnesota Multiphasic Personality Inventory (MMPI) before and after surgery, they showed marked psychological improvement even if they did not show significant weight loss.[9] There was a clear distinction between the psychological profiles of obese men and women independent of the procedure. This is a strong indicator that obese men and women respond differently to their obesity and to the surgery.[10] In general there was a change in self-assessment concerning physical appearance and reports that the patients had experienced an improvement in current relationships and sexual functioning.[11] Yet there was little change in eating habits, although the results clearly showed behavioral change subsequent to weight loss.[12]

The media attention to gastric stapling has turned this procedure into the magic bullet that can "save" the morbidly obese. One does not have to do anything but expose oneself to the surgeon's scalpel. Today a number of procedures can be used. In one form of the surgery the food passes from the small upper stomach into the lower stomach. This is called a vertical banded gastroplasty (VBG). In the small pouch gastric bypass (SPGB), or "Roux-en-Y gastric bypass," the food is rerouted around the stomach by connecting the pouch directly to the intestine. Avoiding major abdominal surgery, laparoscopic gastric banding, recently approved by the Food and Drug Administration, is less invasive. Each approach reduces the amount of food that can be processed at any given time. The cost of such procedures runs from thirty-five thousand dollars for the more extensive surgery to about fifteen thousand dollars for the less invasive. Each demands a very high level of compliance and careful monitoring if the patient is to be successful in obtaining weight loss and maintenance. The dangers associated with these procedures are clear. Side effects can be devastating, including vitamin deficiency, electrolyte depletion, and liver failure, all the result of limited food intake.[13] Medicaid has declared that these procedures do not meet the provision of being medically necessary, but some private insurers recently have begun to cover them. They are "cosmetic" by their very nature and are not covered by the federal insurance program even if, as one study claims, they can cure a version of the "Pickwickian syndrome."[14]

These procedures seem to force the fat boy to correct his lack of will by short-circuiting his metabolic system and radically reducing what he can eat. Indeed descriptions of such procedures sound much like those of Disulfiram (Antabuse), a drug prescribed to alcoholics that makes them nauseous and likely to vomit when they drink. The fat boy whose stomach has been reduced in size is described as suffering from an intense bout of nausea, diarrhea, or vomiting when he attempts to overeat. If he continues to tolerate the overeating and its negative effects, the small upper pouch may grow too large, due to continuous overeating to the point of being "full," and vitiate the entire operation.

Recently, a series of high-profile accounts of men undertaking gastric bypass surgery has been publicized. In *Men's Health* in July/August 2002 Jonathan Wander provided an autobiographical account of his journey to surgery.[15] Weighing 360 pounds before surgery, he (in 2002) weighed 180 pounds. A fat boy, Wander had a childhood of public humiliation: "I couldn't run (the teacher used to make me race against a kid who had one leg)." Most embarrassing, however, was his sense of gender confusion: "If you're a twelve-year-old boy with breasts, you'd rather die than suffer the embarrassment of running up the court topless." As an adult, he has no sex life even though he "lusted after girls." When he goes to New York he winds up "in my hotel room alone with . . . a pastrami sandwich from the Carnegie Deli." He undertakes all of the diet cures, and even though his "health, for the most part, was good," decides to undertake the bariatric procedure because his "moderate good health was sure not to last." Thus, his anxiety about longevity compels this man in his late thirties to undertake a radical restructuring of his body: "I couldn't recall seeing many old men schlepping around 360 pounds." In a last gastronomic splurge he goes on an eating spree right before his surgery, driving from Pittsburgh to Cleveland for a corned beef sandwich! To put the nature of the surgery into the perspective of a fat boy dilemma, he tells the reader he was informed that more than 80 percent of his surgeon's patients are women. The surgeon tells him that "women are usually first to try a method of treating obesity. . . . Men tend to get in touch with us when they're older and the health problems of their obesity have caught up with them." Concerns about "health" (i.e., longevity) rather than "beauty" structure the male response to bariatric surgery.

Wander chooses laparoscopic surgery and is able to eat solid food after about a month. Clearly, however, he has to radically change his relationship to food, because eating too much or eating the wrong kind of food (a hot dog at a baseball game) makes him very, very ill: "Alex was understanding about needing to leave the baseball game. The part he didn't like was the drive home. I had one hand on the wheel and the other holding a Pirates souvenir cup into which I was slowly coughing up my wiener." He can no longer eat sweets, and alcohol is quickly and suddenly absorbed, so even a small drink has an overwhelming effect. This results in a type of behavior modification, and he "learns" to be thin. In another life-altering choice, perhaps a by-product of the procedure, he divorces and marries a woman who tells him that she would not have looked at him when he was fat: "I would have said, 'You're fat. It's disgusting. Go for a walk!' " He becomes a new person, the fat boy now part of his past (like his first marriage to a woman he met in a diet group, who had the same surgery): "The fat buffer between me and the public world is gone." He and his wife are now expecting a baby, and that child "will never know what it's like to have a fat dad." The masculine role as father and husband is defined by the newly slim body of the surgical patient.

Certainly the most recent case of the fat boy made slim is that of Al Roker, the weatherman on NBC's *Today Show*. By the beginning of 2002, Roker had lost 100 pounds from his high of 320 — a third of his body weight. Wander's weight was 180; he had become "exactly half the man I used to be." It is as if the fat man has left and only the thin man within remains. Roker, according to his account, also had a history of overeating as a child but sees part of his tendency as inherited: "We're from the Caribbean, we're stocky, we're low to the ground. We're built to survive hurricanes."[16] He also sees overeating as an addiction "no different than alcoholism or chemical dependency." He was exposed to humiliation as a child, however, when Bill Cosby's character "Fat Albert" appeared on television and his friends saw Roker as embodying him. He initially saw the prospect of surgery as further humiliation. His wife, ABC News 20/20 correspondent Deborah Roberts, had suggested the surgery to him after interviewing the female singer Carnie Wilson about her own surgery. It seemed to him "such an admission of failure. . . . You think people will look at you like, 'You weak son of a pup.' " Failure of the will is a sign of the absence of the real man in control of his body! Roker's attempts at weight loss through diet before the surgery were a failure, but they also reflected his public persona. Someone at a gym told him, "Hey, you don't want to lose too much weight, 'cause that's who you are — you're the funny, fat weather guy." Roker had no problem with being funny but could not see it as a simple reflex of his obesity. He decides to go ahead with the surgery in spite of the public perception because of questions about his health quite familiar to William Banting: "It's taking me 10 minutes to get up four flights of stairs, but that's normal, isn't it?" Roker at last accepts the idea that his obesity is a disease that can be cured by surgery: "If you had heart disease and you had a bypass, nobody would think anything of it. Well, this isn't that different." Like Wander, Roker has to learn to eat through negative reinforcement.

234

He hosts a barbecue segment on the *Today Show* and finds that he has the "dumping syndrome." He also continues to see himself as "fat" even as he loses weight. It is only when he is confronted with his 285-pound wax double at Madame Tussaud's wax museum that he sees himself as having a new body: "It's done. I'm never going back."

Following Roker's public announcement of his surgery, Jerrold Nadler, a member of the U.S. House of Representatives for Manhattan, also revealed that he had had bariatric surgery.[17] At 338 pounds and five feet four inches tall, he was proportionally the heaviest of these three fat boys. The popularity of such procedures is clear. Roker's portrait graced the cover of *People* magazine, and he was featured on a program on NBC; Nadler's weight loss made the front page of the *New York Times*. As with the other former fat boys, his central stated motivation for the surgery was longevity: "I want to live to see my grandchildren grow up. How many grossly overweight 80-year-olds do you know?" The warning indicator Nadler describes is one we know well from Roker but also from Banting. Nadler could not "make it up even a single flight of stairs to the second floor of the Capitol to vote on the House floor." Yet the humiliation of his weight also played a role. When Alfonse D'Amato, then a senator from New York, referred to him as "Jerry Waddler," he was "wounded": "You try to ignore it. But, of course, it's hurtful." The cause, for Nadler, is genetics, "since his identical twin brother is also obese" and since he too had tried all types of diets. Genetic or not, his consumption of food was extraordinary. He would "consume a salad, a rib-eye-steak with french fries, vegetables, bread and butter and a dessert — all washed down with diet Coke" for dinner. Now after the operation he has begun to lose weight: "I was extremely, morbidly obese. Now I am only morbidly obese. I'm getting there." This image of the fat boy "getting there" is paralleled by a shift in the image of the fat boy in American popular culture.

In the 2000–2001 TV season the popular comedy-drama *Ed* debuted. It concerns a lawyer who returns to a small town, discouraged by the crush of modern life in the big city, and opens a bowling alley that quickly becomes a bowling alley/ law practice. In the sixteenth episode, "Live Deliberately," the grossly overweight figure of Mark Vanacore (played by Michael R. Genadry), a student at Stuckeyville High, is introduced, quickly becoming a recurring figure on the show. He is ironic about his ability to eat and drink. "God blessed me with a hearty constitution," he comments when asked about his overindulgence in food and drink. As with Al Roker's comments, in Mark's mind his ancestry determines his psychology and his girth: "My grandparents were Russian. We're world-weary people." In his mind irony and his obese body are clearly linked: "The hungrier I am, the more I need to make up for it with bitter sarcasm." Yet his character is clearly determined by his outsider status: "When you meet with the Lord," he tells a student who has found religion, "can you tell him I got a little screwed over here?!" He, as a fat boy, attempts to make this status into his own, ironic identity: "I like being a loser because we can brood and feel things deeply and make fun of the winners." Still, he never quite succeeds in becoming autonomous, rather than fringe. In the summer of 2002 the character underwent a gastric bypass operation (as did the actor who played him). He was reintroduced in the 2003 season as a figure some one hundred pounds lighter, now dealing with his new body and a new personality.

Is there a difference between the response to gastric bypass surgery on the part of women and men? Certainly the surgery is coded "female." "Real" men seem not to be able to admit to a failure of will that would necessitate such surgery until they are at a point where they begin to question their own mortality. Death, not attractiveness, forms their response. "Ann," a twenty-two-year-old woman who weighs 260 pounds and is a candidate for gastric bypass surgery, writes: "If I had a man that could love me, things would be a lot better. The kind of man I want couldn't want me — he wouldn't climb professionally if he had a heavy woman. You know it is hard to stick to a diet and think about these things all the time. I eat and it takes my mind off these things." "Betty" says that that she is having the surgery out of "desperation. I did not want to live any more. I just know there's another person inside you and you can't get it out yourself." "Donna" notes, "I have a wonderful husband. He will accept me the way I am — I can't." These women are often convinced of their own powerlessness and project this onto the external world: "Prayer has gotten me through all of this, my marriage, my pregnancy, a lot of decisions." The fault lies always in themselves: "My ideals are so high. . . . I am my own worse critic."[18] This sentiment is absent in the case of the men cited above. Also absent is any sense of the loss of an existing personality. Roker confirms that he is really the same man he was when he was fat. He is the typical "thin man" hidden within the fat boy that we have seen in the past. In contrast, Camryn Manheim, an actress who lends a certain status to being overweight, notes that whenever she dieted she lost her essential identity: "When I'd lost the weight, I had lost myself."[19] Fat boys, on the other hand, seem to wish to liberate the thin man within.

Fat boys are different from fat girls in the way they articulate the meaning of their body size and weight. They may share similar concerns expressed in different ways. From both genders' responses to gastric stapling, it is evident that the fat boy has a different sense of self-awareness — or at least of how this awareness will be presented to a broad reading public. The assumption in these narratives is that men are different from women. Are they biologically different, or are they socialized differently? How can we tease this apart? If they are not to be separated, how, indeed, does the meaning of the fat male body shift within the world of therapy over time? What is actually "cured" through gastric bypass surgery? If all of the claims about the rights of the disabled, including now the obese, shift, what qualities are ascribed to the fat man? Is the man with a gastric bypass really the same as the one with a heart bypass, even though one is socially coded as a result of lack of will and the other as a sign of a type-"A" personality? Mortality as a result of obesity is projected to surpass deaths from smoking and will become the leading cause of death for both men and women in the United States unless action is taken.[20] However, the social perception is that women are obese due to a lack of self-control (which they themselves feel to be the case), while men attribute their obesity to outside factors beyond their reach (i.e., genetics). However, there do appear to be physiological differences pertaining to weight loss in both cases, outside of social considerations. In one recent study of gastric bypass patients a surprising difference was found between men and women a year after surgery. While both men and women had lost substantial amounts of weight, only the men studied showed a reduction in adipose tissue metabolism along with weight reduction. After surgery women continued to transmute lipids into fat tissue.[21] Clearly, there are differences not only in gender roles but also in physiology.

In defining the body (and the psyche) the anthropologist Mary Douglas observes: "The human body is always treated as an image of society and . . . there can be no natural way of considering the body that does not involve at the same time a social dimension. Interest in its apertures depends on the preoccupation with social exits and entrances, escape routes and invasions. If there is no concern to preserve social boundaries, I would not expect to find concern with bodily boundaries."[22] The central social boundaries of the fat boy are those of gender. This is the reason that fat boys come to have a wider place in the vocabulary of images that determine how the male human body is seen and made acceptable, or seen as pathological. For modern shifts in gender categories reshape the meaning associated with the fat male body. If Judith Butler in *Gender Trouble* is correct, gendered subjectivity is "a history of identifications, parts of which can be brought into play in given contexts and which, precisely because they encode the contingencies of personal history, do not always point back to an internal coherence of any kind."[23] Male obesity is part of the performance of gender as it defines the limits and possibilities of bodies in general. In an early essay Butler sees gender as "a sculpting of the original body into a cultural form."[24] Clearly this notion of sculpting bodies into gender categories holds for the fat boy whose body is always imagined as a work in progress. This claim is greater than Susan Bordo's view that "obesity is an extreme capacity to capitulate to desire (consumerism in control)." It is "rooted in the same consumer-culture construction of desire as overwhelming and overtaking the self."[25] This is certainly true, but as this volume has shown, obesity is a category in no way limited to the contemporary consumerist world. It has always been a means of seeing the fluidity of bodies by defining their ultimate, pathological state. And this is ultimately the world of the fat boy.

Notes

PREFACE

1. After the completion of this manuscript Lucian Boia's *Forever Young: A Cultural History of Longevity* (London: Reaktion, 2003) appeared.

INTRODUCTION

1. The literature on the topic of women and fat is extensive and expanding: Anne Scott Beller, *Fat and Thin: A Natural History of Obesity* (New York: Farrar, Straus, and Giroux, 1977); Gerald R. Adams and Sharyn M. Crossman, *Physical Attractiveness: A Cultural Imperative* (Roslyn Heights NY: Libra, 1978); Marcia Millman, *Such a Pretty Face: Being Fat in America* (New York: Norton, 1980); Lois W. Banner, *American Beauty* (Chicago: University of Chicago Press, 1983); Robin Tolmach Lakoff and Raquel L. Scherr, *Face Value: The*

Politics of Beauty (New York: Routledge and Kegan Paul, 1984); Wendy Chapkis, *Beauty Secrets: Women and the Politics of Appearance* (Boston: South End Press, 1986); Sabra Wald-fogel, "The Body Beautiful, The Body Hateful: Feminine Body Image and the Culture of Consumption in Twentieth-Century America" (Ph.D. diss., University of Minnesota, 1986); Arthur Marwick, *Beauty in History: Society, Politics, and Personal Appearance* (London: Thames and Hudson, 1988); Roberta Pollack Seid, *Never Too Thin: Why Women Are at War with Their Bodies* (New York: Prentice Hall, 1989); Camille Paglia, *Sexual Personae: Art and Decadence from Nefertiti to Emily Dickinson* (New Haven: Yale University Press, 1990); Naomi Wolf, *The Beauty Myth: How Images of Female Beauty Are Used against Women* (New York: Morrow, 1991); Susan Bordo, *Unbearable Weight: Feminism, Western Culture, and the Body* (Berkeley and London: University of California Press, 1993); Sara Halprin, *Look at My Ugly Face: Myths and Musings on Beauty and Other Perilous Obsessions with Women's Appearance* (New York: Viking, 1995); Kaz Cooke, *Real Gorgeous: The Truth about Body and Beauty* (London: Bloomsbury, 1995); Leslie Heywood, *Dedication to Hunger: The Anorexic Aesthetic in Modern Culture* (Berkeley: University of California Press, 1996); Nancy Friday, *The Power of Beauty* (New York: Harper Collins, 1996); Richard Sartore, *Body Shaping: Trends, Fashions, and Rebellions* (Commack NY: Nova Science Publishers, 1996); Sharlene Hesse-Biber, *Am I Thin Enough Yet: The Cult of Thinness and the Commercialization of Identity* (New York: Oxford University Press, 1996); Frida Kerner Furman, *Facing the Mirror: Older Women and Beauty Shop Culture* (New York: Routledge, 1997); Ruth Raymond Thone, *Fat — A Fate Worse Than Death: Women, Weight, and Appearance* (New York: Haworth Press, 1997); Sarah Blaffer Hrdy, *Mother Nature: A History of Mothers, In-*

fants, and Natural Selection (New York: Pantheon Books, 1999); Venise T. Berry, *All of Me: A Voluptuous Tale* (New York: Dutton, 2000); Rose E. Frisch, *Female Fertility and the Body Fat Connection* (Chicago: University of Chicago Press, 2002).

2. Susie Orbach, *Fat Is a Feminist Issue: How to Lose Weight Permanently without Dieting* (New York: Paddington Press, 1978).

3. Kim Chernin, *The Obsession: Reflections on the Tyranny of Slenderness* (New York: Harper and Row, 1981). See also Greg Critser, *Fat Land: How Americans Became the Fattest People in the World* (New York: Houghton Mifflin, 2003).

4. S. Weir Mitchell, *Fat and Blood and How to Make Them* (Philadelphia: Lippincott, 1877), 15.

5. Sanjida O'Connell, "Land of Hope and Obesity," *The Independent*, 4 May 2002, *Review*, 8.

6. See the recent anthology on obesity and poverty in the Americas: Manuel Peña and Jorge Bacallao, eds., *Obesity and Poverty: A New Public Health Challenge* (Washington DC: Pan American Health Organization, 2002).

7. Antoine de Baecque, "Le Discours anti-noble (1787–1792) aux origines d'un slogan: 'Le Peuple contre les gros,'" *Revue d'Histoire Moderne et Contemporaine* 36 (1989): 3–28.

8. Henri Béraud, *Le Martyre de l'obèse* (Paris: Albin Michel, 1922).

9. Evelyn Nieves, "San Francisco Ordinance Outlaws Size Discrimination," *New York Times*, 9 May 2000, A16.

10. Grant Pick, "What's Wrong with This Picture?" *Chicago Tribune Magazine*, 9 July 2000, 17.

11. Hillel Schwartz, *Never Satisfied: A Cultural History of Diets, Fantasies, and Fat* (New York: Free Press, 1986), 17.

12. "Diseases of the Heart," *Godey's Lady's Book* 87 (1873): 282.

13. "What Causes Obesity?" *Journal of the American Medical Association* 83 (1924): 1003.

14. Harold Dearden, *Exercise and the Will* (London: William Heinemann, 1927), 93.

15. Robert Kemp, *Nobody Need Be Fat* (London: William Heinemann, 1959), 33.

16. Elmer Wheeler, *The New Fat Boy's Diet Book* (1950; rev. ed., New York: Paperback Library, 1968), 15.

17. Laura Kipnis, "Fat and Culture," in *In Near Ruins: Cultural Theory at the End of the Century*, ed. Nicholas B. Dirks (Minneapolis: University of Minnesota Press, 1998), 199–220. See also Beate Hoftadler and Birgit Buchinger, *Körper Normen — Körper Formen* (Wien: Turia and Kant, 2001).

18. Lynne Daroff, "French Fries, Make Mine Double"; available at http://www.crowmagazine.com/fat_issue. html (last accessed 2001).

19. Harrison G. Pope Jr., Katharine A. Phillips, and Roberto Olivardia, *The Adonis Complex: The Secret Crisis of Male Body Obsession* (New York: Free Press, 2000).

20. Arnold Andersen, Leigh Cohn, Tom Holbrook, and Thomas M. Holbrook, *Making Weight: Healing Men's Conflicts with Food, Weight, and Shape* (New York: Gurze Designs and Books, 2000).

21. Marika Tiggemann and Esther Rothblum, "Gender Differences in Social Consequences of Perceived Overweight in the United States and Australia," *Sex Roles* 18.1–2 (1988): 75–86, here 76. Subsequent references will appear in the text.

22. Richard Morgan, "The Men in the Mirror," *Chronicle of Higher Education,* 27 September 2002, A53–55.

23. Youfa Wang, "Is Obesity Associated with Early Sexual Maturation? A Comparison of the Association in American Boys Versus Girls," *Pediatrics* 110 (2002): 903–10.

24. Hilde Bruch, *The Importance of Overweight* (New York: Norton, 1957), 109.

25. E. Annie Proulx, *The Shipping News* (New York: Touchstone, 1994), 2. Subsequent references will appear in the text.

26. Peter Carey, *The Fat Man in History and Other Stories* (New York: Vintage, 1993), 11. See also David Callahan, "Whose History Is the Fat Man's? Peter Carey's *The Fat Man in History*," *Journal of the South Pacific Association for Commonwealth Literature and Language Studies* 40 (1995): 34–53.

27. Joanne Ikeda and Priscilla Naworski, *Am I Fat? Helping Young Children Accept Differences in Body Size* (New York: ETR Associates, 1992), 1.

28. Randle Cotgrave, *A Dictionarie of the French and English Tongues* (London: Adam Islip, 1611).

29. Tobias Venner, *Via recta ad vitam longam; Or, a plaine philosophicall demonstration of the nature, faculties, and effects of all such things as by way of nourishments make for the preservation of health, with divers necessary dieticall observations; as also of the true use and effects of sleepe, exercise, excretions and perturbations, with just applications to every age, constitution of body, and time of yeere . . . Whereunto is annexed a necessary and compendious treatise of the famous baths of Bathe/Lately published by the same author* (London: Printed by Felix Kyngston for Richard Moore and sold at his shop in Saint Dunstans Churchyard in Fleetstreet, 1628), 196. Subsequent references to the 1628 edition will appear in the text.

30. The nineteenth-century German term is *Fettleibigkeit*, which is the term of choice to replace the Latin *adiposa*; see Enoch Heinrich Kisch, *Die Fettleibigkeit (Lipomatosis universalis) auf Grundlage zahlreicher Beobachtungen* (Stuttgart: Enke, 1888).

31. Richard Klein, *Eat Fat* (New York: Pantheon, 1996).

32. Peter Stearns, quoted in "Analysis Facing the Fats," transcript of a recorded documentary; presenter: Felipe Fernandez-Armesto, producer: Zareer Masani, editor: Nicola Meyrick (BBC London; broadcast date: 22 August 2002).

33. Thomas F. Cash and Robin E. Roy, "Pounds of Flesh: Weight, Gender, and Body Images," in *Interpreting Weight: The Social Management of Fatness and Thinness*, ed. Jeffery Sobal and Donna Maurer (New York: Aldine de Gruyter, 1999), 209–28.

34. Michel Foucault, *Discipline and Punish: The Birth of the Prison*, trans. Alan Sheridan (New York: Vintage, 1977), 227.

35. Carol Midgley, "Fat Chance of Success," *The Times* (London) 16 February 2001.

36. K. D. Hopkins and E. D. Lehmann, "Successful Medical Treatment of Obesity in Tenth Century Spain," *Lancet* 346 (1995): 452.

37. John Lascaratos, "Medical Management of Obesity in Fourteenth Century Byzantium," *Lancet* 346 (1995): 54–55.

38. Richard Godfrey and Mark Hallett, *James Gillray: The Art of Caricature* (London: Tate Gallery, 2002); Gillian Russell, "Burke's Dagger: Theatricality, Politics, and Print Culture in the 1790s," *British Journal for Eighteenth-Century Studies* 20 (1997): 1–16; Lora Rempel, "Carnal Satire and the Constitutional King: George III in James Gillray's Monstraws at a New Coalition Feast," *Art History* 18 (1995): 4–23; Max Hasse, "Spott mit dem Spott treiben: Bildzitate in der Karikatur des ausgehenden 18. Jahrhunderts," *Zeitschrift für Kunstgeschichte* 47 (1984): 523–34.

39. Edmund Blunden, *Leigh Hunt's "Examiner" Examined* (London: Harper and Brothers, 1931), 23.

40. J. Bate, "Shakespearean Allusion in English Caricature

in the Age of Gillray," *Journal of the Warburg and Courtauld Institute* 49 (1986): 196–210; Albert Boime, "Jacques-Louis David, Scatological Discourse in the French Revolution, and the Art of Caricature," *Arts Magazine* 62 (1988): 72–81; Michael Dobson, "Falstaff after John Bull: Shakespearean History, Britishness, and the Former United Kingdom," *Shakespeare-Jahrbuch* 136 (2000): 40–55.

41. Schwartz, *Never Satisfied*, 4.

42. Jean Comaroff, "Medicine and Culture: Some Anthropological Perspectives," *Social Science and Medicine* 12 (1978): 247–54.

43. Virginia W. Chang and Nicholas A. Christakis, "Medical Modeling of Obesity: A Transition from Action to Experience in a Twentieth Century American Medical Textbook," *Sociology of Health and Illness* (2002): 151–77.

44. Derek Chadwick and Gail Carden, eds., *The Origins and Consequences of Obesity* (New York: Wiley, 1996).

45. *Americans with Disabilities Act of 1990* (July 1990), 104 STAT. 327

46. *Equal Employment Opportunity Commission Compliance Manual* §902.2(c)(5).

47. *Clemons v. Big Ten Conference* (1997), WL 89227 (N.D. Ill. 1997).

48. National Institutes of Health, *Clinical Guidelines on the Identification, Evaluation, and Treatment of Overweight and Obesity in Adults: The Evidence Report* (Bethesda: U.S. Department of Health and Human Services, 1998).

49. Milt Freudenheim, "Employers Focus on Weight as Workplace Health Issue," *New York Times*, 6 September 1999, A11.

50. William R. Miller, ed., *The Addictive Behaviours: Treatment of Alcoholism, Drug Abuse, Smoking, and Obesity* (Oxford: Pergamon Press, 1980); Jon D. Kassel and Saul Schiff-

man, "What Can Hunger Teach Us about Drug Craving? A Comparative Analysis of the Two Constructs," *Advanced Behavior Research Therapy* 14 (1992): 141–67.

51. "Killjoy Woz Here," *The Economist*, 8 March 2003, 75.

52. A. H. Mokdad, M. K. Serdula, W. H. Dietz, B. A. Bowman, J. S. Marks, and J. P. Koplan, "The Spread of the Obesity Epidemic in the United States, 1991–1998," *Journal of the American Medical Association* 282 (1999): 1519–22.

53. "The Human Genome," *The Economist*, 1 July 2000, 7.

54. H. Tristram Engelhardt Jr. et al., "The Philosophy of Medicine: A New Endeavor," *Texas Reports on Biology and Medicine* 3 (1973): 443–52, here 446.

55. Tobias Venner, *Via recta ad vitam longam, or a plaine philosophical discourse of the nature . . . and effects of all such things, as by way of nourishments and dieteticall obseruations make for the preseruation of health . . . Wherein also . . . the true vse of our famous Bathes of Bathe is . . . demonstrated* (London: Printed by Edward Griffen for Richard Moore, 1620), 11–12.

56. Jeffery Sobal, Barbara S. Rauschenbach, and Edward A. Frongillo Jr., "Marital Status, Fatness, and Obesity," *Social Science and Medicine* 35.7 (1992): 915–23. Subsequent references will appear in the text. Compare Linda J. Waite and Maggie Gallagher, *The Case for Marriage: Why Married People Are Happier, Healthier, and Better off Financially* (New York: Broadway Books, 2001).

57. Immanuel Kant, "Von der Macht des Gemüts, durch den blossen Vorsatz seiner krankhaften Gefühle Meister zu sein," in *Werkausgabe*, vol. 11, *Schriften zur Anthropologie, Geschichtsphilosophie, Politik, und Pädagogik, I*, ed. Wilhelm Weischedel (Frankfurt: Suhrkamp, 1991), 371–93, here 376–77. Subsequent references will appear in the text.

58. Kingsley Amis, *One Fat Englishman* (New York: Summit, 1963), 18.

59. Salman Rushdie, *Grimus* (London: Granada, 1977), 12–13. Subsequent references will appear in the text.

60. John Kennedy Toole, *A Confederacy of Dunces* (New York: Grove Press, 1980), 13–14. Subsequent references will appear in the text.

61. See http://www.iglou.com/info/santa/sec2-1.html (last accessed 1996).

62. Neda Ulaby, "Roscoe Arbuckle and the Scandal of Fatness," in *Bodies out of Bounds: Fatness and Transgression*, ed. Jana Evans Braziel and Kathleen LeBesco (Berkeley: University of California Press, 2001), 153–65, here 156.

63. Edna Ferber, "The Gay Old Dog," in *One Basket* (Chicago: Peoples Book Club, 1947), 11–28. Subsequent references will appear in the text.

64. Richard Collier, *Masculinity, Law, and the Family* (London: Routledge, 1995), 29. See also K. O'Donovan, *Sexual Divisions in Law* (London: Weidenfeld and Nicholson, 1985); N. Naffine, *Law and the Sexes: Explorations in Feminist Jurisprudence* (Sydney: Unwin Hyman, 1990).

65. Rosemarie Garland Thompson, *Extraordinary Bodies: Figuring Physical Disability in American Culture and Literature* (New York: Columbia University Press, 1997).

66. *Nova Mink v. Trans-Canada Airlines* (1951), 2 D.L.R. 241 at 254 *per* McDonald J.

67. *Arland v. Taylor* (1955), O.R. 131 at 142.

68. *Blyth v. Birmingham Waterworks Co.* (1856), 11 Ex. 781 at 784.

69. *Hall v. Brooklands Auto-Racing Club* (1933), 1 K.B. 205 at 224 *per* Green, L.J.

70. A. L. Linden, *Canadian Tort Law*, 4th ed. (Toronto: Butterworths, 1987).

71. *The Uncommon Law*, 7th ed. (London: Methuen, 1952), 1–6.

72. Douglas Degher and Gerald Hughes, "The Adoption and Management of a 'Fat' Identity," in *Interpreting Weight: The Social Management of Fatness and Thinness*, ed. Jeffery Sobal and Donna Maurer (New York: Aldine de Gruyter, 1999), 11–27.

73. BBC *Newsnight*, 15 June 2000.

74. Jean Frumusan, *The Cure of Obesity*, trans. Elaine A. Wood (London: John Bale, Sons, and Danielsson, 1930), 30–31.

75. Cecil Webb-Johnson, *Why Be Fat?* (London: Mills and Boon, 1923), 27.

76. Roger Bacon, *The Cure of Old Age and the Preservation of Youth*, ed. and trans. Richard Browne (London: Thomas Flesher and Edward Evets, 1683), here Browne's introduction, A4v.

77. Kenneth F. Ferraro and Yan Yu, "Body Weight and Self-Ratings of Health," *Journal of Health and Social Behavior* 36 (1995): 274–84.

78. Schwartz, *Never Satisfied*, 137.

79. Jean Baudrillard, "The Obese," in *Fatal Strategies*, trans. Jim Fleming (London: Pluto Press, 1999), 27–34. Subsequent references will appear in the text.

80. Woody Allen, *Getting Even* (New York: Random House, 1971), 62–67.

81. David Koenig, "Airlines under Fire for Making Obese Passengers Buy Two Tickets," *Detroit News*, 20 June 2002.

82. John Ciardi, "Washing Your Feet," in *The Tyranny of the Normal: An Anthology*, ed. Carol Donley and Sheryl Buckley (Kent: Kent State University Press, 1996), 143–44.

83. Ciardi, "Washing Your Feet," 145–46.

84. Jack Coulehan, "The Six Hundred Pound Man," in

The Tyranny of the Normal: An Anthology, ed. Carol Donley and Sheryl Buckley (Kent: Kent State University Press, 1996).

85. J. G. Fleming, *The Law of Torts*, 7th ed. (Sydney: The Law Book Company, 1987), 97.

86. For "the best he knew how," see *Vaughan v. Menlove* (1837), 3 Bing. N.C. 468 at 475. For "does not attempt to see men as God sees them," see Oliver Wendell Holmes, *The Common Law* (1881; reprint, New York: Dover, 1991), 108. The quotation is from Linden, *Canadian Tort Law*, 117.

87. Leslie A. Fiedler, "The Tyranny of the Normal," in *The Tyranny of the Normal: An Anthology*, ed. Carol Donley and Sheryl Buckley (Kent: Kent State University Press, 1996), 3–10, here 9. Subsequent references will appear in the text.

88. Steven F. Kruger, " 'GET FAT, Don't Die!' Eating and AIDS in Gay Men's Culture," in *Eating Culture*, ed. Ron Scapp and Brian Seitz (Albany: State University of New York Press, 1998), 36–59.

89. Julien S. Murphy, *The Constructed Body: AIDS, Reproductive Technology, and Ethics* (Albany: State University of New York Press, 1995), 15.

90. Murphy, *The Constructed Body*, 67.

91. See Sander L. Gilman, *Health and Illness: Images of Difference* (London: Reaktion Books, 1995), 51–66.

92. "Analysis Facing the Fats."

1. FAT BOYS IN THE CULTURAL HISTORY OF THE WEST

1. See Philip J. van der Eijks, *Diocles of Carystus: A Collection of the Fragments with Translation and Commentary* (Leiden and Boston: Brill, 2000), 1:246–49.

2. "Aphorisms," in *Hippocrates, Volume IV, Nature of Man. Regimen in Health. Humours. Aphorisms. Regimen 1–3. Dreams. Heracleitus. On the Universe*, trans. W. H. S. Jones (Cambridge: Harvard University Press, 1931). All references

to Hippocrates' *Aphorisms* are to this edition and will be indicated by section and roman numeral in the text.

3. H. Orth, "Die Behandlung der Fettleibigkeit in der griechisch-römische Antike," *Medizinischer Monatsspiegel* 9 (1960): 193–98.

4. Matthew Fox, "The Constrained Man," in *Thinking Men: Masculinity and Its Self-Representation in the Classical Tradition*, ed. Lin Foxhall and John Salmon (London and New York: Routledge, 1998), 6–22.

5. "On Length and Shortness of Life," in *Aristotle, Volume VIII, On the Soul. Parva Naturalia. On Breath*, trans. W. S. Hett (Cambridge: Harvard University Press, 1936), 403.

6. Aristotle, "On Length and Shortness of Life," 403.

7. Aristotle, "On Length and Shortness of Life," 407.

8. See Aristophanes, *The Frogs*, ed. Sir Kenneth Dover (Oxford: Clarendon Press, 1997), and the standard Greek etymological resource *A Greek-English Lexicon*, ed. Henry George Liddell, Robert Scott, and Sir Henry Stuart Jones (Oxford: Oxford University Press, 1968), 339.

9. This is true as late as Herophilus, who notes "excessive fat in the hips" as a cause of difficult childbirth. Herophilus, *The Art of Medicine in Early Alexandria*, ed. and trans. Henrich von Staden (Cambridge: Cambridge University Press, 1989), 298.

10. See *Timaeus*, in *Plato, Volume IX, Timaeus, Critias, Cleitophon, Menexenus, Epistles*, trans. R. G. Bury (Cambridge: Harvard University Press, 1942), 183–85.

11. M. Montaigne, *Essays* (London: Penguin Books, 1958), 336.

12. See Cicero, *De Fato*, cited by Thomas Cooper, "Observations Respecting the History of Physiognomy," *Memoirs of the Literary and Philosophical Society of Manchester* 3 (1790): 414–15.

13. Robin Osborne, "Sculpted Men of Athens: Masculinity and Power in the Field of Vision," in *Thinking Men: Masculinity and Its Self-Representation in the Classical Tradition*, ed. Lin Foxhall and John Salmon (London and New York: Routledge, 1998), 23–42. This was not much different for the Victorians; see Joseph A. Kestner, *Masculinities in Victorian Painting* (Aldershot: Scolar, 1997).

14. Maud W. Gleason, *Making Men: Sophists and Self-Presentation in Ancient Rome* (Princeton: Princeton University Press, 1995), 84–87.

15. Georg Simmel, *Einleitung in die Moralwissenschaft*, *Gesamtausgabe IV*, ed. Klaus Christian Köhnke (Frankfurt: Suhrkamp, [1989]), 96 (my translation).

16. Eric P. Widmaier, *Why Geese Don't Get Obese (and We Do)* (New York: W. H. Freeman, 1998).

17. Werner Jaeger, *Paideia: The Ideals of Greek Culture*, trans. Gilbert Highet (New York: Oxford University Press, 1944), 3:34.

18. Celsus, *De medicina*, trans. W. G. Spencer (Cambridge: Harvard University Press, 1935), 1:97.

19. Celsus, *De medicina*, 1:3, cited in *The Seven Books of Paulus Aegineta*, trans. Francis Adams (London: Sydenham Society, 1844), 1:81.

20. On the theories and representation of obesity see Iris Ritzmann, "Adipositas: Diskriminerung und Leidensausdruck" (Ph.D. diss., University of Zürich, 1991); Christoph Klotter, *Adipositas als wissenschaftliches und politisches Problem: Zur Geschichtlichkeit des Übergewichts* (Heidelberg: Roland Asanger, 1990); Simone Moses, "Spannenlanger Hansel — nudeldicke Dirn. Eßstörungen un der frühren Neuzeit und im Zeitalter der Aufklärung" (Stuttgart: Diplom-Arbeit, 1997), 73–110; and "Mäßig und gefräßig: Eine Ausstellung," comp. Annemarie Hürlimann and Alexandra Reininghaus,

MAK — Österreichisches Museum für angewandte Kunst (Vienna: Skira, 1996). See also K. Y. Guggenheim, "Galen of Pergamon on Obesity," *Koroth* 9 (1988): 555–56.

21. Galen, *De Sanit. Tuenda*, vi, 8, cited in *The Seven Books of Paulus Aegineta*, trans. Francis Adams (London: Sydenham Society, 1844), 1:81.

22. *The Seven Books of Paulus Aegineta*, 1:81.

23. Edward Dickinson, *Regimen of Health and Longevity: A Poetical Invitation* (London: Printed for the author, 1820), 21.

24. Jeffrey Steingarten, *The Man Who Ate Everything* (New York: Random House, 1998), 177.

25. Ossi Rahkonen, Olle Lundberg, Eero Lahelma, and Minna Huuka, "Body Mass and Social Class: A Comparison of Finland and Sweden in the 1990s," *Journal of Public Health Policy* 19 (1998): 88–105, here 88–89.

26. *Regimen sanitatis salernitanum*, trans. P. Holland, reprinted in *The Code of Health and Longevity*, ed. John Sinclair (Edinburgh: Arch. Constable and Co., 1806), 3:5–46, here 3:35.

27. See Franz Rosenzweig, *Understanding the Sick and the Healthy: A View of World, Man, and God*, trans. Nahum Glatzer (Cambridge: Harvard University Press, 1999), 35–36.

28. Kelly D. Brownell and Thomas A. Wadden, "Obesity," in *Kaplan and Sadock's Comprehensive Textbook of Psychiatry*, 7th ed., ed. Benjamin J. Sadock and Virginia A. Sadock (Baltimore: Williams and Wilkins, 1998), 25.3.

29. Julius Preuss, *Biblical and Talmudic Medicine*, trans. Fred Rosner (New York: Sanhedrin Press, 1978), 215.

30. Jon L. Berquist, *Controlling Corporeality: The Body and the Household in Ancient Israel* (New Brunswick: Rutgers University Press, 2002), 34–35.

31. Samuel S. Kottek, "On Health and Obesity in Talmudic

and Midrashic Lore," *Israel Journal of Medical Sciences* 32 (1996): 509–10.

32. *Das diätetische Sendschreiben des Maimonides (Rambam) an den Sultan Saladin*, ed. and trans. D. Winternitz (Wien: Braumüller und Seidel, 1843). Compare Fred Rosner, *The Medical Legacy of Moses Maimonides* (Hoboken NJ: KTAV, 1998), 58.

33. Maimonides, *Medical Writings: The Art of Cure — Extracts from Galen*, ed. and trans. Uriel S. Barzel (Haifa: Maimonides Research Institute, 1992), 175–76.

34. Toby Gelfand, " 'Mon Cher Docteur Freud': Charcot's Unpublished Correspondence to Freud, 1888–1893," *Bulletin of the History of Medicine* 62 (1988): 563–88, here 574.

35. George Henry Lane Fox Pitt-Rivers, *The Clash of Culture and the Contact of Races* (London: Routledge, 1927), 82.

36. Frumusan, *The Cure of Obesity*, 9.

37. Robert Saundby, "Diabetes mellitus," in *A System of Medicine*, ed. Thomas Clifford Allbutt (London: Macmillan, 1897), 197–99.

38. W. F. Christie, *Obesity: A Practical Handbook for Physicians* (London: William Heinemann, 1937), 31.

39. M. J. Oertel, "Obesity," in *Twentieth Century Practice*, ed. Thomas J. Stedman (London: Sampson Low, Marston, and Co., 1895), 3:626–725, here 3:647–48.

40. C. v. Noorden, *Die Fettsucht* (Wien: Alfred Hölder, 1910), 63.

41. Leonard Williams, *Obesity* (London: Humphrey Milford/Oxford University Press, 1926), 53.

42. See Jean Leray, *Embonpoint et obésité* (Paris: Masson et cie, 1931), 11–12. See also W. F. Christie, *Surplus Fat and How to Reduce It* (London: William Heinemann, 1927), which begins with a long discussion of racial predisposition to fat (1–8).

43. W. H. Sheldon, S. S. Stevens, and W. B. Tucker, *The Varieties of Human Physique* (New York: Harper, 1940), 221.

44. On fat Jews and fasting Jews see "Who Fasts on Yom Kippur?" chapter 10 of Stanley Schachter, *Emotion, Obesity, and Crime* (New York: Academic Press, 1971), 124–34.

45. K. Schmidt-Nielsen et al., "Diabetes Mellitus in the Sand Rat Induced by Standard Laboratory Diets," *Science* 143 (1964): 689, cited in Richard M. Goodman, *Genetic Disorders among the Jewish People* (Baltimore: Johns Hopkins University Press, 1979), 334–41. See also A. E. Mourant, Ada C. Kopec, and Kazimiera Domaniewska-Sobczak, *The Genetics of the Jews* (Oxford: Clarendon Press, 1978).

46. See http://www.davidmargolis.com/journalism__fat .html (last accessed 2001).

47. See the work of Daniel Boyarin, *A Radical Jew: Paul and the Politics of Identity* (Berkeley: University of California Press, 1994), and *Carnal Israel: Reading Sex in Talmudic Culture* (Berkeley: University of California Press, 1993). Daniel Boyarin makes a compelling case for understanding the Pauline letters themselves as sites of a thoroughly allegorical anthropology. Among the binary oppositions of Pauline allegory stand the analogous pairs flesh-spirit, literal-figurative, and signifier-signified, in which the first element is a mere pointing to the privileged second element. So for Paul the Torah is but a pointing to its fulfillment in Christ.

48. Hector Avalos, *Health Care and the Rise of Christianity* (Peabody MA: Hendrickson, 1999). For a later moment see Louise Mirrer, "Representing 'Other' Men: Muslims, Jews, and Masculine Ideals in Medieval Castilian Epic and Ballad," in *Medieval Masculinities: Regarding Men in the Middle Ages*, ed. Clare A. Lees (Minneapolis: University of Minnesota Press, 1994), 169–86.

49. Erin Sawyer, "Celibate Pleasures: Masculinity, Desire,

and Asceticism in Augustine," *Journal of the History of Sexuality* 6 (1995): 1–29.

50. St. Augustine, *Confessions*, trans. R. S. Pine-Coffin (London: Penguin Books, 1961), 235–37. Subsequent references will appear in the text. See also Mary Harlow, "In the Name of the Father: Procreation, Paternity, and Patriarchy," in *Thinking Men: Masculinity and Its Self-Representation in the Classical Tradition*, ed. Lin Foxhall and John Salmon (London and New York: Routledge, 1998), 155–69. Subsequent references will appear in the text.

51. St. Augustine, *The City of God* (Cambridge: Harvard University Press, 1957–72), 2:247, 3:37.

52. See Brian E. Daley, *The Hope of the Early Church: A Handbook of Patristic Eschatology* (Cambridge: Cambridge University Press, 1991), 144.

53. See the discussion in Sander L. Gilman, *Seeing the Insane* (New York: Wiley, 1982), 22–24.

54. W. F. Toal, ed., *The Sunday Sermons of the Great Fathers*, 4 vols. (Chicago: Regnery, 1957–63), 3:315.

55. Caroline Walker Bynum, *Holy Feast and Holy Fast: The Religious Significance of Food to Medieval Women* (Berkeley: University of California Press, 1987). A counterargument is found in Rudolph M. Bell, *Holy Anorexia* (Chicago: University of Chicago Press, 1985). On modern women and pathological thinness see Joan Jacobs Brumberg, *Fasting Girls: The Emergence of Anorexia Nervosa as a Modern Disease* (Cambridge: Harvard University Press, 1988).

56. Lorraine Daston and Katharine Park, *Wonders and the Order of Nature, 1150–1750* (New York: Zone, 1998), 192. See also Jeffrey Jerome Cohen, *Of Giants: Sex, Monsters, and the Middle Ages* (Minneapolis: University of Minnesota Press, 2002).

57. Michel Jeanneret, *A Feast of Words: Banquets and Table*

Talk in the Renaissance, trans. Jeremy Whitely and Emma Hughes (Chicago: University of Chicago Press, 1991).

58. Jeffrey Jerome Cohen and Bonnie Wheeler, eds., *Becoming Male in the Middle Ages* (New York: Garland, 1997).

59. Nathaniel Strout, "A Biblical Framework for Orgoglio's Fall: A Note on *The Faerie Queene*, I.viii.22," *Notes and Queries* 32 (1985): 21–23; Douglas Waters, "Duessa and Orgoglio: Red Crosse's Spiritual Fornication," *Renaissance Quarterly* 20 (1967): 211–20.

60. *Luther's Works*, ed. Jaroslav Pelikan (St. Louis: Concordia Publishing House, 1973), 28:196. Subsequent references to this volume, which contains the *Commentary on 1 Corinthians 15*, will appear in the text.

61. Thomas Cornfield, "Luther, Paracelsus, and the Spirit" (Ph.D. diss., University of Chicago, 1996).

62. Isaiah Shachar, *The Judensau: A Medieval Anti-Jewish Motif and Its History*, Warburg Institute Surveys, no. 5 (London: Warburg Institute, 1974).

63. *Luther's Works*, ed. Jaroslav Pelikan (Philadelphia: Fortress Press, 1971), 47:268–93, here 47:274.

64. Julia Kristeva, *Powers of Horror: An Essay on Abjection*, trans. Leon S. Roudiez (New York: Columbia University Press, 1982), 185.

65. Erik H. Erikson, *Young Man Luther: A Study in Psychoanalysis and History* (New York: Norton, 1958), 208.

66. Svetlana Alpers, *The Making of Rubens* (New Haven: Yale University Press, 1995).

67. Johann Sigismund Elsholtz, *Diaeteticon* (1682; reprint, Leipzig: Edition Leipzig, 1984).

68. La Bruyère, *Characters*, trans. Jean Stewart (Baltimore: Penguin, 1970), 208.

69. Christopher William Hufeland, *The Art of Prolonging Life* (London: J. Bell, 1797), 1:169. This is a fairly accurate

translation of his *Die Kunst das menschliche Leben zu verläng-ern* (Jena: Akademische Buchhandlung, 1797).

70. Thomas Jameson, *Essays on the Changes of the Human Body, at Its Different Ages* (London: Longman, Hurst, Bees, Orme, and Brown, 1811).

2. FAT BOYS WRITING AND WRITING FAT BOYS

1. Edward Jukes, *On Indigestion and Costiveness: A Series of Hints To Both Sexes . . .* (London: John Churchill, 1833), 293.

2. See Luigi Cornaro, *The Art of Living Long* (Milwaukee: William F. Butler, 1903). Subsequent references will be to this translation and will appear in the text. For an earlier English translation see *Discourses on a Sober and Temperate Life* (London, Cadell and Davies [etc.], 1798). On the background of the work see Gerald J. Gruman, "The Rise and Fall of Prolongevity Hygiene, 1558–1873," *Bulletin of the History of Medicine* 35 (1961): 221–29; Gerald J. Gruman, *A History of Ideas about the Prolongation of Life: The Evolution of Prolongevity Hypotheses to 1800* (Philadelphia: American Philosophical Society, 1966); William B. Walker, "Luigi Cornaro, a Renaissance Writer on Personal Hygiene," *Bulletin of the History of Medicine* 28 (1954): 525–34; Mark Benecke, *The Dream of Eternal Life: Biomedicine, Aging, and Immortality*, trans. Rachel Rubenstein (New York: Columbia University Press, 2002).

3. Cited by Nancy G. Siraisi, *The Clock and the Mirror: Girolamo Cardano and Renaissance Medicine* (Princeton: Princeton University Press, 1997), 79. On Cornaro see 79–85. Subsequent references will appear in the text.

4. See the comparison in Carol Houlihan Flynn, *The Body in Swift and Defoe* (Cambridge: Cambridge University Press, 1990), 46–50.

5. Ulrich von Hutten, "From the Book of Dialogues: Fever

the First," in *German Humanism and Reformation*, ed. Reinhold Becker (New York: Continuum, 1982), 235–43.

6. Erasmus, *Concerning the Eating of Fish* (1526), in *The Essential Erasmus*, ed. and trans. John P. Dolan (New York: Mentor-Omega, 1964). Subsequent references will appear in the text.

7. Bacon, *The Cure of Old Age*, 54.

8. See William Shakespeare's *Hamlet*, in *The Riverside Shakespeare*, ed. G. Blakemore Evans (Boston: Houghton Mifflin, 1974), 2.2.174.

9. Johann Baptista van Helmont, *Aufgang der Artzney-Kunst, das ist: noch nie erhörte Grund-Lehren von der Natur . . .* , trans. Christian Knorr von Rosenroth (Sultzbach: Johann Andrae Enders sel. Söhne, 1683), 144–45. Subsequent references will appear in the text.

10. Leonard Lessius, *Hygiasticon*, trans. Timothy Smith (London: Charles Hitch, 1742), 40. Subsequent references to this edition will appear in the text, unless noted. For the nineteenth century see John Burn Bailey, *Modern Methuselahs; Or, Short biographical sketches of a few advanced nonagenarians or actual centenarians who were distinguished in art, science, literature, or philanthropy. Also, brief notices of some individuals remarkable chiefly for their longevity* (London: Chapman and Hall, 1888), which pairs Cornaro with Titian, Fontenelle, and Sir Moses Montefiore, among many others.

11. Hufeland, *The Art of Prolonging Life*, 1:175–76. See also his *Die Kunst das menschliche Leben zu verlängern: Hufelands Makrobiotik* (Frankfurt am Main: Insel, 1995). Also see Ortrun Riha, "Diät für die Seele: Das Erfolgsrezept von Hufelands Makrobiotik," NTM 9 (2001): 80–89.

12. Lewis Cornaro, Dr. Franklin, and Dr. Scott, *The immortal mentor; Or, Man's unerring guide to a healthy, wealthy,*

and happy life. In three parts (Philadelphia: Printed for the Rev. Mason L. Weems by Francis and Robert Bailey, no. 116, High-Street, 1796).

13. Jukes, *On Indigestion and Costiveness*, 240–42.

14. Miguel de Cervantes Saavedra, *The Adventures of Don Quixote*, trans. J. M. Cohen (Harmondsworth: Penguin Books, 1986). Subsequent translated references will be to this edition and will appear in the text.

15. Miguel de Cervantes Saavedra, *Obras completas*, ed. Angel Vanbuena Prat (Madrid: Aguilar, 1960), 1062. Subsequent untranslated references will be to this edition and will appear in the text.

16. Jean Villechauvaix, *Cervantes: Malade et médecin*, Thèse, Faculté de médecine de Paris (Paris: Société d'Éditions Scientifiques, 1898); Jerome R. Head, "Medical Allusions in Don Quixote," *Annals of Medical History* 6 (1934): 169–79; Horacio Caballero Palacios, *El pensamiento médico en Don Quijote* (San Luis Potosí, México: Editorial de las Manzanas, 1977), 52–56, 101–16; José Manuel Reverte Coma, *La antropología médica y el Quijote* (Madrid: Rueda, 1980); Antonio López Alonso, *Molimientos, puñadas, y caídas acaecidos en el Quijote* (Alcalá de Henares: Universidad de Alcala de Henares, 1996), 49–51, 55–57, 129–32.

17. P. J. García Ruiz and L. Gulliksen, "Did Don Quixote Have Lewy Body Disease?" *Journal of the Royal Society of Medicine* 92 (1999): 200–201.

18. Harold López Méndez, *La medicina en el "Quijote" Colección de autores hispanoamericanos 1* (Madrid: Editorial Quevedo, [1969]), 345.

19. *Regimen sanitatis salernitanum*, 3:5–46, here 3:13.

20. Bacon, *The Cure of Old Age*, 139, 150.

21. Everard Maynwaringe, *Vita Suva and Longa, the Preser-*

vation of Health and the Prolongation of Life Proposed and Proved (London: J. D., 1670), 60. Subsequent references will appear in the text.

22. Elsholtz, *Diaeteticon*, 148–49.

23. Here one can cite the extensive literature on Stan Laurel and Oliver Hardy and their many replacements. The most recent study is by the novelist Simon Louvish, *Stan and Ollie: The Roots of Comedy* (New York: Thomas Dunne, 2002).

24. Mendle Mocher Seforim, *The Travels and Adventures of Benjamin the Third*, trans. Moshe Spiegel (New York: Schocken, 1949). Subsequent references will appear in the text. See Dan Miron, *A Traveler Disguised: The Rise of Modern Yiddish Fiction in the Nineteenth Century* (Syracuse: Syracuse University Press, 1996).

25. Heinrich Singer, *Allgemeine und spezielle Krankheitslehre der Juden* (Leipzig: Benno Konegen, 1904), 9 (my translation).

26. Hans Gross, *Kriminal-Psychologie* (Leipzig: F. C. W. Vogel, 1905), 121 (my translation).

27. Adolf Jellinek, *Der jüdische Stamm: Ethnographische Studien* (Vienna: Herzfeld und Bauer, 1869), 89–90 (my translation).

28. Laurence Sterne, *The Life and Opinions of Tristram Shandy, Gentleman*, ed. Graham Petrie, intro. Christopher Ricks (London: Penguin Books, 1967). Subsequent references will appear in the text. See also Ronald Saul Hafter, "Sterne's Affective Art and Eighteenth-Century Psychology" (Ph.D. diss., Brandeis, 1970); Deborah Anderson, "Reproduction and the New Science: Identity Production in *Tristram Shandy*," *Mentalities* 15 (2001): 7–16.

29. Arthur H. Cash, *Laurence Sterne: The Early and Middle Years* (London: Methuen, 1975), 180.

30. Bacon, *The Cure of Old Age*, 140.

31. Johannes Joachim Becher, *Chymisches Laboratorium, oder Unter-erdische Naturkündigung* (Frankfurt: Johann Haaß; 1680), 668–84. Also see Pamela H. Smith, *The Business of Alchemy: Science and Culture in the Holy Roman Empire* (Princeton: Princeton University Press, 1994); Harold J. Cook, "A Material Man: The Alchemy of Money in J.J. Becher's Writings," *Studies in History and Philosophy of Science* 27 (1996): 387–96.

32. Friedrich Nicolai, *Geschichte eines dicken Mannes worin drei Heiraten und drei Körbe nebst viel Liebe* (Weimar: Gustav Kiepenheuer, 1972). See Alexander Kosenina, "Friedrich Nicolai's Satires on Philosophy," *Monatshefte* 93 (2001): 290–99.

33. Stanley W. Jackson, *Melancholia and Depression from Hippocratic Times to Modern Times* (New Haven: Yale University Press, 1986), 284.

34. *The Letters of David Hume*, ed. J. Y. T. Grieg (Oxford: Clarendon Press, 1932), 1:12–18.

35. This view continues well into the nineteenth century. See Robert James Culverwell, *The confessional . . . An analysis of the causes and cure of melancholy, nervousness, mental and physical debility, arising from ill health, worldly anxiety . . . To which is added an essay on corpulency-obesity . . . A sketch of choice in marriage, phrenologically considered . . . and a few comments on drunkenness* (London: Sherwood, 1841).

36. Sanctorius Sanctorius, *De statica medicine*, reprinted in *The Code of Health and Longevity*, ed. John Sinclair (Edinburgh: Arch. Constable and Co., 1806), 3:122–230, here 3:129.

37. Nicholaus Joseph von Jacquin, *Hortus Botanicus Vindobonensis* (Vienna: Leopold Johann Kaliwoda, 1770), 1, table 42.

38. Samuel Johnson, *Diaries, Prayers, and Annals*, ed. E. L. McAdam Jr., D. Hyde, and M. Hyde (New Haven: Yale

University Press, 1958), 1:301. Also see in this context Robert Eberwein, "Samuel Johnson, George Cheyne, and the 'Cone of Being,'" *Journal of the History of Ideas* 36 (1975): 153–58.

39. See *Dr. Samuel Johnson and Eighteenth Century Medicine*, exhibition catalog, the Wellcome Institute for the History of Medicine (n.d.); and Milo Keynes, "The Miserable Health of Dr. Samuel Johnson," *Journal of Medical Biography* 3 (1995): 161–69.

40. James Boswell, *Life of Johnson*, ed. R. W. Chapman (Oxford: Oxford University Press, 1980), 958. This is also very different from Boswell's own sense of his manly body; see Philip Carter, "James Boswell's Manliness," in *English Masculinities, 1660–1800*, ed. Tim Hitchcock and Michèle Cohen (London: Longman, 1999), 111–30. See also John Tosh, "The Old Adam and the New Man: Emerging Themes in the History of English Masculinities, 1750–1850," in *English Masculinities, 1660–1800*, ed. Tim Hitchcock and Michèle Cohen (London: Longman, 1999), 217–38.

41. Boswell, *Life of Johnson*, 958.

42. Boswell, *Life of Johnson*, 1121.

43. Pat Rogers, "Fat Is a Fictional issue: The Novel and the Rise of Weight-Watching," in *Literature and Medicine during the Eighteenth Century*, ed. Marie Mulvey Roberts and Roy Porter, Wellcome Institute Series in the History of Medicine (London: Routledge, 1993), 168–87. See also Marguerite M. Regan, "The Roasting of John Bull: Vegetarian Protest in Eighteenth-Century English Literature" (Ph.D. diss., University of Arkansas, 2001).

44. George Cheyne, *The English Malady; Or, a Treatise of nervous diseases of all kinds, as Spleen, Vapours, Lowness of Spirits, Hypochondrical, and Hysterical Distempers* (London: G. Strahan, 1733). Subsequent references will appear in the text.

45. Henry Fielding, *Joseph Andrews*, ed. H. Goldberg (New York: Norton, 1987), 127.

46. William Macmichael, *The Golden-Headed Cane* (London: John Murray, 1828), 56–57.

47. Anita Guerrini, *Obesity and Depression in the Enlightenment: The Life and Times of George Cheyne* (Norman: University of Oklahoma Press, 2000); D. E. Shuttleton, "Methodism and Dr. George Cheyne's 'More Enlightening Principles,'" *Clio Medica* 29 (1995): 316–35; K. French and A. Wear, *The Medical Revolution of the Seventeenth Century* (Cambridge and New York: Cambridge University Press, 1989); G. S. Rousseau, "Mysticism and Millenarianism: The Immortal Dr. Cheyne," in *Millenarianism and Messianism in English Literature and Thought, 1650–1800*, ed. Richard Popkin (Leiden: Brill, 1988), 81–126; Ginnie Smith, "Prescribing the Rules for Health: Self Help and Advice in the Eighteenth Century," in *Patients and Practitioners*, ed. Roy Porter (Cambridge: Cambridge University Press, 1985), 249–82; L. S. King, "George Cheyne, Mirror of Eighteenth-Century Medicine," *Bulletin of the History of Medicine* 48 (1974): 517–39; G. Bowles, "Physical, Human, and Divine Attraction in the Life and Thought of George Cheyne," *Annals of Science* 31 (1974): 473–88; Trevor H. Howell, "George Cheyne's Essay on Health and Long Life," *The Gerontologist* 9 (1969): 226–28. See also Roy Porter, introduction to *The English Malady*, by George Cheyne (1733; reprint, London: Routledge, 1991).

48. Georg Forster, *Voyage around the World*, ed. Nicolas Thomas and Oliver Berghof (Honolulu: University of Hawaii Press, 2000), 1:164–65.

49. Jean Anthelme Brillat-Savarin, *The Physiology of Taste; Or, Meditations on Transcendental Gastronomy*, trans. M. F. K. Fisher (Washington: Counterpoint, 1999), 239, 241. This work's first translation into English was as *The Handbook*

of Dining; Or, Corpulency and Leanness, trans. L. F. Simpson (New York: D. Appelton, 1865). This earlier translation draws upon the "so-called Banting system" (3) to frame the earlier text solely as a text on obesity and diet. See also Jean Armand-Leroche, *Brillat-Savarin et la médecine* (Paris: Le Francois, 1931); Roland Barthes, "Reading Brillat-Savarin," in *The Rustle of Language* (New York: Hill and Wang, 1986), 165–82.

50. Hufeland, *The Art of Prolonging Life*, 1:169. This is a fairly accurate translation of his *Die Kunst das menschliche Leben zu verlängern* (Jena: Akademische Buchhandlung, 1797).

51. Edwin James, *Early Western Travels*, vol. 15, *Part II of James's Account of S. H. Long's Expedition, 1819–1820*, ed. Reuben Gold Thwaites (Cleveland: A. H. Clark Co., 1905), 68.

52. John B. Wyeth, *Early Western Travels*, vol. 21, *Wyeth's Oregon: Or, a Short History of a Long Journey, 1832: Townsend's Narrative of a Journey across the Rocky Mountains, 1834*, ed. Reuben Gold Thwaites (Cleveland: A. H. Clark Co., 1905), 307.

53. Cited by Bernard Mandeville, *A Treatise of the Hypochonriak and Hysterick Diseases* (London: J. Graves, J. Hooke, and T. Jeffries, 1724), 162.

54. William Thackeray, *Vanity Fair* (Oxford: Oxford University Press, 1983), 55. Subsequent references will appear in the text.

55. Harriet Ritvo, *The Platypus and the Mermaid and Other Figments of the Classifying Imagination* (Cambridge: Harvard University Press, 1997), 148–49. See also Leslie A. Fiedler, *Freaks: Myths and Images of the Secret Self* (New York: Simon and Schuster, 1978), 128–29.

56. David T.-D. Clarke, *Daniel Lambert*, Leicestershire Museums Publication, no. 23 (1981), 3.

57. Jan Bondeson, *The Two-Headed Boy and Other Medical Marvels* (Ithaca: Cornell University Press, 2000), 237–60, here 243.

58. T. Coe, "A Letter . . . Concerning Mr. Bright, the Fat Man at Malden in Essex," *The Royal Society: Philosophical Transactions* 47 (1751–52): 188–89. Subsequent references will appear in the text.

59. German E. Berrios, *The History of Mental Symptoms: Descriptive Psychopathology since the Nineteenth Century* (Cambridge: Cambridge University Press, 1996), 351–68. See also John H. Smith, "Abulia: Sexuality and Diseases of the Will in the Late Nineteenth Century," *Genders* 6 (1989): 102–24.

60. John Locke, *An Essay Concerning Human Understanding* (New York: Dover, 1959), vol. 2, chap. 11, para. 5.

61. John Sinclair, ed., *The Code of Health and Longevity* (London: Sherwood, Gilbert, and Piper, 1833), 369.

62. Thomas Reid, *Works*, ed. William Hamilton (Edinburgh: Maclachan and Stewart, 1854), essay II, chap. 1.

63. Brillat-Savarin, *The Physiology of Taste*, 245.

64. William Wadd, *Comments on Corpulency* (London: John Ebers, 1829), 39–77.

65. I quote from the third (the first commercial) edition: William Banting, *Letter on Corpulence, Addressed to the Public*, 3d ed. (London: Harrison, 1864). Subsequent references will appear in the text. On Banting see Joyce L. Huff, "A 'Horror of Corpulence': Interrogating Bantingism and Mid-Nineteenth-Century Fat-Phobia," in *Bodies out of Bounds: Fatness and Transgression*, ed. Jana Evans Braziel and Kathleen LeBesco (Berkeley: University of California Press, 2001), 39–59.

66. William Banting, *Letter on Corpulence, Addressed to the Public*, 2d ed. (London: Harrison, 1863), 28.

67. William E. Aytoun, "Banting on Corpulence," *Blackwood's Edinburgh Magazine* 96 (November 1864): 607–17, here 609.

68. Brillat-Savarin, *The Physiology of Taste*, 245.

69. William Harvey, *On Corpulence in Relation to Disease: With Some Remarks on Diet* (London: Henry Renshaw, 1872), 69. Subsequent references will appear in the text.

70. A. W. Moore, *Corpulency, i.e., Fat, or Embonpoint, in Excess* (London: Printed for the Author by Frederick William Ruston, 1857), 12–13.

71. Watson Bradshaw, *On Corpulence* (London: Philip and Son, 1864), iii. Subsequent references will appear in the text.

72. "A London Physician," *How to Get Fat; Or, the Means of Preserving the Medium between Leanness and Obesity* (London: John Smith, 1865).

73. Mitchell, *Fat and Blood and How to Make Them*, 16.

74. Aytoun, "Banting on Corpulence," 609.

75. Felix von Niemeyer, *Lehrbuch der speciellen Pathologie und Therapie: Mit Besonderer Rücksicht auf Physiologie und pathologische Anatomie* (Berlin: Hirschwald, 1871).

76. Joshua Duke, *Banting in India with Some Remarks on Diet and Things in General* (Calcutta: Thacker, Spink, and Co., 1885). Subsequent references will appear in the text.

77. Brillat-Savarin, *The Physiology of Taste*, 237.

78. Henry S. Kahn and David F. Williamson, "Abdominal Obesity and Mortality Risk among Men in Nineteenth-Century North America," *International Journal of Obesity* 18 (1994): 686–91.

3. PATIENT ZERO

1. Stuart M. Tave, *The Amiable Humorist: A Study in the Comic Theory and Criticism of the Eighteenth and Nineteenth Centuries* (Chicago: University of Chicago Press, 1960), 187.

2. Bruce Thomas Boehrer, "Renaissance Overeating: The Sad Case of Ben Jonson," *Publications of the Modern Language Association* 105 (1990): 1071–82. See also his *The Fury of Men's Gullets: Ben Jonson and the Digestive Canal* (Philadelphia: University of Pennsylvania Press, 1997).

3. William C. Carroll, *Fat King, Lean Beggar: Representations of Poverty in the Age of Shakespeare* (Ithaca and London: Cornell University Press, 1996). See also Jonathan Gil Harris, *Foreign Bodies and the Body Politic: Discourses of Social Pathology in Early Modern England* (Cambridge: Cambridge University Press, 1998).

4. William Hazlitt, *Characters of Shakepear's Plays* (London: C. H. Reynell, 1817). Hazlitt's analysis of Falstaff in *Henry IV* occurs on 145–52, in *Henry V* on 155, and in *Merry Wives* on 250–51.

5. Robert Burton, *The Anatomy of Melancholy* (New York: Vintage, 1977), 1:136, 150, 376, 430; 2:124; 3:56.

6. All quotations from Shakespeare are from the Riverside edition: *The Riverside Shakespeare*, ed. G. Blakemore Evans (Boston: Houghton Mifflin, 1974). Subsequent references will appear in the text.

7. See Jon Arrizabalaga, John Henderson, and Roger French, *The Great Pox: The French Disease in Renaissance Europe* (New Haven: Yale University Press, 1997), 38–55.

8. Kristen Poole, "Facing Puritanism: Falstaff, Martin Marprelate, and the Grotesque Puritan," in *Shakespeare and Carnival: After Bakhtin*, ed. Ronald Knowles (Houndmills UK: Macmillan–St. Martin's, 1998) 97–122.

9. See John Crawford Adams, *Shakespeare's Physic* (London: Royal Society of Medicine Press, 1989), 59–60.

10. Pierre Boaistuau, *Theatrum Mundi, The Theatre or rule of the world, wherein may be sene the running race and course of euerye mans life, as touching miserie and felicity . . .*

*whereunto is added a learned, and maruellous worke of the ex-
cellencie of mankinde. Written in the Frenche/Latin tongues by
P. Boaystuau, and translated into English by Iohn Alday* (London: Printed by Henry Bynneman for Thomas Hacket, 1574),
213. See Ruth E. Sims, "The Green Old Age of Falstaff," *Bulletin of the History of Medicine* 13 (1943): 144–47. For a recent
overview of the literature on this topic see David Womersley,
"Why Is Falstaff Fat?" *Review of English Studies* 47 (1996): 1–
22. See also Saul Jarcho, "Falstaff, Kittredge, and Galen," *Perspectives in Biology and Medicine* 39 (1987): 197–200. In general on Falstaff see J. Dover Wilson, *The Fortunes of Falstaff*
(Cambridge: Cambridge University Press, 1979).

11. Henry Cuffe, *The Differences of the ages of mans life together with the originall causes, and end thereof* (London:
Printed by Arnold Hatfield for Martin Clearke, 1607), 113.

12. See Greg W. Bentley, *Shakespeare and the New Disease:
The Dramatic Function of Syphilis in* Troilus and Cressida,
Measure for Measure, *and* Timon of Athens (New York: Peter
Lang, 1989), 27.

13. See Laura Keyes, "Hamlet's Fat," in *Shakespeare and
the Triple Play: From Study to Stage to Classroom*, ed. Sidney
Homan (Lewisburg PA: Bucknell University Press, 1988), 89–
104; Greg W. Bentley, "Melancholy, Madness, and Syphilis in
Hamlet," *Hamlet Studies: An International Journal of Research on* The Tragedie of Hamlet, Prince of Denmarke 6
(1984): 75–80.

14. Quoted in Bentley, *Shakespeare and the New Disease*, 27.

15. Ernst Kretschmer, *Körperbau und Charakter* (Berlin:
Springer, 1921).

16. Leonard Lessius, *Hygiasticon; Or, the Right Course of
Preserving Life and Health unto extream old Age* (Cambridge:
Printers of the Universitie of Cambridge, 1636), 16. Subse-
quent references to this edition will appear in the text. This

volume also contains a contemporary translation of Cornaro's texts.

17. Burton, *The Anatomy of Melancholy*, 1:2, 376, citing Botaldus.

18. *Fracastoro's Syphilis*, ed. and trans. Geoffrey Eatough (Liverpool: Francis Cairns, 1984), 65. See also Bruce Thomas Boehrer, "Early Modern Syphilis," *Journal of the History of Sexuality* 1 (1990): 197–214.

19. On Falstaff and the medical theory of his day see John M. Steadman, "Falstaff's 'Facies Hippocrita': A Note on Shakespeare and Renaissance Medical Theory," *Studia Neophilogica* 29 (1957): 130–35; and R. F. Fleissner, "Putting Falstaff to Rest: 'Tabulating' the Facts," *Shakespeare Studies* 16 (1983): 57–70.

20. La Fontaine, "Le Tableau," in *Oeuvres*, ed. Henri de Régnier (Paris: Enoch frères snf Costallat, 1883–92), 5:587, 1:86.

21. Wendy Gibson, "Attitudes towards Obesity in Seventeenth-Century France," *Seventeenth-Century French Studies* 13 (1991): 215–29, here 220.

22. See John Crawford Adams, *Shakespeare's Physic*, 158–83.

23. Quoted from D. J. Enright, ed., *Ill at Ease: Writers on Ailments Real and Imagined* (London: Faber and Faber, 1989), 4–5. See also Michael Schoenfeldt, *Bodies and Selves in Early Modern England: Physiology and Inwardness in Spenser, Shakespeare, Herbert, and Milton* (Cambridge: Cambridge University Press, 1999); Michael Schoenfeldt, " 'That Spectacle of Too Much Weight': The Poetics of Sacrifice in Donne, Herbert, and Milton," *Journal of Medieval and Early Modern Studies* 31 (2001): 561–84.

24. Francis Toye, *Giuseppe Verdi: His Life and Works* (New York: Horizon, 1983), 234.

25. Cited in *"Falstaff," commedia lirica in tre atti di Arrigo Boito, musica di Guiseppe Verdi* (Milan: Ricordi, [1893]), 48. See also James A. Hepokoski, *Guiseppe Verdi: "Falstaff"* (Cambridge: Cambridge University Press, 1983), 138–44; Julian Budden, "Falstaff: Verdi e Shakespeare," in *Falstaff: Città de Parma, Teatro Regio (Stagioni lirica, 1994–1995)* (Parma: Teatro Regio, 1994–95), 41–47.

26. Noorden, *Die Fettsucht*, 65–72, 110–11.

27. See here the recent discussion by Emanuele Senici, "Verdi's *Falstaff* in Italy's Fin de Siècle," *The Musical Quarterly* 85 (2001): 274–311; on Wagner see 299–302.

28. All references are to the score: Giuseppe Verdi, *Falstaff* (1893; reprint, New York: Dover, 1980), here 47–50. Subsequent references will appear in the text.

29. Patricia Parker, *Literary Fat Ladies: Rhetoric, Gender, Property* (London and New York: Methuen, 1987), 14.

30. Conrad Rieger, *Die Castration in rechtlicher, socialer und vitaler Hinsicht* (Jena: Gustav Fischer, 1900), 106.

31. Richard Krafft-Ebing, *Psychopathia sexualis*, trans. Harry E. Wedeck (New York: G. P. Putnam, 1965), 68–69.

32. See Sander L. Gilman, "Love + Marriage = Death," in *Sex Positives? The Cultural Politics of Dissident Sexualities*, ed. Thomas Foster, Carol Siegel, and Ellen E. Berry (New York and London: New York University Press, 1997), 197–224.

33. Emil Kraepelin, *Psychiatrie: Ein Lehrbuch für Studierende und Ärtze*, 8th ed. (Leipzig: Johannes Ambrosius Barth, 1910), 2.1:392–94. Subsequent references will appear in the text.

34. Luigi Galvani, *De Viribus Electricitatus in Motu Musculari Commentarius*, trans. Robert Montraville Green (Cambridge MA: Elizabeth Licht, 1953), 75.

35. Albert von Haller, *First Lines of Physiology*, trans. Wil-

liam Cullen (1786; reprint, New York: Johnson Reprints, 1966).

36. Cesare Taruffi, *Hermaphrodismus und Zeugungsunfähigkeit: Eine systematische Darstellung des Missbildungen der menschlichen Geschlechtsorgane*, trans. R. Teuscher (Berlin: H. Barsdorf, 1903), 96–103.

37. Taruffi, *Hermaphrodismus und Zeugungsunfähigkeit*, 97.

38. Ferdinand-Valére Faneau de la Cour, *Du Féminisme et de l'infantilisme chez les tuberculeux* (Paris: A. Parent, 1871).

39. Henri Meige, "L'Infantilisme, féminisme, et les hérmaphrodites antiques," *L'Anthropologie* 15 (1895): 257–64.

40. Wilhelm Ebstein, *Die Fettleibigkeit (Corpulenz) und ihre Behandlung nach physiologischen Grundstätzen*, 6th ed. (Wiesbaden: J. F. Bergmann, 1884), 2, cited in *Corpulence and Its Treatment on Physiological Principles*, trans. A. H. Keane (London: H. Grevel, 1884), 9. Subsequent references to the translated edition will appear in the text.

41. Max von Gruber, *Hygiene of Sex* (Baltimore: Williams and Wilkins, 1926), 82.

42. Hilde Bruch, "Psychiatric Aspects of Obesity in Children," *American Journal of Psychiatry* (March 1943): 752–57. Subsequent references will appear in the text. The follow-up study to this is Flemming Quaade, *Obese Children: Anthropology and Environment* (Copenhagen: Danish Science Press, 1955). It is answered by Julius Bauer's claim that Bruch's children all showed genetic anomalies; see Bauer's "Some Conclusions from Observations on Obese Children," *Archives of Pediatrics* 57 (1940): 631–40.

43. See Leonid Kotkin's *Eat, Think, and Be Slender* (New York: Hawthorn, 1954; Blackpool: A. Thomas, 1955), which argues that obesity is a form of neurosis.

44. The physiological explanation is argued by Israel

Bram, "Psychic Factors in Obesity," *Archives of Pediatrics* 67 (1950): 543–52, here 543–44.

45. Bruch, *The Importance of Overweight*, 35.

46. John S. Sullivan, "The Medical History of Shakespeare's Sir John Falstaff," *Medical Heritage* 2 (1986): 391–401. Subsequent references will appear in the text.

47. Alvin Rodin and Jack Key, "Falstaff's Obesity," *Ohio Medicine* 86 (1990): 222.

48. Abraham Verghese, "The 'Typhoid State' Revisited," *American Journal of Medicine* 79 (1985): 370–72.

49. Herbert S. Donow, " 'To Everything There Is a Season': Some Shakespearean Models of Normal and Anomalous Aging," *Gerontologist* 32 (1992): 733–38, here 736.

50. Henry Buchwald and Mary E. Knatterud, "Morbid Obesity: Perceptions of Character and Comorbidities in Falstaff," *Obesity Surgery* 10 (2000): 402–8.

51. Jack J. Adler, "Did Falstaff Have the Sleep-Apnea Syndrome?" *New England Journal of Medicine* 308 (1983): 404.

52. K. Tjoorstad, "Pickwick-syndromet. Fra litteraere spekulasjoner til sovnforskning," *Tidsskr Nor Laegeforen* 115 (1995): 3768–72; Uwe Henrik Peters, *Das Pickwick-Syndrom: Schlafänfalle und Periodenatmung bei Adiposen* (München: Urban und Schwarzenberg, 1976). See also C. Sidney Burwell, Eugene D. Robin, Robert D. Whaley, and Albert G. Bickelman, "Extreme Obesity Associated with Alveolar Hypoventilation: A Pickwickian Syndrome," *American Journal of Medicine* 21 (1956): 811–18.

53. On naming in medicine see Charles E. Rosenberg and Janet Golden, eds., *Framing Disease: Studies in Cultural History* (New Brunswick: Rutgers University Press, 1992).

54. Juliet McMaster, *Dickens the Designer* (Totowa NJ: Barnes and Noble, 1987), 25, 88. Subsequent references will appear in the text.

55. Thomas Love Peacock, *Nightmare Abbey [and] Crotchet Castle*, ed. Raymond Wright (1831; Harmondsworth: Penguin, 1986), 364. See also Douglas Hewitt, "Entertaining Ideas: A Critique of Peacock's 'Crotchet Castle,' " *Essays in Criticism* 20 (1971): 200–212; James Mulvihill, "Peacock's *Crotchet Castle*: Reconciling the Spirits of the Age," *Nineteenth-Century Fiction* 38 (1983): 253–70.

56. Jukes, *On Indigestion and Costiveness*, 287. Subsequent references will appear in the text.

57. Charles Dickens, *The Pickwick Papers*, ed. James Kinsley (Oxford: Clarendon Press, 1986), 61.

58. Wadd, *Comments on Corpulency*, 53.

59. John Tosh, *A Man's Place: Masculinity and the Middle-Class Home in Victorian England* (New Haven: Yale University Press, 1999), 4.

60. Louis Robinson, "Darwinism in the Nursery," *Nineteenth Century* 30 (1891): 831.

61. "The Evolution of Fatness," *Punch*, 25 March 1903, 203.

62. Yiying Zhang, Ricardo Proenca, Margherita Maffei, Marisa Barone, Lori Leopold, and Jeffrey M. Friedman, "Positional Cloning of the Mouse Obese Gene and Its Human Homologue," *Nature* 372 (1994): 425–31. This is a key paper for any further research in this field because it specifies the exact code of this gene. Its central importance and credibility in this particular field of research stem from the fact that any researcher wanting to study this gene in *ob* mice must have information about the gene itself. Knowing the exact code allows hypotheses to be set up about whether the physiological problem is a defect in the protein that the *ob* gene makes or perhaps a defective receptor of *ob*. In this case, as subsequent studies were able to confirm, there are in fact multiple ways of having an obese phenotype (i.e., a fat mouse). In some cases the *ob*

gene itself is defective, and in others the receptor gene (a different one, called *db*) is defective. Of course, other genes entirely can also cause obesity. Zhang et al.'s paper is the starting point for any closer examination of what the gene products resulting in obesity are and how they interact. The paper is credible as the techniques used to determine this sequence were based on a standard, universally accepted genetic method for finding genes. This standard method is as follows: first, recombination studies are done. This means that researchers allow mice to breed in large numbers and then look for inheritance patterns that do not necessarily follow Mendelian patterns. By comparing numbers of fat to lean offspring in relation to some other genetically related trait (molecular markers), it is possible to determine approximately where on a chromosome (and on which chromosome) a mutation is. The chromosome and the gene's approximate location were already known to Zhang et al. The next step is to continue to narrow down where on the chromosome a particular gene (here *ob*) is by comparing it to other genes close to it (by making a genetic map, which gets increasingly specific). After this researchers have a very small (comparatively) region of DNA that they know contains the gene. By insetting the region via recombinant techniques in bacteria and growing them, they can see which parts are expressed and are therefore part of the gene. Furthermore, the sequences are compared to standard DNA libraries to see if homology to other genes exists. In the case of Zhang et al. this technique worked because the product of the gene, a protein called Leptin, was already known, so researchers only had to compare the region of DNA and its putative gene product to the protein Leptin to see whether they had the right region. These methods are entirely standard, and there is no reason to doubt the report's veracity. Thus, not

276

only is this paper central because it is entirely within the bounds of standard genetic research, but it is also the starting point for any further work. However, its genetic credibility does not absolve its scientific weaknesses, namely that it equates obesity with bad health and considers obesity the cause rather than the symptom of other illnesses.

63. Ellen Ruppel Shell, *The Hungry Gene: The Science of Fat and the Future of Thin* (New York: Atlantic Monthly Press, 2001).

64. Wadd, *Comments on Corpulency*, 131–36.

65. Johannes Joachim Becher, *Medicinische Schatz-Kammer* (Leipzig: Christoff Hülsen, 1700).

66. A. Stayt Dutton, *The National Physique* (London: Baillière, Tindall, and Cox, 1908), 64–65.

67. Alexandra Minna Stern, "Beauty Is Not Always Better: Perfect Babies and the Tyranny of Pediatric Norms," *Patterns of Prejudice* 36 (2002): 68–78.

68. The debate between Hilde Bruch (neurosis) and Israel Bram (metabolic error) is typical. They both agree that fat babies are ill but only differ on why. See Bruch, "Psychiatric Aspects of Obesity in Children," 752–57; and Israel Bram, "The Fat Youngster," *Archives of Pediatrics* 40 (1943): 239–49.

69. William Golding, *Lord of the Flies* (New York: Berkley, 1954), 180. Subsequent references will appear in the text.

70. Derrick Brian and E. F. Jelliffe, "Fat Babies: Prevalence, Perils, and Prevention," *Journal of Pediatrics* 21 (1975): 123–59.

71. Lise Belkin, "Watching Her Weight," *New York Times Magazine*, 8 July 2001, 30–33.

72. P. Potvliege, "Le Syndrome 'de Pickwick': Priorité de sa description par le duc de Saint-Simon (1675–1755)," *Nouvelle Presse Médicale* 11 (1982): 2360.

73. Hilde Bruch, *Eating Disorders: Obesity, Anorexia Nervosa, and the Person Within* (London: Routledge and Kegan Paul, 1974), 137. Subsequent references will appear in the text.

74. R. P. Junghans, "Falstaff Was Drunker Than He Was Fat," *New England Journal of Medicine* 308 (1983): 1483.

4. HOW FAT DETECTIVES THINK

1. Steven Shapin, "The Philosopher and the Chicken: On the Dietetics of Disembodied Knowledge," in *Science Incarnate: Historical Embodiments of Natural Knowledge*, ed. Steven Shapin and Christopher Lawrence (Chicago: University of Chicago Press, 1998), 21–50.

2. Marsilio Ficino, *Three Books on Life*, ed. and trans. Carol V. Kaske and John R. Clark (Binghamton NY: The Renaissance Society of America, 1989), 109.

3. See the two basic studies by Irving Kenneth Zola, "The Portrayal of Disability in the Crime Mystery Genre," *Social Policy* 17 (1987): 34–39, and the longer essay " 'Any Distinguishing Features?': The Portrayal of Disability in the Crime-Mystery Genre," *Policy Studies Journal* 15 (1987): 485–513. See also Nancy Harrowitz, "The Body of the Detective Model: Charles S. Peirce and Edgar Allan Poe," in *The Sign of Three: Dupin, Holmes, Peirce*, ed. Umberto Eco and Thomas A. Sebeok (Bloomington: Indiana University Press, 1983), 179–97.

4. David R. Anderson, *Rex Stout* (New York: Frederick Ungar, 1984), 113.

5. Michel Foucault, *The Use of Pleasure*, trans. Robert Hurley (New York: Vintage, 1990), 86–87.

6. Gerhart von Graevenitz, "Der Dicke im schlafenden Krieg: Zu einer Figur der europäischen Moderne bei Wilhelm Raabe," *Jahrbuch der Raabe-Gesellschaft* (1990): 1–21; Konstantin Imm and Joachim Linder, "Verdächtige und Täter: Zuschreibung und Kriminalität in Texten der 'schönen Lit-

eratur' am Beispiel des Feuilletons der Berliner *Gerichts-Zeitung*, der Romanreiche *Eisenbahn-Unterhaltungen* und Wilhelm Raabes *Horacker* und *Stopfkuchen*," in *Zur Sozialgeschichte der deutschen Literatur von der Aufklärung bis zur Jahrhundertwende*, ed. Günter Hantzschel and John Ormrod (Tübingen: Niemeyer, 1985), 21–96.

7. Wilhelm Raabe, *Novels*, ed. Volkmar Sander, trans. Barker Fairly (New York: Continuum, 1983), 174. Subsequent references will appear in the text.

8. Hubert Ohl, "Eduards Heimkehr oder Le Vaillant und des Riesenfaultier: Zu Wilhelm Raabes *Stopfkuchen*," *Jahrbuch der Deutschen Schiller-Gesellschaft* 8 (1964): 247–79.

9. H. R. Klieneberger, *The Novel in England and Germany: A Comparative Study Source* (London: Wolff, 1981), and "Charles Dickens and Wilhelm Raabe," *Oxford German Studies* 4 (1969): 90–117.

10. James Joyce, *Ulysses*, ed. Hans Walter Gabler (New York: Random House, 1986), 154. See also Zack Bowen, "Joyce's Endomorphic Encomia," *James Joyce Quarterly* 34 (1997): 259–65.

11. "An Eye-Witness," in *Readings on the Character of Hamlet, 1661–1947*, ed. Claude C. H. Williamson (London: Allen, 1950), 55.

12. Ferdinand Freiligrath, "Hamlet," in *Freiligraths Werke in einem Band* (Berlin: Aufbau, 1967), 73–75 (my translation).

13. Gottfried Benn, *Gedichte* (Frankfurt: Fischer, 1982), 47 (my translation).

14. Theodor Adorno, "Reconciliation under Duress," in *Aesthetics and Politics*, ed. Frederic Jameson (New York: Verso, 1980), 170.

15. D. F. Rauber, "Sherlock Holmes and Nero Wolfe: The Role of the 'Great Detective' in Intellectual History," *Journal of Popular Culture* 6 (1972): 483–95.

16. James D. Smead, "The Landscape of Modernity: Rationality and the Detective," in *Digging into Popular Culture: Theories and Methodologies in Archeology, Anthropology, and Other Fields*, ed. Ray B. Browne and Pat Browne (Bowling Green OH: Popular, 1991), 165–71.

17. Duke, *Banting in India*, 55.

18. Ronald R. Thomas, "Minding the Body Politic: The Romance of Science and the Revision of History in Victorian Detective Fiction," *Victorian Literature and Culture* 19 (1991): 233–54.

19. Thomas M. Sobottke, "Speculations on the Further Career of Mycroft Holmes," *The Baker Street Journal* 2 (1990): 75–77; Robert S. Pasley, "The Greek Interpreter Interpreted: A Revisionist Essay," *The Baker Street Journal* 35 (1985): 106–11; Bruce R. Beaman, "Mycroft Holmes, Agoraphobe," *The Baker Street Journal* 26 (1976): 91–93; William W. Propp, "A Study in Similarity: Mycroft Holmes and C. Auguste Dupin," *The Baker Street Journal* 28 (1978): 32–35.

20. *The Original Illustrated Sherlock Holmes* (New York: Castle, n.d.), 294. This is a facsimile edition of the serial publication of the Holmes stories. Subsequent references will appear in the text.

21. Heta Pyrönen, *Mayhem and Murder: Narrative and Moral Problems in the Detective Story* (Toronto: University of Toronto Press, 1999), 31–64.

22. Vance Thompson, *Eat and Grow Thin* (New York: Dutton, 1914), 17.

23. Wilkie Collins, *The Woman in White*, ed. John Sutherland (Oxford: Oxford University Press, 1996). Subsequent references will appear in the text.

24. Brillat-Savarin, *The Physiology of Taste*, 243–44.

25. Joseph Conrad, *The Secret Agent* (New York: Penguin, 1996). Subsequent references will appear in the text.

26. *Original Illustrated Sherlock Holmes*, 143. See also Brian McKinley, "Free Love and Domesticity: Lizzie M. Holmes, Hagar Lyndon (1893), and the Anarchist-Feminist Imagination," *Journal of American Culture* 13 (1990): 55–62.

27. Dashiell Hammett, *Complete Novels*, ed. Steven Marcus (New York: Library of America, 1999), 480.

28. On the history of myelin see especially Edwin Clarke and C. D. O'Malley, *The Human Brain and Spinal Cord: A Historical Study Illustrated by Writings from Antiquity to the Twentieth Century*, 2d ed. (San Francisco: Norman, 1996). See also F. Wohlrab and U. Henoch, "Carl Weigert (1845–1904) in Leipzig, 1878–1885," *Zentralblatt für Allgemeine Pathologie* 138 (1988): 743–51; M. Bessis and G. Delpech, "Sickle Cell Shape and Structure: Images and Concepts (1840–1980)," *Blood Cells* 8 (1982): 359–435; W. Stoeckenius, "From Membrane Structure to Bacteriorhodopsin," *Journal of Membrane Biology* 139 (1994): 139–48; L. C. Mokrasch, "Myelin. I. Historical Introduction," *Neuroscience Research Program Bulletin* 9 (1971): 445–51.

29. Two excellent studies that show the relationship between literary narratives and theories of nervousness are Peter Melville Logan, *Nerves and Narrative: A Cultural History of Hysteria in Nineteenth-Century British Prose* (Berkeley: University of California Press, 1997); and Janet Oppenheim, *"Shattered Nerves": Doctors, Patients, and Depression in Victorian England* (New York: Oxford University Press, 1991).

30. Cited in Daniel Boyarin, "The Great Fat Massacre: Sex, Death, and the Grotesque Body in the Talmud," in *People of the Body: Jews and Judaism from an Embodied Perspective*,

ed. Howard Eilberg-Schwartz (Albany: State University of New York Press, 1993), 69–100; here 88. I am using Boyarin's rather contemporary translation.

31. Clarke and O'Malley, *The Human Brain and Spinal Cord*, 46–52.

32. Timothy O. Lipman, "Vitalism and Reductionism in Justus von Liebig's Physiological Thought," *Isis* 58 (1967): 167–85; K. Y. Guggenheim, "Johannes Müller and Justus Liebig on Nutrition," *Koroth* 8 (1985): 66–76.

33. Jameson, *Essays on the Changes of the Human Body*, 91. This is very much in line with the older view that fat combats melancholy. See *Laugh and Be Fat: Or, an Antidote against Melancholy* (London: Printed by A. W. for A. Bettesworth, 1724).

34. Clarke and O'Malley, *The Human Brain and Spinal Cord*, 78–80.

35. German E. Berrios and J. I. Quemada, "Multiple Sclerosis," in *A History of Clinical Psychiatry: The Origin and History of Psychiatric Disorders*, ed. German E. Berrios and Roy Porter (New York: New York University Press, 1995), 174–92.

36. Clarke and O'Malley, *The Human Brain and Spinal Cord*, 845–48.

37. Clarke and O'Malley, *The Human Brain and Spinal Cord*, 547–53.

38. Eric L. Santner, *My Own Private Germany: Daniel Paul Schreber's Secret History of Modernity* (Princeton: Princeton University Press, 1996), 70–77.

39. Sigmund Freud, *Standard Edition of the Complete Psychological Works of Sigmund Freud*, ed. and trans. J. Strachey, A. Freud, A. Strachey, and A. Tyson (London: Hogarth, 1955–74), 1:299–300. Subsequent references will appear in the text.

40. Mitchell, *Fat and Blood and How to Make Them*, 15. Subsequent references will appear in the text. See also Barbara Will, "Nervous Systems, 1880–1915," in *American Bodies*, ed. Tim Armstrong (New York: New York University Press, 1996), 86–100.

41. Martha J. Cutter, "The Writer as Doctor: New Models of Medical Discourse in Charlotte Perkins Gilman's Later Fiction," *Literature and Medicine* 20 (2001): 151–82.

42. D. Rang, *Pharmacology* (London: Churchill Livingstone, 1995), 105.

43. On Father Brown and Sherlock Holmes see Owen Dudley Edwards, "The Immortality of Father Brown," *The Chesterton Review* 15 (1989): 295–325; Walter Raubicheck, "Father Brown and the 'Performance' of Crime," *The Chesterton Review* 19 (1993): 39–45.

44. Frederick Isaac, "Enter the Fat Man: Rex Stout's *Fer-de-Lance*," in *In the Beginning: First Novels in Mystery Series*, ed. Mary Jean DeMarr (Bowling Green OH: Popular, 1995), 59–68. See also Mia I. Gerhardt, " 'Homicide West': Some Observations on the Nero Wolfe Stories of Rex Stout," *English Studies* 49 (1968): 107–27.

45. John McAleer, *Rex Stout: A Biography* (Boston: Little, Brown, 1977), 552.

46. Rex Stout, *Fer-De-Lance* (1934; reprint, New York: Bantam, 1984), 2.

47. Stout, *Fer-De-Lance*, 2.

48. Stout, *Fer-De-Lance*, 164.

49. Rex Stout, *Over My Dead Body* (1939; reprint, New York: Bantam Books, 1994), 119.

50. David R. Anderson, *Rex Stout*, 23.

51. Maud Ellmann, *The Hunger Artists: Starving, Writing, and Imprisonment* (Cambridge: Harvard University Press, 1993).

52. Franz Kafka, *The Diaries, 1910–1913*, ed. Max Brod, trans. Joseph Kresh (New York: Schocken, 1948), 160.

53. Stout, *Fer-De-Lance*, 4–5.

54. Rex Stout, *Not Quite Dead Enough* (1944; reprint, New York: Bantam Books, 1992), 13.

55. Stout, *Not Quite Dead Enough*, 81.

56. Rex Stout, *In the Best of Families* (1950; reprint, New York: Bantam, 1993), 142. See also Neil Brooks, "Not Just a Family Affair: Questioning Critical and Generic Orthodoxies through the Nero Wolfe Mysteries," *Clues* 20 (1999): 121–38.

57. *Orson Welles: Interviews*, ed. Mark W. Estrin (Oxford: University Press of Mississippi, 2002), 34.

58. Jerry Mosher, "Setting Free the Bears: Refiguring Fat Men on Television," in *Bodies out of Bounds: Fatness and Transgression*, ed. Jana Evans Braziel and Kathleen LeBesco (Berkeley: University of California Press, 2001), 166–93.

59. Tom Gunning, "Tracing the Individual Body: Photography, Detectives, and Early Cinema," in *Cinema and the Invention of Modern Life*, ed. Leo Charney and Vanessa R. Schwartz (Berkeley: University of California Press, 1995), 15–45.

60. One can note that there is a fat female detective in Barbara Neely's *Blanche* series from the 1980s. She is a black detective of large proportions.

61. Rachel Adams, " 'Fat Man Walking': Masculinity and Racial Geographies in James Mangold's *Copland*," *Camera Obscura* 42 (1999): 5–28, here 9.

62. Lynda Gorov, "Sly Remakes Himself," *The Boston Globe*, 10 August 1997, N1.

63. Gorov, "Sly Remakes Himself," N1.

64. Scott Adams, *Bring Me the Head of Willy the Mailboy!* (Kansas City: Andrews and McMeel, 1995), 82.

5. FAT BALLPLAYERS AND THE BODIES OF FAT MEN

1. M. E. Chryssafis, "La Médicine sportive chez Hippocrate," in *II. Internationaler Sportärzte-Kongress Berlin 1936*, ed. A. Mallwitz (Leipzig: Georg Thieme, 1937), 229–31, here 230. See more recently Jack W. Berryman, ed., *Sport, Exercise, and American Medicine, Journal of Sport History* 14.1 (1987; special issue).

2. Wadd, *Comments on Corpulency*, 48.

3. J. G. P. Williams, "Nutrition and the Athlete," in *Sports Medicine* (London: Edward Arnold, 1962), 332–44, here 332.

4. W. E. Tucker, "Fitness and Training," in *Injury in Sport*, ed. J. R. Armstrong and W. E. Tucker (London: Staples, 1964), 82–93, here 83.

5. Thomas Dutton, *Indigestion Clearly Explained, Treated, and Dieted* (London: Henry Kimpton, 1892), 77.

6. Greg R. McLathie, "Diet in Sport," in *Essentials of Sports Medicine* (Edinburgh: Churchill Livingston, 1986), 48–59, here 56.

7. "American College of Sports Medicine Roundtable: Physical Activity in the Prevention and Treatment of Obesity and Its Comorbidities," *Medicine and Science in Sports and Exercise* 31 (1999; supplement): 497–667.

8. Jan Jarvis, "Obesity Epidemic for Children Brings Pain of Diseases, Social Stigma," *Fort Worth Star-Telegram*, 3 May 2002.

9. Philip M. Teigen, "Sore Arms and Selective Memories: Alexander H. P. Leuf and the Beginning of Baseball Medicine," *Journal of the History of Medicine and Allied Sciences* 50 (1995): 391–408. On pitching injuries see Alexander H. P. Leuf, *Hygiene for Base Ball Players: Being a Brief Consideration of the Body as Mechanism, the Art and Science of Curve Pitching, a Discussion of the Causes and Treatment of the Dis-*

abilities of the Players, with a Few Practical Hints to Club Managers (Philadelphia: A. J. Reach, 1888). Leuf advocates galvanism for muscle injuries. He was director of physical education at the University of Pennsylvania in 1888. Only after World War I was there a resurgence of interest in medicine and baseball.

10. Quoted in John G. Robertson, *The Babe Chases Sixty* (Jefferson NC: McFarland, 1999), 161.

11. Marshall Smelser, *The Life That Ruth Built: A Biography* (New York: Quadrangle/New York Times Books, 1975), 135.

12. Smelser, *The Life That Ruth Built*, 171.

13. Brother Gilbert, *Young Babe Ruth*, ed. Harry Rothgerber (Jefferson NC: McFarland, 1999), 32.

14. Smelser, *The Life That Ruth Built*, 134.

15. Robert W. Creamer, *Babe: The Legend Comes to Life* (New York: Penguin, 1974), 21.

16. Michael Oriard, *Dreaming of Heroes: American Sports Fiction, 1869–1980* (Chicago: Nelson-Hall, 1982), 128.

17. Creamer, *Babe*, 320.

18. Geoffrey C. Ward and Ken Burns, *Baseball: An Illustrated History* (New York: A. A. Knopf, 1994), 155.

19. Creamer, *Babe*, 321–22.

20. Creamer, *Babe*, 21.

21. Jimmy Powers, *Baseball Personalities* (New York: Rudolf Field, 1949), 113.

22. Alfred H. Fuchs, "Psychology and the 'Babe,'" *The Journal of the History of the Behavioral Sciences* 35 (1998): 153–65.

23. Hugh S. Fullerton, "Why Babe Ruth Is the Greatest Home-Run Hitter," *Popular Science Monthly* 99 (1921): 19–21, 110, here 110.

24. On Babe Ruth's health see A. Voisin, D. B. Elliott, and

D. Regan, "Babe Ruth: With Vision Like That, How Could He Hit the Ball?" *Optometry and Vision Science* 74 (1997): 144–46. See David A. Goss, "Babe Ruth Did Not Have Amblyopia When He Played Baseball," *Hindsight* 30 (1999): 11–13, on Ruth's amblyopia.

25. Smelser, *The Life That Ruth Built*, 304–7.

26. *New York Times*, 15 January 1926, 24.

27. *New York Times*, 18 January 1926, 19.

28. George Herman Ruth, *Babe Ruth's Own Book of Baseball* (1928; reprint, Lincoln: University of Nebraska Press, 1992), 276. Subsequent references will appear in the text.

29. Creamer, *Babe*, 324.

30. See N. B. Bikhazi, A. M. Kramer, J. H. Spiegel, and M. I. Singer, "Babe Ruth's Illness and Its Impact on Medical History," *Laryngoscope* 109 (1999): 1–3, on Ruth's nasopharyngeal neoplasms.

31. Roger Ebert, "The Babe," *Chicago Sun-Times*, 17 April 1992, 24.

32. Jack Scher, "Lou Gehrig: The Man and the Legend," in *Twelve Sport Immortals*, ed. Ernest V. Heyn (New York: Bartholomew, 1949), 9–32, here 18. Subsequent references will appear in the text.

33. Ray Robinson, *Iron Horse: Lou Gehrig in His Time* (New York: Norton, 1990), 37.

34. Edward J. Kasarskis and Mary Winslow, "When Did Lou Gehrig's Personal Illness Begin?" *Neurology* 39 (1989): 1243–45. See also Harold L. Klawans, *Why Michael Couldn't Hit: And Other Tales of the Neurology of Sports* (New York: W. H. Freeman, 1996).

35. Dana Cavicke and J. Patrick O'Leary, "Lou Gehrig's Death," *American Surgeon* 67 (2001): 393–95, here 395.

36. Robinson, *Iron Horse*, 259.

37. R. G. Cutler, W. A. Pedersen, S. Camandola, J. D.

Rothstein, and M. P. Mattson, "Evidence That Accumulation of Ceramides and Cholesterol Esters Mediates Oxidative Stress-Induced Death of Motor Neurons in Amyotrophic Lateral Sclerosis," *Annals of Neurology* 52.4 (2002): 448–57.

38. N. Scarmeas, T. Shih, Y. Stern, R. Ottman, and L. P. Rowland, "Premorbid Weight, Body Mass, and Varsity Athletics in ALS," *Neurology* 59.5 (2002): 773–75.

39. Tom Verducci, "A Farewell to Skinny Arms," *Sports Illustrated*, 23 March 1998, 67–71.

40. Lydia Hamburg and Terence M. Hines, "Correlations for Weight, Height, and Two Measures of Batting Performance," *Perceptual and Motor Skills* 88 (1999): 466–68.

41. Albert Reibmeyer, *Kurze Anleitung zur mechanisch-physikalischen Behandlung der Fettleibigkeit* (Leipzig: Franz Deuticke, 1890), 27–34.

42. Mark Harris, *Bang the Drum Slowly* (New York: Alfred A. Knopf, 1956). Subsequent references will appear in the text. See C. Kenneth Pellow, "Baseball in Fiction and Film: Mark Harris's *Bang the Drum Slowly,*" *Arete: The Journal of Sport Literature* 4 (1987): 57–67; Robert Cochran, "Bang the Drum Differently: The Southpaw Slants of Henry Wiggen," *Modern Fiction Studies* 33 (1987): 151–59.

43. Douglass Wallop, *Damn Yankees* (New York: Norton, 1984); published as *The Year the Yankees Lost the Pennant* in 1954. Subsequent references will appear in the text. On baseball fiction see also David McGimpsey, *Imagining Baseball: America's Pastime and Popular Culture* (Bloomington: Indiana University Press, 2000); Timothy Morris, *Making the Team: The Cultural Work of Baseball Fiction* (Urbana: University of Illinois Press, 1997); Deeanne Westbrook, *Ground Rules: Baseball and Myth* (Urbana: University of Illinois Press, 1996).

44. Quoted by Edward G. White, *Creating the National Pastime* (Princeton: Princeton University Press, 1996), 258.

45. John R. Tunis, *Keystone Kids* (New York: Harcourt, Brace, and Company, 1943). Subsequent references will appear in the text.

46. Anatole Leroy-Beaulieu, *Israel among the Nations: A Study of the Jews and Antisemitism*, trans. Frances Hellman (New York: G. P. Putnam's Sons, 1895), 258. First published as Anatole Leroy-Beaulieu, i.e., Henry Jean Baptiste Anatole, *(Les) Juifs et l'antisémitisme: Israël chez les nations* (Paris: Lévy, 1893). See also Sander L. Gilman, *The Jew's Body* (New York: Routledge, 1991).

47. Irwin Shaw, *Voices of a Summer Day* (New York: Dial, 1965), 69–72. Subsequent references will appear in the text.

48. On what it meant to be one of the first (and the most prominent) Jews in baseball of the day see Hank Greenberg, *The Story of My Life*, ed. Ira Berkow (New York: Times Books, 1989), 22–23, 44–45, 56–61.

49. Philip Roth, *American Pastoral* (Boston: Houghton Mifflin, 1997). Subsequent references will appear in the text.

50. Ernest Hemingway, *The Sun Also Rises* (New York: Charles Scribner's Sons, 1954), 4. See Michael S. Reynolds, The Sun Also Rises: *A Novel of the Twenties* (Boston: Twayne Publishers, 1995).

51. Philip Roth, *The Great American Novel* (New York: Holt, Rinehart, and Winston, 1973), 110. Subsequent references will appear in the text. See Kerry Ahearn, " 'Et in arcadia excrementum': Pastoral, Kitsch, and Philip Roth's *The Great American Novel*," *Aethlon* 11 (1993): 1–14.

52. Bernard Malamud, *The Natural* (1952; reprint, New York: Perennial Classics, 2000). Subsequent references will appear in the text. See Gerry O'Connor, "Bernard Malamud's

The Natural: 'The Worst That Ever Was in the Game,'" *Arete* 3 (1986): 37–42; Patrick Keats, "Hall of Famer Ed Delehanty: A Source of Malamud's *The Natural*," *American Literature* 62 (1990): 102–4; Kathleen Sullivan Porter, "Women as 'Goddess' Archetypes in Baseball Fiction," *Aethlon* 15 (1997): 63–70.

53. Ruth Tarson, "*The Natural*: The Movie about Robert Redford, and God, and Baseball, and What If the World Were Flat," *Aethlon* 4 (1997): 17–20.

54. Garrison Keillor, "Herb Johnson, the God of Canton," in *The Book of Guys* (New York: Viking Penguin, 1993), 213–23. Subsequent references will appear in the text.

55. Kretschmer, *Körperbau und Charakter.*

56. Davydd J. Greenwood, *Taming of Evolution: The Persistence of Non-evolutionary Views in the Study of Humans* (Ithaca: Cornell University Press, 1984); Stephen H. Gatlin, "William H. Sheldon and the Culture of the Somatotype" (Ph.D. diss., Virginia Polytechnic Institute and State University, 1997).

57. W. H. Auden, *Nones* (New York: Random House, 1951), 63.

58. Sante Naccarati and H. E. Garrett, "The Relation of Morphology to Temperament," *Journal of Abnormal and Social Psychology* 19 (1924): 254–63.

59. Christopher Lawrence and George Weisz, eds., *Greater Than the Parts: Holism in Biomedicine, 1920–1950* (New York: Oxford University Press, 1998).

60. W. H. Sheldon, "Some Relations between Certain Physical, Mental, and Social Traits" (Ph.D. diss., University of Chicago, 1926), 61. Subsequent references will appear in the text.

61. Sheldon, Stevens, and Tucker, *The Varieties of Human Physique.* Subsequent references will appear in the text.

62. Ian J. MacQueen, "The Significance of Somatotype in Sport and Athletics," *Essentials of Sports Medicine*, ed. Greg R. McLathie (Edinburgh: Churchill Livingston, 1986), 94–104. These categories remain standard within sports medicine today. See the entries in Michael Kent, ed., *Oxford Dictionary of Sports Science and Medicine* (Oxford: Oxford University Press, 1994).

63. W. H. Sheldon, *Atlas of Men: A Guide for Somatotyping the Adult Male of All Ages* (New York: Harper, 1954).

64. George L. Mosse, "Fascist Aesthetics and Society: Some Considerations," *Journal of Contemporary History* 31 (1996): 245–52, here 246–47.

65. W. H. Sheldon, *The Varieties of Temperament* (New York: Harper Brothers, 1942), 31–95. Subsequent references will appear in the text.

CONCLUSION

1. Katharine A. Phillips, *The Broken Mirror: Understanding and Treating Body Dysmorphic Disorder* (New York: Oxford University Press, 1998).

2. Harvey J. Sugerman, "Obesity Surgery," *Surgical Clinics of North America* 81 (2001): 1001–198.

3. Preuss, *Biblical and Talmudic Medicine*, 215.

4. Oertel, "Obesity," 3:626.

5. H. A. Kelly, "Excessive Growth of Fat," *Bulletin of the Johns Hopkins Hospital* 10 (1899): 197. A detailed follow-up on Kelly's patient is to be found in Lindsay Peters, "Resection of the Pendulous, Fat Abdominal Wall in Cases of Extreme Obesity," *Annals of Surgery* 33 (1901): 299–304.

6. C. Schulz, *Eine operative Behandlung der Fettleibigkeit. Grenzgebiete der Medizin und Chirugie* (Jena: Fischer, 1908).

7. Brownell and Wadden, "Obesity," 25.3.

8. On the pathologies of fat distribution see Denis Crad-

dock, *Obesity and Its Management* (Edinburgh: E. and S. Livingstone, 1969), 12–13.

9. E. C. Saltzstein and M. C. Gutmann, "Gastric Bypass for Morbid Obesity: Preoperative and Postoperative Psychological Evaluation of Patients," *Archive of Surgery* 115 (1980): 21–28.

10. S. F. Johnson, W. M. Swenson, and C. F. Gastineau, "Personality Characteristics in Obesity: Relation of MMPI Profile and Age of Onset of Obesity to Success in Weight Reduction," *American Journal of Clinical Nutrition* 29 (1976): 626–32.

11. P. C. Chandarana, P. Conlon, R. L. Holliday, T. Deslippe, and V. A. Field, "A Prospective Study of Psychosocial Aspects of Gastric Stapling Surgery," *Psychiatric Journal of the University of Ottawa* 15 (1990): 32–35.

12. R. H. Bull, W. D. Engels, F. Engelsmann, and L. Bloom, "Behavioural Changes Following Gastric Surgery for Morbid Obesity: A Prospective, Controlled Study," *Journal of Psychosomatic Research* 27 (1983): 457–67.

13. See the editorial by C. Gollobin and W. Y. Marcus, "Bariatric Beriberi," *Obesity Surgery* 12 (2002): 6–11.

14. J. W. Lee, "Recurrent Delirium Associated with Obstructive Sleep Apnea," *General Hospital Psychiatry* 20 (1998): 120–22.

15. Jonathan Wander, "Fat Boy Slim," *Men's Health* (July/August 2002): 128–31.

16. Michelle Tauber and Mark Dagostino, "One Hundred and Counting," *People*, 2 November 2002, 104–10.

17. Raymond Hernandez, "Politician, as Last Resort, Sheds Weight by Surgery," *New York Times*, 16 November 2002, A1, A15.

18. All of the quotes are from Robert E. Hockley, "Toward an Understanding of the Obese Person," *Journal of Religion*

and Health 18 (1979): 120–31. This is a psychoanalytic reading, based on the work of Hilde Bruch, of seven women preparing to undergo gastric bypass surgery.

19. Camryn Manheim, *Wake Up, I'm Fat* (New York: Broadway Books, 1999), 85.

20. P. E. O'Brien and J. B. Dixon, "The Extent of the Problem of Obesity," *American Journal of Surgery* 184 (2002): S4–8.

21. M. Kolehmainen, H. Vidal, J. J. Ohisalo, E. Pirinen, E. Alhava, and M. I. J. Uusitup, "Hormone Sensitive Lipase Expression and Adipose Tissue Metabolism Show Gender Difference in Obese Subjects after Weight Loss," *International Journal of Obesity* 26 (2002): 6–16.

22. Mary Douglas, *Natural Symbols* (New York: Pantheon Books, 1970), 70.

23. Judith Butler, *Gender Trouble* (New York: Routledge, 1990), 33.

24. Judith Butler, "Variations on Sex and Gender: Beauvoir, Wittig, and Foucault," in *Contemporary Literary Criticism: Literary and Cultural Studies*, ed. Robert Con Davis and Ronald Schleifer (New York: Longman, 1998), 611–23, here 614.

25. Bordo, *Unbearable Weight*, 201.

Index

Abbott, George, 207
Abdisu, 132
Achilles, 39
Adams, Scott, 191
addiction, food as, 66, 234
Addison, Joseph, 73
Adler, Jack J., 142, 150
Adler, Richard, 207
Adorno, Theodore, 163
aesthetic surgery, 228–39. *See also* gastric bypass surgery; stomach stapling
Aguero, Doctor Pedro Recio de, 76–77
Alcibiades, 39
Alderson, Baron, 24

Allen, Woody, 28
ALS. *See* amyorophic lateral sclerosis
Althoum, 132
America, 31. *See also* obesity: as American problem
American Obesity Association, 29
American Pastoral (1997), 211–13
Americans with Disabilities Act (1990), 14–15
Amis, Kingsley, 20
amyorophic lateral sclerosis (ALS), 203–4. *See also* Gehrig, Lou

animals, 37–38
Anne, Queen, 90
Applegate, Mr., 207–9
Apronius, Consul L., 228
Aquinas, St. Thomas, 52
Arbuckle, Fatty (Roscoe), 23
Arbuthnot, John, 90
Aristophanes, 38
Aristotle, 37, 45, 87; golden mean of, 44–45, 60
Arnald of Villanova, 43
Arnold, Edward, 186
Arthur, King, 54
askesis, 40. *See also* exercise
Athanadoros of Rhodes, 40
the athlete, xi, 40, 41, 193–95, 204, 219–20, 223, 226; acceptable body of, 220–21, 225; and diet regime, 194–95, 204; as ideal American, 211–12; as thin, 196, 204–5; distinction between fat and ill, 207, 224. *See also* baseball; Hippocrates
Augustine, St., 31, 51–52, 60, 65, 68, 73, 75, 97, 113, 121
autobiography, 61, 64, 65, 67, 68, 70–71, 74, 80, 82, 90, 91–92, 97, 101, 105, 107, 112, 117, 199–200
Aytoun, William E., 106

Baader, Franz von, 28
Baal, John, 213
Bacchus. *See* Dionysus

Bacon, Roger, 72, 78, 87
Bakunin, Mikhail, 167
Balzac, Honoré de, 135
Bang the Drum Slowly (1956), 205–6
Banting, William, 101–7, 108, 109, 191, 234, 235
Bardolph, 186
baseball: as cure for obesity, 195, 206; as masculine, 196–97
baseball players: 193, 195–220; fat, as healthy, 206, 211, 214; fat, as ill, 198–200, 204, 208, 211, 218, 226; as giant, 195–96, 199, 201, 213; ideal, 201, 202–3, 214, 225; Jewish (*see* Jews: in baseball); as thin, 196, 200, 204–5. *See also* the athlete
basso, comic, 124–28, 130–33
Baudrillard, Jean, 28
beauty, ix, 39–41, 83, 195, 224; corpulence as, 105, 144; health as, 102
Becher, Johann Joachim, 87, 88, 147
Benjamin, 80–81. See also *The Travels and Adventures of Benjamin the Third*
ben Yose, Ishamel, 46
Bembo, Cardinal Pietro, 67
Bendix, William, 201
Benn, Gottfried, 163
Béraud, Henri, 3

Bernard, Claude, 104
Bishop, Henry Rowley, 125–26
black bile, 35. *See also* humors
blas, 85–86, 88
blood, 35, 180. *See also* humors
Bobadill, 112
Bochco, Steven, 189–90
body, xi, 54–55, 239; self-
  perception of, 7, 26–27
body dysmorphic disorder,
  27, 228
Bogart, Humphrey, 155
Boito, Arrigo, 123, 127–28,
  131–33, 137, 138
Bordo, Susan, 239
Boswell, James, 90
Bougainville, 93
Boyarin, Daniel, 170
Boyd, Joe, 207–9
Bradshaw, Watson, 104–5
Branagh, Kenneth, 154
Brando, Marlon, 33
Bretzner, Christoph
  Friedrich, 124
Bright, Edward, 98
Brillat-Savarin, Jean Anthelme,
  94, 101, 103, 107, 166
British Disability Discrimina-
  tion Act (1995), 14
Brown, Father, 182
Browne, Richard, 27
Bruch, Hilde, 139–40, 150–51
Buchwald, Henry, 141
Budd, Superintendent, 182
Buddha, 21

Bull, John, 13
Buntz, Norman, 190
Burr, Raymond, 189
Burton, John, 83, 113, 119
Burwell, C. Sidney, 142,
  149, 150
Butler, Judith, 239
Byrd, Paul Richard (Horse),
  206

Caelius Aurelianus, 37
Callahan, George, 201
Canadian Charter of Rights and
  Freedoms (1994), 14
Cannon, Frank, 188
Cantini of Naples, 138
Carcano, Giulio, 128
Cardano, Girolamo, 64–65
caricatures, 12–13
castration, 124–25, 137; social,
  124, 134, 136. *See also* sexual-
  ity: and castration
Celsus, 41
Cervantes, Miguel de, 9, 74–81,
  82, 83, 84, 91, 93, 97, 108–9
Chalmers, Duddington Pell,
  182
Charcot, Jean Martin, 47, 174
Chernin, Kim, 1
Chesterton, G. K., 182
Cheyne, George, 88, 90–93,
  95–97
Chiari, Walter, 187
Chicago Size Acceptance
  Group, 4

Christ, 21, 115
Christianity. *See* Pauline
    Christianity
Christie, W. F., 48
chymoi, 35
Ciardi, John, 29–31
Cicero, 39
Clito, 59
Cobb, Ty, 195–96
cocaine: as mental stimulant,
    164; as treatment, 109
Coe, Dr T., 98
Cohn, Robert, 212
Collins, Wilkie, 166
Coltrane, Robbie, 154
Comaroff, Jean, 14
Conrad, Joseph, 167–68
Conrad, William, 188
Cook, Bonnie, 3
Cook, Captain James, 93
Cooper, Gary , 203
Corden, James, 2
Cornaro, Alvise (Luigi), 13, 64–
    74, 76, 78, 79, 91–92, 93, 96,
    97, 104, 109, 117, 186
corpulence, 149, 164; as
    disease, 105–6; as healthy,
    32, 62, 114, 119, 137–38, 144,
    180–81
Costner, Kevin, 201
Coulehan, Jack, 30–31

D'Amato, Alfonse, 235
Damn Yankees. See *The Year
    the Yankees Lost the Pennant*

Daroff, Lynn, 6
Daston, Lorraine, 53
Dearden, Harold, 5
decay of body, xi, 58, 61–62,
    113, 116, 121–22, 132, 139;
    as pathological, 128, 130,
    133, 137
Dedalus, Stephen, 160
Dedo II, Count, 228
Defoe, Daniel, 96–97
Defranceschi, Carlo
    Prospero, 125
Degher, Douglas, 26
Demme, Jonathan, 32
DeNiro, Robert, 190, 206
detectives, ix, xi, 153–54; as
    active, 155–56, 164–65; as
    empathetic, 154, 162, 189–90;
    fat, as thinking body, 180–83,
    185, 189, 191–92; fat of, as
    mental facilitator, 153, 155–
    56, 176–79, 181; as intuitive,
    155–56, 162, 170–71, 179–80,
    182, 189; as observers, 157,
    158–60, 164–65; as passive,
    162, 164, 181; as sedentary,
    155–56, 162, 189; as thin, 155–
    56, 164, 165
diabetes, 27, 47–50, 81, 104, 141,
    147, 230
Diatectica, 36
Dickens, Charles, 109, 142, 144,
    147, 150, 151, 159, 166
Dickinson, Edward, 43
Diderot, Denis, 93

diet, 36, 41, 59, 60, 64–65, 67, 88, 90, 92–3, 95–6, 99, 104, 105, 109, 172, 185, 194. *See also* Banting, William

dietetics, x, 28, 54, 59, 60–61, 71, 72, 97, 115

Din, Gunga, 107

Dionysus, 22, 38

Dionysus of Carystus, 36

Discourses on a Sober and Temperate Life (Discorsi della vita sobria) (1558), 64–67, 69–71. *See also* Cornaro, Alvise (Luigi)

Dogbert, 191–92

Donizetti, Gaetano, 126

Donlan, Ray, 191

Don Quixote (1605), 74–75, 109. *See also* Cervantes, Miguel de

Dostoevski, Fyodor, 29

Douglas, Mary, 238

Downey, Morgan, 29

Doyle, Sir Arthur Conan, 164–65, 166, 182

Drake, Paul, 189

Duessa, 54

Duke, Joshua, 107–9, 164

Dupin, C. Auguste, 155

Ebert, Roger, 201

Ebstein, Wilhelm, 137–40, 151, 160

Eckstein, Soho, 210

Edward VII, of Great Britain, 12

Ehud, 45–46

El'azar, Rabbi, 170

Eleazar ben Simeon, 46

elements: of Aristotle, 35, 87; of Paracelsus, 87. *See also* Aristotle; Paracelsus

Elgar, Edward, 127, 140

Elgon, King of Moab, 45–46

Elsholtz, Johann Sigismund, 58

Engelhardt, Tristram, 17

Englinton, John, 160

the Enlightenment, xi, 39, 59, 96

Ent, Roscoe, 208

Epicureans, 52

Equal Employment Opportunity Commission, 3

Erasmus, Desiderius, 71–72

Erikson, Erik, 57

Esquirol, J. E. D., 101

exercise, 40–42, 48, 59, 60, 103, 204–5

Falstaff, operas of, 123, 125–37

Falstaff, Sir John, 91, 111–17, 119–133, 150–51, 154, 159, 186, 187–88, 227; asexuality of, 134–38; diet of, 115, 118, 120; as medical case study, 139–42; proposed sleep apnea of, 142; retrospective diagnosis of, 140–41. *See also* obesity: as comic

fasting, 53, 71, 184

Fat Joe, 142–45, 147, 149–50, 159, 166, 227

fatty degeneration, 137–38

Fat Underground, 2

Faust, 207–8

Federer, Benjamin, 211

feminism. *See* obesity: as feminist issue

Ferber, Edna, 23

Ferraro, Kenneth F., 27

Ficino, Marsilio, 153

Fiedler, Leslie A., 31

Fielding, Henry, 91, 109

fish, 69, 71–73

Fitzgerald, Eddie (Cracker), 154–55, 162, 165

Flechsig, Paul Emil, 174–77

Fleming, J. G., 30

Flockhart, Calista, 20

Flynt, Larry, 22–23

Folliet, Dr., 143

food, as medicine, 36, 43, 51

Forman, Milos, 22

Forster, Georg, 93–94

Fosco, Count, 166–67

Fosse, Bob, 207

Foucault, Michel, 11, 54, 156

four ages of man, 35

Fox, Charles James, 12

Fracastoro, Girolamo (Hieronymus Fracastorus), 67–68, 119

Franklin, Benjamin, 74

Franz, Dennis, 189–90

Freilingrath, Ferdinand, 161

Freud, Sigmund, 47, 175, 177–79, 181

Friedman, Jeffrey, 146

Gaedel, Eddie, 208

Galen, 41–42, 43–44, 53, 59, 77

Galenic baths, 12

Galenic medicine, 43, 46, 65, 71

Gall, Franz Joseph, 170, 175

Gallico, Paul, 196

Galvani, Luigi, 135

Garden, George, 97

Gargantua, 54. *See also* giants

gastric bypass surgery, x, xi, 236, 238; difference of, for women and men, 236–38; negative effects of, 231–32, 233. *See also* stomach stapling

Gavalas, John, 12

Gehrig, Lou (Henry Louis), 197, 201–4, 206, 208, 220, 225

Genadry, Michael R., 236

gender, 6–8, 10, 18–20, 38, 61, 239

George IV, of England, 13

germs, 68

Gertrude, 117

giants, 53–54, 65, 98. *See also* obesity: distinction of, from giantism

Gielgud, Sir John, 188

Gillray, James, 12–13

Gilman, Charlotte Perkins, 180

Giotto, Ambrogio Bondone, 53

gluttony, 31, 59, 68–69, 75, 88, 89, 93, 113, 115, 118, 135; as cause for illness, 65–66
Glyde, Sir Perceval, 166
God, 21, 24, 31, 55, 58
Goethe, Johann Wolfgang von, 207
Golding, William, 148
Goodman, John, 201
Goodwin, Archie, 183
gout, 65, 96, 97, 115
Gray, Stephen, 26
Greece, Ancient, 35–41. *See also* Hippocrates
Greek Medicine, 36–37, 40
Greeks, ix, x, xi, 12, 38–39, 44, 156, 199, 220. *See also* beauty; ideal body
Greenberg, Hank, 211
Gross, Hans, 81
Gross, Otto, 81
Grünewald, Mathis, 21
Gut, Mr. *See* Panza, Sancho
Gutman, Casper, Esq., 169

Hagen, 132
Hagesandros of Rhodes, 40
Hal, Prince, 115–16, 142
Hamlet, 72, 117, 158, 160–61
Hammett, Dashiell, 155, 169, 187
Hancock, John, 206
Hanks, Tom, 32
Harbin, Beth, 29

Hardy, Joe, 208–9
Harrelson, Woody, 22
Harris, Mark, 205–6, 213
Hartright, Walter, 166
Harvey, William, 103–6
Hazlitt, William, 113
health, xi, 26–28, 43; fat as, 32, 44, 62, 179. *See also* corpulence
Helfin, Freddy, 190
Hemingway, Ernest, 212
Henry II, of Great Britain, 12
Henry IV, 111, 113–17, 136, 140, 188
Henry VIII, of Great Britain, 11
Herbert, A. P., 25
Herodes, 132
Herodicus of Selymbria, 41
Hertz, Jo, 23–24
Heston, Charlton, 187
Hiller, Arthur, 201
Hippocrates, 11, 35–37, 41, 59, 193, 199, 219–20
Hippocratic Corpus, 35, 37, 77
Hippocratic medicine, 42, 43
Hisdai ibn Shaprut, 12
HIV/AIDS, 31–32
Hobbs, Roy, 214–18
Hogarth, William, 83, 87
Holmes, Mycroft, 164–65, 166, 181, 182
Holmes, Sherlock, 155, 164–65, 166
Honig, Donald, 195

Hooper, Harry, 196–97
Hufeland, Christoph Wilhelm, 59–61, 74, 147
Hughes, Gerald, 26
Hugo, Victor, 128
Hume, David, 88, 90
humors, 35, 38, 42, 44, 62, 82, 84, 118, 122, 227; imbalance of, 36–37, 42
Hunter, Tab, 208

Ibn Sina, 46
ideal body, 39–40, 51–52, 199, 224. *See also* Greeks
identity, fat as, 26–27, 186, 236
infertility, 36–37, 38
International Obesity Task Force, 32
Ironside, Robert, 189

Jackson, Shoeless Joe, 218
James, Edwin, 94
James, Philip, 32
Jameson, Thomas, 62, 172
Jarvis, Jan, 195
Jellinek, Adolf, 81
Jewish Diaspora, 47
Jews, 45–51; in baseball, 209–10, 212, 220; body stereotypes of, 49, 56, 210–12, 222; diet of, 47–50; as effeminate, 38, 81–82; as marginalized, 173; perceived predisposition of, to obesity, 41, 46–48, 80, 210
John, Elton, 8

Johnson, Samuel, 90
Jones, Virgil, 20
Jonson, Ben, 112
Joslin, Elliot, 48
Joyce, James, 160
Jukes, Edward, 64, 74, 144
Junghans, R. P., 150

Kafka, Franz, 32, 184
Kant, Immanuel, 19, 60–62, 100
Keillor, Garrison, 219
Keitel, Harvey, 190
Kelly, Howard A., 228
Kemp, Robert, 5
Kentridge, William, 210
Key, Jack, 141
King's Evil. *See* scrofula
Kipling, Rudyard, 107
Kipnis, Laura, 6
Klein, Jocko, 209–10
Klein, Richard, 10
Klump, Sherman, 24
Knatteraud, Mary E., 141
Kraepelin, Emil, 135
Krawinkel, Lenard Fritz, 194
Kretschmer, Ernst, 117; body categories of, 220–21
Kristeva, Julia, 56

La Bruyère, Jean de, 59
labor: as ability, 38, 60, 97; as treatment, 59
Laidlaw, J. A., 24
Lambert, Daniel, 98–99, 106, 108

The Laocoon, 40
laparoscopic gastric banding,
    231, 233. *See also* gastric
    bypass surgery
Leggett, Jay, 20
Leigh, Mike, 2
Lesages, Alain-René, 91
Lessing, Gotthold Ephraim, 40
Lessius, Leonard, 73, 117–19
Levinson, Barry, 218
Levov, 211–12
Lewis, Jerry, 24
Lichtenberg, Georg
    Christoph, 160
Linden, A. L., 30
Locke, John, 100
Lombroso, Cesare, 167–68
longevity, xi, 19, 37, 45, 60–61,
    64–65, 67, 73, 78, 83, 86–87,
    90–91, 92, 100, 232–33
Lou Gehrig's disease. *See*
    amyorophic lateral sclerosis
Louis XIV, of France, 12
Love, Buddy, 24
Luther, Martin, 49, 54–58
Lycurgus, 39
Lysippos, 39
Lyttleton, Lord, 91

madness, 135
Maimonides, Moses (Moshe
    ben Maimun), 46
Malamud, Bernard, 213, 216
Mangold, James, 190
Manheim, Camryn, 237

Mantle, Mickey, 208
Margolis, David, 50
marriage, 19–21
Martial, 77
Marx, Karl, 167, 174
masculinity, ix, 6, 10–11, 18–20,
    33, 38–39, 62, 63, 74, 82, 90,
    97, 101, 114, 128, 151, 223, 233,
    239; obesity as antithesis of,
    107–8, 114, 120, 145, 150; and
    reason, 153–55, 173, 181. *See
    also* gender; longevity; sexual-
    ity; syphilis
Mason, Perry, 189
Mattson, Mark, 203
Maudsley, Henry, 101
Maynwaringe, Everard, 78, 118
McBeal, Ally, 20
McCabe, J. L. (Fatman), 188–89
McCowan, George, 188
McIntyre, John T., 182
McKnight, Fred, 188
McMaster, Juliet, 142, 144
McSherry, John, 204
Meige, Henry, 137
melancholy, 88–89, 92, 96,
    117–19, 134
Mendoza, Daniel, 210
Mercy, Max, 215
The Merry Wives of Windsor
    (1602), 111–13, 120–21, 138,
    188; as opera, 126; Nicolai's,
    137. *See also* Falstaff, Sir John
Meynert, Theodor, 175
Michaelis, 167–69

Micheldene, Roger, 20

Milch, David, 189–90

Milton, John, 122, 151

Mime, 132

Minkoff, Myrna, 21

Minnesota Multiphasic Personality Inventory (MMPI), 230

Mitchell, S. Weir, 2, 105, 179–81

Monostatos, 124–25, 139

Montaigne, Michel de, 39

Montfleury, 119

Moore, A. W., 104

Moore, Clement Clarke, 21

Moore, Marianne, 195

Moore, Mavor, 187

morality, xi, 59–61; decay of, 120; obesity as lack of, 27, 59, 99, 136, 147, 148

Moreau, Jeanne, 188

Moriarty, Michael, 206–7

Moriarty, Professor, 166

Mosenthal, S. H., 126

Mosse, George L., 224

Mozart, Wolfgang Amadeus, 124

Müller, Johannes, 106, 169, 173

Murphy, Eddie, 24

Murphy, Julian, 32

myelin, 169, 171–72, 174–77, 179, 180

NAAFA. *See* National Association to Advance Fat Acceptance

Naccarati, Sante, 221–22

Nadler, Jerrold, 235

Nast, Thomas, 21

National Association to Advance Fat Acceptance, 1, 4

National Association to Aid Fat Americans. *See* National Association to Advance Fat Acceptance

The Natural (1952), 214–18

nervous system, 169–70; and fat, 171–79, 183

Newman, Paul, 207

Newton, Isaac, 154

Nicolai, Friedrich, 88

Nicolai, Otto, 126, 127, 137

Niemeyer, Felix, 106

Nietzsche, Friedrich Wilhelm, 74

norm, ix, x, 31; as inaccessible, 11

normal man, 24–26, 30–31, 45, 60

obesity, ix, x, xi, 2, 8–9, 12–14; as American problem, 2, 6; as asexual, x, 21, 24, 58, 139; associated with old age, 103, 104, 132, 135, 136, 186, 209; as bloated, 55–57, 108, 142, 162, 167; British representations of, 12–13; as castrated, 124, 134; as caused by society, 93, 94; as cause of illness, 102; as cheery, 27, 142, 144, 172; childhood, 8, 45, 48, 60, 144–45, 195, 147–49;

obesity (*cont.*)

Christian attitudes toward, 51–58, 66; as class status, 49, 97, 109; as comic, 111–14, 120, 123–28, 135, 138, 142, 144–45 (*see also* Falstaff, Sir John); as cowardly, 114, 116; as cultural problem, 17; cure for, 65–66, 67, 92, 238; as damned, 58; as danger, 5, 62, 107, 112, 134, 144, 169; definition, 15–16; as deviant, 20, 97; as disability, 3, 14–17, 103; as disease, 26–28, 64, 101, 105, 106, 113, 114, 144; as dishonest, 9, 45; distinction of, from giantism, 53–54; as effeminate, 80–82, 120, 136–37, 155, 182 (*see also* Jews: as effeminate); as epidemic, x, 32, 195; etymology, 9–10; as evil, 9; as failure of will, 100, 106, 228, 231, 234; as feminist issue, 3, 50; French perspective toward, 3, 13; genetics as cause of, 235, 238; as global concern, 32, 229; as graceful, 196; Greek treatments for, 36, 38, 41–42; as harmless, 168; as hypersexual, x, 125, 139; as insulation, 170, 183; as illness, 27–36, 94; Jewish attitudes toward, 46; as Jewish issue, 46–51; Jewish treatments for, 46; as lack of self-control, 46, 231, 234; as lazy, 9, 37, 44, 45, 145; medicalized, 109; morbid, 11, 15, 32, 138, 139, 141, 172, 236; and national identity, 3, 160–61; as nervous, 167; of nobility, 3, 11–12; as pandemic, 32; as pathological, 9, 18, 28, 30, 35–38, 41, 43–44, 49, 53, 59, 62, 63, 88, 89, 102, 105–6, 108, 113, 115, 128, 141, 148, 228, 239; as phlegmatic, 36–37, 42, 44, 62, 94, 112, 114; as physiological condition, 106, 228, 238; as potential for disease, 41, 46, 47, 117; as potential for illness, 27, 88, 108, 141; as primitive, 145–47, 158, 163–64, 175–78, 181–84, 191, 223; as prophylaxis against disease, 179–80; as prosperous, 163; as protection, 183, 185; psychiatric treatment for, 228; psychology associated with, 228, 230–31; qualities of, 30; as result of emotional deprivation, 140, 150; risk of, 61; as scientific problem, 5, 27; shift of, from male to female body, 4, 63; as sign of disease, 28, 41, 119–20, 134; as solid, 55, 57; stigma associated with, 102–3, 204; as stupid, 37, 39, 45, 145, 191; as ugly, 9, 20, 38–41; as unreason or obesity (*cont.*)

    madness, 30, 139; as violation of constraint, 37, 117; as weakness, 12; as woman's issue, 1, 3–6, 14, 95, 101

obesity gene, 146–47, 227

Ochs, Baron, 132

Oertel, Max, 48

Olivas, Richard, 195

Olympic Games, 40, 193

opera, 123–26

Orbach, Susie, 1

Orbeyi, Hakan, 194

Orgoglio, 54

Osmin, 124–25, 127, 132, 139

O'Toole, Delores, 20

Panza, Sancho, 74–81, 82, 84, 108, 144; as caricature, 12; medicalized, 77

Paracelsus, 85, 87

Park, Katharine, 53

Pastorelli, Robert, 155

Pauline Christianity, 51–52, 54, 58

Paul of Aegina, 42

Paul of Tarsus, 52, 55, 66

Peacock, Thomas Love, 143

Pearson, Bruce, 206–7

Penthesilea, 39

Perez, Gil, 91

Petrie, Daniel, 207

Pfitzner, Hans, 132

phlegm, 35–7, 84. See also humors

Pickwick, Samuel, 142–47

Pickwickian syndrome. *See* sleep apnea

The Pickwick Papers, 159–60

Piggy, 148–49

Pippen, Harry, 20

Pitt-Rivers, George, 47

Pizzi, Italo, 123

plague. *See* syphilis

Plato, 38, 39, 53

Platonic body, 41, 51–52

Plautus, 111

Pliny the Elder, 228

plumpness, as healthy, 32, 142–44; as indication of prosperity, 11

Poe, Edgar Allen, 155

poetry, 29–31

Poitier, 56

Polonius, 72, 78

Polydros of Rhodes, 40

Polysarkia, 37, 42

Pope, Alexander, 91

poverty, 2

pox, 113–15

Praxiteles, 39

Presley, Elvis, 33

psychiatry, 100–101

Puccini, Giacomo, 132

Puntarvolo, 112

Pyrönen, Heta, 165

Quinlan, Detective, 188
Quixote, Don, 74–76, 78–80, 81, 88, 96, 144

Raabe, Wilhelm, 156, 159, 160–62, 176, 182
Rabelais, François, 53, 58, 65
Ranvier, Louis, 173–74
reason, 30–31, 38, 60. *See also* normal man
Red Cross Knight, 54
Redford, Robert, 218
the Reformation, 54
Regino, Anamarie, 149
Reibmeyer, Albert, 205
Reid, Thomas, 100
Reilly, Ignatius J., 21
Remak, Robert, 171, 173, 174
Renaissance, xi, 53, 113, 135, 153
Reynolds, Frederic, 125
Rhotonet, 228
Ribera, Jusepe de, 58
Ribot, Theodor, 101
Richardson, Samuel, 90, 109
Rieger, Conrad, 134
Roberts, Deborah, 234
Robin, Michael, 189
Robinson, Louis, 145
Robinson, Phil Alden, 201
Rodin, Alvin, 141
Roker, Al, 233–35, 236, 237
Rosenzweig, Franz, 45
Ross, Jerry, 207

Rossini Gioacchino, 126
Roth, Phillip, 211–13
Rothblum, Esther, 7
Roux-en-Y gastric bypass, 231. *See also* gastric bypass surgery
Rubens, Peter Paul, 58, 63
Runyon, Brad, 187
Rushdie, Salman, 20
Ruth, Babe (George Herman), 195–201, 203, 205, 206, 207, 208, 214, 220, 224–25, 227; cancer of, 200–201; diets of, 198, 200; as glutton, 196–97; as hypersexual, 197
Ruth, Roy Del, 201

Salerno medical school, 43
Salieri, Antonio, 125
Salmi, Albert, 207
Sancho I, of Leon, 12
Sanctorius Sanctorius, 89
Sansfoy, 54
Santa Claus, 17, 21–23
Satan, 55, 57–58, 151
Satlof, Ron, 188
savages, 93–95
Schaumann, Heinrich (Tubby), 157–59, 160–63, 164–65, 166, 181, 185, 189, 227
Schikaneder, Emanuel, 124
Schlegel, Friedrich, 126
Schoenberg, Arnold, 132
Schreber, Daniel Paul, 175

Schulz, C., 228
Schwartz, Hillel, 4, 13, 27
Schwimmer, Rusty, 20
science: of athletics, 219; of dietetics, 60, 97; of medicine, 61; of obesity, 27, 59, 60, 84–85, 87–88, 204
scrofula, 90
Sedley, Joseph (Jos), 97, 99–100, 106
Seforim, Mendele Mosher, 80–81, 82
Selinus, 22
Senderel, 80–81, 82
Sesit, Mike, 202
seven deadly sins, 51–52, 113; *acedia*, 52, 119; *gula*, 51, 59. *See also* gluttony; obesity: as lazy; sloth
sexuality, x, 19–24, 56, 58, 68, 113, 122, 125, 133–34, 139; and castration, 124–25, 131; decay from, 139; negation of, 112, 131, 134; as pathological, 132. *See also* gender; masculinity
sexually transmitted disease, 113, 121, 135. *See also* syphilis
Shafer, Robert, 207
Shakespeare, William, 111–14, 120–21, 125, 126, 127, 130, 137, 142, 151, 188
Shandy, Tristram, 82–84, 88
Shandy, Walter, 83, 86, 88, 89
Shapin, Steven, 153–54
Sharp, Becky, 97, 99–100

Shaw, Irwin, 211
Sheldon, William, 49, 221–25
Silenus, 39, 58
Simmel, Georg, 40
Sims, Ethan Allen, 146–47
sin, 31, 51–53, 58–59, 65, 66, 145. *See also* seven deadly sins
Sinclair, John, 100
Singer, Heinrich, 81
Sipowicz, Andy, 189–90
sleep apnea, 142, 150, 230–31
Slop, Dr., 83, 87
sloth, 31, 47, 52, 88, 145, 158, 162, 164, 179, 181. *See also* obesity: as lazy; seven deadly sins
small pouch gastric bypass (SPGB), 231. *See also* gastric bypass surgery
Smart, J. Scott, 187
Smollett, Tobias, 109
Sobal, Jeffrey, 18
Socrates, 37, 39, 58, 196
somatotypes, 221–25
Soughers, Carolyn, 3
soul, 97, 113, 119, 121
Southwest Airlines, 29
Spade, Sam, 155, 187, 188
Spenser, Edmund, 54
Spurzheim, Johann Caspar, 170
Stallone, Sylvester, 190–91
Stanley, Sir Henry Morton, 164
state, male body as metaphor for, 114, 119

Stearns, Peter, 11
Steinbrenner, George, 204
Steingarten, Jeffrey, 43
Stephanie, Gottlob, Jr., 124
Sterne, Laurence, 82–91, 93, 97, 109
St. Nicholas. *See* Santa Claus
Stoics, 52, 61
stomach stapling, 230–31, 237
Stone, Oliver, 22
Stout, Rex, 182–83, 185, 188
Strauss, Richard, 132
Suetonius, 9
Sullivan, John, 140–41, 142, 151
sumo wrestlers, 194
Swedish Act Concerning Support and Services for Persons with Certain Functional Impairments (1993), 14
Sydenham, Thomas, 88
syphilis, 3, 68, 74, 113, 117–19, 121, 134–35, 147; feminization as result of, 136–37

Taft, William Howard, 12
Taupin, Bernie, 8
Tave, Stuart M., 111
Teitelbaum, Felix, 210
temperance, 65–67, 98
Thackeray, William Makepeace, 97, 99–100, 107
Thersites, 39
thinness, 31–32; as cause for hysteria, 179; as cause for illness, 75, 180; as ideal, 10; as libera-

tion from obesity, 237; and philosophers, 153–54; as sign of illness, 32, 184. *See also* detectives
Thompson, Rosemarie Garland, 24
Thompson, Vance, 165
Tieck, Ludwig, 126
Tiggermann, Marika, 7
Tilden, Moe, 190
Timias, 54
Tinker, Mark, 189
Titchener, Edward Bradford, 222
tobacco, 16–17, 87, 164
Toole, John Kennedy, 21
The Travels and Adventures of Benjamin the Third (1885), 80–81
Tristram Shandy (1759–67), 82–83. *See also* Sterne, Laurence
Trulliber, 91
Tubby Schaumann, 156–59
Tunis, John R., 209, 213
Tupman, Mr., 159

Udall, Nicholas, 112

Vanacore, Mark, 236
Van Helmont, Johannes Baptista, 73, 78, 84, 85–88
Vanity Fair (1847–48), 97, 99
Veeck, Bill, 208
Veloc, 168–69
Venner, Tobias, 10, 18, 72, 78

Verdi, Giuseppe, 123–34, 135, 137, 138, 151
Verdon, Gwen, 208
Verghese, Abraham, 141
Verner, Gerald, 182
vertical banded gastroplasty (VBG), 231. *See also* gastric bypass surgery
villains: as obese, 165–69. *See also* detectives
Virgil, 58
virtue, 41, 53
Vlady, Marina, 187
von Gruber, Max, 139
von Haller, Albrecht, 136, 172
von Hofmannthal, Hugo, 132
von Hutten, Ulrich, 68
von Liebig, Justus, 172

Wadd, William, 101, 145, 149, 194
Wagner, Richard, 126, 132
Wallop, Douglass, 207
Walston, Ray, 207
Wander, Jonathan, 232–34
Wang, Youfa, 7
Wardel, Mr., 142, 149, 159
Watson, Dr. John, 164
Weigert, Carl, 174
weighing, 89
Weller, Sam, 144, 147, 149
Welles, Orson, 33, 187–88

Wheeler, Elmer, 5, 8
Wieland, Christop Martin, 126
Wiggen, Henry Whittier, 205–7
will, disease of, 100–101, 108, 216. *See also* obesity: as disease; obesity: as illness
Williams, Ralph Vaughan, 127
William the Conqueror, 12
Wilson, Carnie, 234
Winckelmann, Johann Joachim, 40
Wolfe, Nero, 182–89
Wolsey, Thomas Cardinal, 11
women, xi, 3, 6, 7, 8, 36–38, 179, 237, 238; difference from male body, 230, 237–38. *See also* gender; obesity: as woman's issue
World Health Organization, 15–16
Wyeth, John, 95

Xenophon, 38

The Year the Yankees Lost the Pennant (1954), 207–9
yellow bile, 35. *See also* humors
Yemenites, 50
Yu, Yan, 27

Zopyrus, 39
Zuckerman, Nathan, 212

Breinigsville, PA USA
01 November 2010
248453BV00001B/3/P